The BEST of ENEMIES

The BEST *of* ENEMIES

Race and Redemption in the New South

Osha Gray Davidson

With a New Introduction by the Author

THE UNIVERSITY OF NORTH CAROLINA PRESS / *Chapel Hill*

© 1996, 2018 by Osha Gray Davidson
Introduction © 2007 by Osha Gray Davidson
All rights reserved

Originally published by Scribner in 1996.
Paperback edition published by the
University of North Carolina Press in 2007.

Designed by Erich Hobbing
Text set in Aster
Manufactured in the United States of America

The paper in this book meets the guidelines for permanence
and durability of the Committee on Production Guidelines for
Book Longevity of the Council on Library Resources.

*The Library of Congress has cataloged the original edition
of this book as follows:*

Davidson, Osha Gray
  The best of enemies: race and redemption in the New South / Osha
Gray Davidson.
     p. cm.
  Includes bibliographical references (p.) and index.
  1. Southern States—Race relations—Case studies. 2. Durham (N.C.)—
Race relations—Case studies. 3. Social change—Southern States—Case
studies. 4. Civil rights workers—Southern States—Case studies. 5. Ku
Klux Klan (1915–)—Southern States—Case studies.   I. Title.
  E185.61.D29   1996
  305.8′009756—dc20   95-45543
                              CIP
ISBN 978-0-8078-5869-1 (cloth: alk. paper)
ISBN 978-1-4696-4660-2 (pbk.: alk. paper)
ISBN 978-1-4696-4661-9 (ebook)

Cover illustration: Motion Picture Artwork © 2018 STX Financing, LLC.
All Rights Reserved.

ACKNOWLEDGMENTS

I first read about the amazing friendship between C. P. Ellis and Ann Atwater in Studs Terkel's book *Race*. The story of two individuals who stepped across the color line was something special—even among the many other moving voices Terkel had coaxed into print. I am deeply indebted, therefore, to Studs Terkel, and not only for bringing this unique tale to my attention. For years, he has been the interviewer I've tried to model myself upon: passionate yet never polemical, probing but entirely respectful, and always fully engaged. He interviews people—not subjects—and it's a distinction I've worked to remember.

Of course, my primary debt is to C.P. and Ann. For over two years, they answered my endless questions, even the painful ones, with an openness and patience that must have been difficult to maintain at times. They took me as I am, an ignorant middle-class Yankee, and taught me about the realities of life in Dixie—good and bad. A heartfelt "thank you" to both of them.

While a great many individuals worked in various ways to produce this book, a few require special mention. Florence Blakely served above and beyond the call of duty, pointing me toward resources I couldn't have otherwise found, introducing me around Durham, hunting down rare photographs, shepherding me through the bureaucratic labyrinth downtown as we sleuthed out decades-old files. Ms. Blakely is known around town as Duke University's chief information librarian (retired) and current vice president of the Durham Historical Preservation Society. To me, she'll always be the Angel of Durham.

For decades, Jack and Joan Preiss have stood at the heart of Durham's true progressive community. As a city councillor during many of the years covered in this book, Jack Preiss fought hard for decency and equality. Joan Preiss (who has walked more miles on picket lines and protest marches over the years than Arnold Palmer has covered on grass) allowed me to sift through her extensive files. Both of them gave generously of their time in recalling past battles and personalities.

Jibreel Khazan, who (as freshman college student Ezell Blair, Jr.) was one of four students who began the lunch-counter movement in February 1960, has been a remarkable source of information and inspiration throughout the writing of this book. Getting to know people like "Easy" is one of the serendipitous joys of writing a book like this.

Many others also deserve recognition for a variety of assistance: Virginia Lee Williams; Joycelyn McKissick; Noah Chandler, research assistant at the Center for Democratic Renewal in Atlanta; Angie Lowry, Klanwatch; Leah McGinnis, graduate student at University of North Carolina, Chapel Hill; Cynthia Lewis, Director of Archives, Martin Luther King, Jr., Center for Nonviolent Social Change, Inc.; Rev. J. C. Cheek and the congregation of the Mount Calvary United Church for Christ, Durham; Dr. Steven Salmony, Chapel Hill; Harold Moore, *Durham Herald-Sun*; Renee Romano, Department of History, Stanford University; Maura Porter, Reference Archivist, John Fitzgerald Kennedy Library, in Boston; Ann Berkley, North Carolina Reference Librarian, and Elizabeth Moorman, Durham County Library; John White, Southern Historical Collection, University of North Carolina, Chapel Hill; Edward Morris, North Carolina Archives, Raleigh; the staff of the Dalton-Brand Research Room, Special Collections Library, Duke University; Holly Carver, the University of Iowa Press; Margaret Andera, the Milwaukee Art Museum; Nicolette Bromberg and Susan Pagani, Visual Reference Archives, State Historical Society of Wisconsin, Madison.

Thanks to the dedicated staff at the Iowa City Public Library—especially to Irene Patil, who, as head of interlibrary loan, has a degree of persistence that Canadian Mounties would envy. She always gets her document.

I appreciate the many helpful suggestions and criticisms from friends and colleagues, particularly from Jack Shelton, Cherry Muhanji, and Theresa Riffe.

ACKNOWLEDGMENTS

I am forever indebted to my editor at Scribner, Hamilton Cain, for performing much-needed liposuction on the manuscript, and to my agent, Alison Picard, for believing in this project.

Also at Scribner, Jennifer Chen handled all the crucial details of the publishing process with competence and grace, and Angella J. Baker and John P. Lynch wielded their red pencils expertly.

And finally to Mary, whose love gets me through the hard parts, thank you, once again.

For Sienna, Sarah, and Liam—

And for Louis E. Austin,
publisher of the *Carolina Times*, 1927–1971

To be born with a dark skin is unforgivable in the South, and only the Negro must forever be assigned a place of hatred in the heart of the southerner. . . . So deep are the roots and so well fertilized have they been by generation after generation of his ancestors that long before he is born, the pattern, the way of life for the white child in the South has already been provided. What it has cost the South economically, politically, socially, and, above all, morally, can never be estimated.

—Louis E. Austin

The South is still the most terrible place in America. Because it is, it is filled with heroes.

—Howard Zinn

The BEST of ENEMIES

INTRODUCTION

Is there anything new to say about race in America? Even a decade ago, critics of President Bill Clinton's call for a national conversation on the subject didn't think so.

It's all been said before, they complained, and with some justification. It is true, for example, that racial incidents, followed by calls for tolerance and understanding, are a more-or-less permanent feature of the American landscape, durable as the Rocky Mountains, familiar as the Mississippi River.

But Clinton's critics were missing the point. With a few significant exceptions, what has been occurring for decades, even for a century or more, has not been a *dialogue* on race, but any number of simultaneous *monologues* on the subject. You want race-talk? Oh, there has been plenty of talk. It's listening that is in short supply. (Not that this observation is original or even vaguely new. Forty years ago—in 1967—the late poet June Jordan covered this same ground, brilliantly, in an article she wrote for the *Nation* entitled "On Listening: A Good Way To Hear.")

One way to read the story of Ann Atwater and C.P. Ellis is as a testimony to the transformative power of listening. Listening is, however, only the first step. What comes next is even more difficult: reconciling the new information with what we already know, or think we do. This feat requires what the early-twentieth-century American writer Sinclair Lewis called a "willingness to sift the sanctified lies," a chore that is hard enough when the "lie" is trivial. Imagine the difficulty of listening to, and then accepting, a truth that overturns everything you believe about the world. And not merely that, but a truth that informs you that "the world is not what you think it is. And, by the way, neither are you." How many of us have

1

the intellectual courage to consider, let alone accept, the truth when it demands so much?

C.P. Ellis did. And he did even knowing that the truth that would set him free would also set him adrift, untethered in a divided society that demanded to know, every day: "Which side are you on?" Deep into the winter of 1994, more than two decades after leaving the Klan, C.P. was driving me around Durham in his old Buick, giving me a tour of the city he had lived in nearly all his life. It was late in the day and cloudy. Neither of us had spoken for several minutes. Suddenly, apropos of nothing beyond what was churning in his head and heart, C.P. said, "I don't feel comfortable here." He added, "I wish I had more friends." There was plenty of regret in his voice, but none, it seemed to me, for the choices he had made, and most especially no remorse over his one big choice, the decision that had left him perpetually uneasy and nearly friendless in his hometown.

A slightly different way to read this story is as a cautionary tale—albeit one with a measure of hope—charting the price we pay for embracing our glorious national myths while ignoring or minimizing the cruel realities of America's past and present. (As if we have only those two choices: "America, the Beautiful" or "America, the Great Satan.")

The myth most pertinent to this story is that America is a classless society, where anyone can rise from humble origins to become whatever he or she aspires to be, limited only by individual ability and level of commitment to work hard. C.P. inherited this myth from his father, Paul Ellis, a mill worker who died of brown lung, worn out and impoverished (despite working two jobs nearly all his life) at the age of forty-eight. "Do right," Paul Ellis taught C.P., "support the police, salute the flag, and good things will happen to you."

But good things were not forthcoming. The harder he worked, the deeper C.P. sank into the very rut that had swallowed his father, even as he watched the less talented and shiftless children of the wealthy prosper. So C.P. turned to another myth to explain the bizarre situation. When, through no fault of their own, whites *didn't* thrive, it was because after the Civil War, a conspiracy between outsiders (Northerners) and Southern blacks had upset the natural order:

> Ignorance, Lust and Hate seized the reins of State, and riot, rapine and universal ruin reigned supreme; the highest form of cultured society was thrust down and its noble neck was forced under the iron heel of pernicious passion who yielded a potent scepter of inquisitorial oppression, and the very blood of the Caucasian race was seriously threatened with an everlasting contamination.

This florid version of the myth is from the *Kloran*, the self-described "sacred book" of the Knights of the Ku Klux Klan, the United Klans of America, the organization in which C.P. found a home and a purpose, and where he rose to become the Exalted Cyclops.

It's unlikely that C.P. would have been drawn to the racial mythologies of the Klan if "respectable" society hadn't mirrored many of these same beliefs. Here's another version of the myth, this time cleaned up for mass consumption, its racism oblique, and tailored to its Cold War audience:

> The Congress of the United States yields to blackmail, and passes socialistic legislation—calling it "progress." It appropriates billions, as directed by the President, on the pretense of helping the poor. The Supreme Court shackles the police, compounds confusion in the legislatures of the states, and turns loose murderers and rapists to repeat their evil deeds upon the innocent and law-abiding members of society. How much of this is the result of communist planning? Who can say? . . . The communists want law and order destroyed in America. . . . They want riots in the streets, and demonstrations on the campus. They want confusion in our courts, and frustration among our states. . . . The name of the game is now survival—and we will either win it or lose it.

These are the words of Jesse Helms, who, before becoming a United States senator, delivered commentaries five nights a week after the news on a Raleigh, North Carolina, television station; the commentaries were then rebroadcast on radio stations and reprinted in newspapers throughout the South. Between 1960 and 1971, Helms read thousands of these monologues, usually dedicated to conspiracy theories and apocalyptic warnings about the Red threat, which he saw everywhere, from the mildest liberal proposals to the civil rights movement as a whole. When speaking on issues of race (which he frequently did), Helms was careful to use code words and phrases that weren't *necessarily* racist, but which his intended audience of Southern white conservatives clearly understood as racial. When, for example, he posed the rhetorical question, "Is survival possible when civilization reverts to the law of the jungle?" his devoted listeners recognized the reference to Africa and African Americans. When Helms railed that "we must decide whether we will be ruled by sanity or ruined by savagery," his audience knew exactly which "savages" Helms meant. Only rarely did he allow an undisguised racist remark to slip through, like the time he referred to "the purely scientific statistical evidence of natural racial distinctions in group intellect."*

The Klan didn't exist in a vacuum, and, in fact, it couldn't have. To appreciate the *Kloran*'s appeal you have to understand the role played by Jesse Helms, George Wallace, Richard Nixon, and all the other respectable leaders who played the race card to advance their own careers, whatever the cost to our nation.

Ann Atwater grew up poor, black, and female in the mid-twentieth-century South, all circumstances that precluded her from buying into the myths that beguiled C.P. She had her own set of beliefs, of course, including the conviction that all whites were simply and unalterably bad. Yes, some of them had a pleasant exterior. But experience had taught her this much: scratch the surface and you'll find the racist.

---

*The extracted quote ("The Congress of the United States . . .") is from *Viewpoint* no. 1829, April 22, 1968. Helms's other comments are quoted in Ernest B. Furguson, *Hard Right: The Rise of Jesse Helms* (New York: W. W. Norton & Co., 1986), pp. 215 ("Is survival possible. . ." and "we must decide . . .") and 217 ("the purely scientific . . .").

Her experience with C.P. taught her something new. A layer of racism may be nearly inevitable among white Americans. Perhaps racism is like DDT, the poison that was banned decades ago, but which, because it persists in the environment, is still found within our bodies. The American experience (not our mythology, but our history) is permeated by racism. Northerners and Southerners alike. How could we avoid ingesting it? (And, besides, unlike DDT, racism is still sold over the counter in America. Slavery was abolished. So was Jim Crow. Racism survives.) But beneath this body-burden of racism, Ann discovered in C.P. something more profound: a recognition of our shared humanity.

The fact that not everyone is willing to dig deep enough to find that core is hardly evidence that it doesn't exist. It's difficult and painful work, and most whites don't want to expose the layer of racism, even to themselves, let alone to others. Some, no doubt unconsciously, fear that Ann was right in her earlier belief, that there's nothing below the racism—except more racism. And if that's true, isn't it better to leave those poisonous thoughts alone? At least they're covered by a veneer of civility.

On the other hand, if what Ann learned from C.P. is true for all of us, then by not digging we condemn ourselves to lives of ignorance and alienation, not just of others, but of ourselves.

When C.P. Ellis died on November 3, 2005, a memorial service was held for family members at a local funeral home. The exception to the family-only rule was Ann Atwater, who was invited because her friendship with C.P. had been so close and lasted for so many years.

Ann happened to arrive first. She sat down in the first row, nearest to the casket holding the body of her friend, grieving in silence. After a minute or two, she was startled by a hesitant cough beside her. She looked up.

"Excuse me," whispered a white man whose face was, at that moment, a deep red. "This service is for Mr. Claiborne Ellis," he told her, nodding toward the casket.

"Yes," Ann replied. "I know."

There was an awkward moment of silence. The man cleared his throat.

"I'm sorry," he said, "but the service is for family members only."

"I know that, too." Ann was growing tired of the interruption.

The man glanced at the exit, perhaps hoping that Ann would take the hint.

"Well, are you a . . . *family* member?"

"Yes," she said, glowering at the man. Another pause.

"Can I ask how you're related to the deceased?"

Ann stared at him for several seconds before answering.

"C.P. was my *bro-ther*," she said, drawing the word out, emphasizing it, allowing it to unroll like one of the red carpets in the aisle.

Without saying anything else, the man hurried out the door.

C.P.'s daughter, Vickie, told me this story, laughing, not long after her father's passing. I remembered the story recently, when I was talking to Ann.

"Did you really say that C.P. was your brother?" I asked her, chuckling.

"Yeah," Ann said without laughing. "Because that's how it was between us."

It was that way between them, because, after years of battling each other, C.P. and Ann took that courageous first step of listening. And having taken that step into the void, they kept on going.

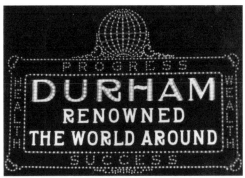

The Durham Commercial Club celebrated its hometown in 1913 with this forty-by-fifty-foot sign, its confident message spelled out in colored electric lights. *(Courtesy of the Durham Historic Photographic Archives, Durham County Library)*

(below) Erwin Cotton Mills, Durham, 1920s. William Erwin, president of the mill, was a benevolent dictator. Like other mill executives, he paid low wages but built an auditorium, a swimming pool, tennis courts, and even a small zoo for "his" workers. At night, Erwin pedaled his bicycle through the mill village enforcing a 10 P.M. "lights-out" rule. *(Courtesy of the Durham Historic Photographic Archives, Durham County Library)*

Louis E. Austin, publisher of the *Carolina Times* newspaper from 1927 to 1971, pictured in the 1950s. Editorials by Austin, an uncompromising advocate of integration and full rights for blacks, had a national audience. In 1933, Austin and a small group of supporters attempted to enroll a black student at the University of North Carolina at Chapel Hill—the first legal challenge to segregation in higher education in America. *(Courtesy of the Durham Historic Photographic Archives, Durham County Library)*

A nattily dressed C. C. Spaulding, 1905. He helped build the North Carolina Mutual into a national business giant. Spaulding represented a new kind of Southern black businessman, eschewing the servile role whites demanded of blacks. A white judge described Spaulding as "lean, Cassius-like, and copper-colored, he seldom smiled. . . . All he asked of life was an open field and a fair chance. He was strictly business." *(Courtesy of the Durham Historic Photographic Archives, Durham County Library)*

Parrish Street, Durham, 1920s, home of the North Carolina Mutual Life Insurance Company (tall building, left of center). The Mutual was the largest black-owned business in the world at the time. Sociologist E. Franklin Frazier called Durham the "Capital of the Black Middle Class," but prosperity never went much beyond Parrish Street. *(Courtesy of Special Collections Library, Duke University)*

A typical Southern mill village, like the one in which C.P. grew up. This one is in Rome, Georgia, photographed in April 1913 by Lewis Hine. (Housing in the Factory's Shadow, *Courtesy of the Milwaukee Art Museum, Gift of Robert Mann*)

C.P., the proud owner of a service station, Durham, early 1960s. He joined the Klan soon after buying the business.

C.P. Ellis, fifteen years old, Main Street, downtown Durham.

Martin Luther King, Jr., at the Woolworth's lunch counter in Durham, shut down by students protesting Jim Crow segregation on February 8, 1960. King had traveled to Durham to announce his support for the lunch-counter movement because of Reverend Douglas Moore, a Durham minister who was a former classmate of King's at Boston University. When King started the 1956 Birmingham bus boycott, Moore had urged his friend to take the action nationwide, but King was not prepared to lead a mass movement at the time. From the left: Ralph Abernathy, King, Douglas Moore, unidentified protester. Photograph taken February 16, 1960. *(Courtesy of Jim Thornton,* Durham Herald-Sun*)*

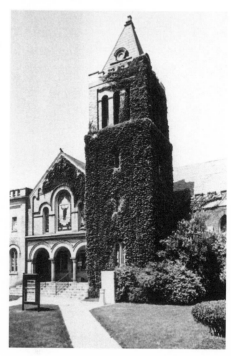

White Rock Baptist Church, where Durham's black elite worshiped. It became one of the "movement churches" after Martin Luther King, Jr., delivered his "Fill Up the Jails" speech there on February 16, 1960. That event marked the beginnings of King's commitment to nonviolent direct action. *(Courtesy of the Durham Historic Photographic Archives, Durham County Library)*

Some 4,000 blacks stage a "sit-in" at the Durham Howard Johnson's, August 12, 1962. It was the largest such protest in the city's history, and it shocked many whites, who believed that blacks desired segregation as much as whites did. *(Courtesy of Harold Moore,* Durham Herald-Sun*)*

Civil rights leaders speaking at the Howard Johnson's protest, August 12, 1962. James Farmer, national director of the Congress of Racial Equality (CORE), with microphone. Behind Farmer, second from the right in the white suit, is Floyd McKissick, the protest organizer and future CORE director. Second from the left is Roy Wilkins, executive director of the NAACP. *(Courtesy of Harold Moore,* Durham Herald-Sun*)*

Durham police arrest anti-segregation demonstrators at Howard Johnson's, May 19, 1963. *(Courtesy of Tony Rumple,* Durham Herald-Sun*)*

After several days of demonstrations against segregation, newly elected mayor Wense Grabarek (second row, extreme left) visited St. Joseph's A.M.E. Zion Church, May 21, 1963. He told the black congregation that whites now understood "the seriousness and sincerity" of their resolve. (*Courtesy of Harold Moore,* Durham Herald-Sun)

Lloyd Jacobs, the president of a splinter Klan organization, in front of Durham's City Hall at a march for open housing, 1967. (*Courtesy of Harold Moore,* Durham Herald-Sun)

(*below*) Howard Fuller (with upraised hand), the charismatic community activist who hired Ann Atwater, speaking to a crowd at a demonstration following the assassination of Martin Luther King, Jr., April 5, 1968. (*Courtesy of Harold Moore,* Durham Herald-Sun)

A policeman stands guard on Main Street after several nights of fire bomb-
ings following the assassination of Martin Luther King, Jr. Jesse Helms, then a
commentator on WRAL television, infuriated the black community by charging
that King's "violent" protest methods might have provoked the assassination.
(Courtesy of Harold Moore, Durham Herald-Sun*)*

C.P. Ellis, Exalted Cyclops of the Durham Ku Klux Klan (behind counter) with Ann
Atwater, leader of United Organizations for Community Improvement, a militant
black protest group, at the opening of the school charrette, an effort to help Durham deal with problems associated with court-ordered school desegregation. C.P.
and Ann, longtime enemies, were named co-chairs of the charrette. S.O.S., "Save
Our Schools," was the program's motto. City leaders stand at left. Photograph taken
July 7, 1971. *(Courtesy of Jim Thornton,* Durham Herald-Sun*)*

C.P. Ellis and Ann Atwater during the early 1970s, when they co-chaired a committee to confront problems associated with court-ordered desegregation in Durham. *(Courtesy of Jim Sparks,* Durham Herald-Sun*)*

C.P. Ellis and Ann Atwater outside of her house, 1995. (Photograph by the author)

CHAPTER ONE

Esse Quam Videri
(To Be Rather Than to Seem)
—North Carolina state motto

Southerners are exposed the most when they boast.
—ROBERT PARRIS MOSES

In the beginning—in 1864—Durham, North Carolina, was a scruffy cluster of shacks with under a hundred residents, surrounded by impoverished farms and linked by rutted dirt lanes that kicked up plumes of choking dust in the summer and became nearly impassable with mud in the winter. But in the span of just a few decades straddling the turn of the twentieth century, in a region still reeling from a bloody civil war and its calamitous aftermath, the town rose from obscurity to become the Jewel of the New South.

Durham transformed itself into a bustling, modern city: Electric trolley cars clattered down broad, tree-lined avenues. Newly successful businessmen erected mansions, filled them with imported objets d'art, hung costly crystal chandeliers in every room, and encircled their properties with groves of graceful maple trees and fragrant magnolias.

On warm summer evenings, entire families rode the open-air trolley out to the Lakewood amusement park, dubbed the "Coney Island of the South" by promoters. It was only a slight exaggeration. At Lakewood, teenagers joined in the new national fad of roller-skating on an indoor wooden rink. Couples danced to the latest hits while fireworks exploded overhead, or they enjoyed light comedies performed by a local stock company, in a theater that served as a casino between productions. For youngsters, there was a merry-go-round. For older children and stouthearted adults, Lakewood boasted a large roller coaster that filled the air with the clacking of metal on wood and the delighted shrieks of its riders. The truly daring, however, gamely climbed into a rattan gondola, felt hats or straw bowlers grasped tightly in hand as a hot-air balloon lofted them skyward. They rose with surprising speed into the clear North Carolina air until the din of Lakewood was a distant murmur and the entire city of Durham lay beneath them. From that altitude the streets and lanes of the city were mere lines on a page, the houses and factories a child's collection of boxes. Hills flattened into nothingness, lowlands rose until they merged with promontories, and every part of Durham was revealed and intelligible in the gelid light.

"Just like a toy village," they reported, breathlessly, to their admiring families upon returning to earth.

By 1900, Durham claimed 7,000 citizens; a decade later, nearly 20,000. The city was home to a large laboring class, a small middle class, and even a few millionaires who regularly packed up their wives and children for the Grand Tour of European capitals. "Everything here is push," wrote a local newspaper editorialist in 1906, "everything is on the move, every citizen is looking out for everything that will make Durham great."

Isolated, torpid, tattered little Durham had become the envy of the South. It was hailed as the "City of Opportunity," the "Chicago of the South," "Foremost City of the New South," and "Type-Town of the Future South."

The town's new status may have struck many Southerners as ironic, for in the years immediately following the Civil War, Durham was known chiefly as the site of one of the Confederacy's final humiliations. On April 26, 1865, General Joseph Eggleston Johnston surrendered the Southern troops to Union general William Tecumseh Sherman at a farmhouse just outside of town. Most Americans date the end of the Civil War with the rendezvous, two weeks earlier, of Generals Robert E. Lee and Ulysses S. Grant at Appomattox Courthouse. Lee had surrendered only the Army of the Potomac. Tens of thousands of rebel soldiers remained in the field all across the South.

True, they were ill fed and ill equipped, suffering from low morale and yearning to return home to their families and farms in time for spring planting. But they were still an army. Although no one considered them capable of winning the war, they could at least draw out the bloody conflict for weeks or months and inflict heavy casualties on Union troops.

After earlier negotiations had broken down, Confederate President Jefferson Davis had ordered Johnston to retreat while the politicians held out for more favorable terms of surrender. Johnston, however, would not wait. He shared the sentiment that his adversary Sherman would later so famously proclaim: that "war is hell." Physically, the Southern general resembled the owner of a dry-goods store more than a career warrior. He was a dozen years older than Sherman, with sparse gray hair and sad brown eyes. Morose by nature, there was little in his present circumstance to give Johnston any cheer. His men were starving. Much of the South already lay in ruins. The dream of an independent Confederate States of America had long since died.

"My men are daily deserting in large numbers," he informed Davis. "My small force is melting away like snow before the sun . . ." Privately, Johnston was even more forceful, telling friends that to continue fighting under such circumstances would be "criminal."

Johnston simply ignored his President's instructions (a courageous act for which Davis branded him a traitor). Seated beside Sherman at a small wooden table inside the farmhouse, he signed articles of surrender and then walked out of the dark room and into the brilliant sunlight of the North Carolina spring. Standing amidst blazing cherry blossoms, he ordered the men under his command—some 88,000 troops in North Carolina, Georgia, and Florida—to lay down their weapons. The South's defeat was official.

Durham's fortunes were about to change, however, and in an unlikely fashion. The seeds of its future magnificence were riding in the pockets and packs of Sherman's exhausted Federal troops. The returning soldiers carried the only booty available in the squalid town: the pale golden leaves of "bright" tobacco. They had looted a small tobacco factory not far from the farmhouse where the two generals thrashed out the terms of surrender. The owner, one John Ruffin Green, was ruined when his inventory of "Best Flavored Spanish Smoking Tobacco" disappeared.

It was the best thing that had ever happened to Green. After four years of eating bug-infested rations, sleeping in cold and damp tents, and slogging night and day through thickets and mud, American men had had enough of rough pursuits. They eagerly traded harsh burley tobaccos then popular for the mild and sweet-tasting bright tobacco they found in Durham. The former soldiers couldn't get enough of it; orders for Green's tobacco soon began pouring in from around the country. Green went from bust to boom in weeks, buying up whatever tobacco was available from his neighbors and shipping it off to New York, Kansas, Ohio, Iowa, Pennsylvania, Maine, California. Casting around for a company symbol, Green chose the profile of a bull. A similar image appeared to work well for another product: a popular brand of mustard. It also seemed like a good omen to Green that the condiment was made in Durham, England. Just four years after the end of the war, his company was shipping 60,000 pounds of "Genuine Bull Durham Smoking Tobacco" annually. In 1883, it sold over five million pounds.

Green started Durham down the tobacco-lined path of prosperity, but another family, of even humbler origins, was responsible for parlaying his good luck into a business empire rivaling the railroad and oil trusts of the North. This was the family of Washington Duke: the elder Duke, his three sons— Brodie, Benjamin, and James—and daughter, Mary. Together, they amassed one of the great American fortunes of their era.

For the first five decades of his life, there was nothing remarkable about Washington Duke. A small farmer before the war, and twice a widower, Duke was always on the edge of ruin, scratching a living from the lean soil of the northern Piedmont. An ardent Methodist, he was an abstemious, plain-spoken man, tall and muscular, with a dry sense of humor. Like many citizens of the upper South, Duke opposed secession. Although he briefly owned one slave, Duke was not known as a supporter of slavery, but in late 1863, when Duke was in his forties, the Confederacy began drafting men his age. Leaving his children with relatives, he went off to do his duty.

Duke was captured after the battle of Richmond and spent a few months as a prisoner before being released at war's end. With just fifty cents in his pocket, he walked 134 miles home to his farm to start life over again, growing and processing tobacco, selling it in bags labeled "Pro Bono Publico" (For the Public Good) from the back of a wagon pulled by a pair of blind mules. The W. Duke and Sons company grew steadily, thanks to the Dukes' hard work and frugality ("Wash" Duke and his sons slept in a single bed set up inside their factory). All the Dukes were involved in the family business in varying degrees, but the real force behind the company was clearly the youngest son, James Buchanan Duke, known to intimates as "Buck." Buck Duke was a man seemingly created for his rough, freewheeling times. As severe as his father, but lacking the older man's sense of humor, the brilliant young industrialist was guided by a near-religious faith in Progress, Business, and Machinery that allowed him to speak without blushing of "business temples" when discussing factories.

In 1881, the innovative Buck added a new product to the Duke line: cigarettes, already popular in Europe, but still relatively untried in America. He hired scores of skilled Jewish cigarette rollers from Poland (by way of New York) and began manufacturing and selling "Duke of Durham" cigarettes. His rivals at Bull Durham—by this time reorganized as the Blackwell Durham Tobacco Company—also made cigarettes and, as the more established company, managed to outsell him. Buck Duke was reminded of that fact several times each day when he heard his rival's huge steam whistle, designed to sound like a bellowing bull. The frustrated Buck likened the task of outselling the "Bull" to running into a stone wall.

Buck's envy of his competitor couldn't be explained in traditional business terms. There was, after all, plenty of money to be made by the two growing tobacco firms, not to mention the several smaller companies in and around Durham at the time.

But there was only one thing that could satisfy Buck Duke and the other leading businessmen of his day—Mellon, Morgan, and Rockefeller: crushing their competition. Absolute control through a monopoly was the goal, not merely building a successful business. This was the new American way of doing business: energetic and ruthless, marked by ingenious new methods of production and technologies, driven by insatiable appetites—and always on a scale as large as the new continent where it was practiced.

Buck Duke helped to shape his times. In 1884, at the age of twenty-seven, he moved to New York City, to be closer to the financial markets that pumped the lifeblood of the new industrial age. A yuppie a century ahead of the herd, Buck read only business reports, wrote almost no letters (even to his family), and for entertainment would walk the streets of New York at night, head down, counting empty cigarette packages to see if there were more of his brands or his hated competitors'. This way of business—and of life—puzzled and distressed Washington Duke.

"There are three things I never could understand," the aging patriarch once confessed. "Electricity, the Holy Ghost, and my son Buck."

It is fitting of both the man and his times that what allowed Buck Duke finally to beat the Bull and to create a true empire was his decision to gamble everything on a new and untried technology: the cigarette-rolling machine. Although the Bonsack cigarette machine could do the work of forty-eight hand rollers when it was operating correctly, in the spring of 1884, when Buck first placed a rolling machine in his Durham factory, its performance was unreliable. Other manufacturers had largely steered clear of the machines because, in addition to questions about the machinery's dependability, it was felt that the public wouldn't accept machine-rolled cigarettes. As always, Duke went his own way. He leased several of the machines, replacing all hand rollers by 1888. Once the bugs were worked out of the Bonsack machines, Duke churned cigarettes out of his factories at an unprecedented rate—823 million in 1889—and at a price his competition couldn't match.

But mechanization wasn't Duke's only weapon in the struggle for market dominance. He was also "an aggressive advertiser," observed a magazine profile of the era, "devising new and startling methods which dismayed his competitors; and always willing to spend a proportion of his profits which seemed appalling to more conservative manufacturers." Duke funneled millions of dollars into promoting his brands through newspaper and magazine advertising, sponsoring athletic teams, giving away free merchandise sporting his brand names, and including with packs of cigarettes small photographs of scantily clad women. The last technique moved his prudish father to fire off a letter complaining about the "lascivious photographs." The elder Duke informed his son that he "always looked upon the distribution of this character of advertisement as wrong in its pernicious effects upon young man- and womanhood, and therefore [it] has not jingled with my religious impulses." The photographs continued, however, as did Buck's faith in the power of advertising. Although some Americans still weren't smoking or chewing his products, "if there is enough [advertising] work put back of them," he declared flatly, "we will make them all consumers."

Even with his machines humming and advertisements for his products insinuating themselves into all aspects of American life, Duke wasn't satisfied with his market share. His competitors soon had their own rolling machines—although Duke had worked out a special arrangement with the machine's makers guaranteeing him a rate 25 percent under the best price charged any other manufacturer. His competitors also advertised heavily. (The makers of Bull Durham had, in fact, blazed the marketing path ahead of Duke, even slapping their emblematic animal on the side of the Great Pyramid in Egypt.)

On April 23, 1889, Buck Duke took the single most important action in his dynamic career. At precisely 3:30 P.M., at the posh Fifth Avenue Hotel in New York City, he convened a meeting with his four largest competitors. There, Duke announced his stunning plan: the men would weld their five companies into a single mammoth holding company. As far back as 1885, Duke had discussed less ambitious joint ventures with some of the individuals in the room, but what he now suggested was on a different scale altogether. Their company would do with tobacco what John D. Rockefeller had done with oil and J. P. Morgan with steel: it would dominate the market and absorb or wipe out virtually all other manufacturers. Although the men gathered in the room saw the benefits to such a system, it took several more meetings to overcome the mutual distrust caused by years of bitter rivalry.

"There were some pretty stormy times," recalled one of the men years after the meeting. "They would break up and wouldn't speak, and then they would get together again . . . there was a great deal of friction among these men and they were very difficult to keep talking any length of time together."

As usual, though, Duke eventually triumphed. Less than a year after the first meeting in New York, the thirty-three-year-old tycoon was named president of the newly incorporated American Tobacco Company (ATC), a sprawling holding company that would eventually swallow up 250 smaller firms, giving Duke control over four-fifths of the country's tobacco industry—excepting only cigars. In 1898, in what must have been a supremely satisfying event for Buck Duke, ATC acquired the Blackwell Durham Tobacco Company, makers of Bull Durham.

A decade later Teddy Roosevelt was in the White House, and trust-busting, not trust-building, was the new American passion. In 1911, the U.S. Supreme Court ordered Duke to carve up his tobacco octopus, but the resourceful businessman had already diversified into textiles and electric power generation. In fact, Duke's interest in his giant holding company waned soon after its creation. The satisfaction lay largely in beating his competition. With that achieved, Duke had turned his enormous talents (and equally immense acquisitiveness) to other areas, and with similar results. By 1899, the Dukes controlled all major textile mills in the Durham area.

The breakup of the ATC had little effect on Durham. Like Duke himself, his native town had long since expanded far beyond cigarette production, turning to millwork first to supply the tobacco industry with cotton bags, and later expanding

22

to manufacture hosiery and other garments. By the turn of the century, textile-mill workers outnumbered tobacco workers in Durham by a margin of two to one. While the country as a whole had endured a torturous depression during the early 1890s, Durham's businesses were so solid that the town experienced merely a slowing down in its normally frantic activity. By the opening of the new century, Durham's economic engine was once again revving at full throttle. During this period, too, the city fathers resolved to change Durham's reputation as a manufacturing center with no culture. They built new schools and improved old ones, endowed libraries, organized a music festival (the first performance was by the New York Symphony), constructed new theaters (including fantastic "picture palaces" for viewing moving pictures), formed three music schools and even a baseball team—the Durham Bulls—which began its rise to the top of the Piedmont League.

In a spasm of self-congratulation for their "Magic City," the Durham Commercial Club celebrated itself in 1913 by erecting a forty-by-fifty-foot sign on top of a downtown building. Running around a model of the globe, and spelled out in more than a thousand flashing colored lights, was a fitting incantation for the industrial age: "Durham Renowned the World Around: Progress, Success, Health, and Wealth." If Durham had earned a solid reputation throughout the nation, black people in the South held it in even higher regard. For them, the city represented something new under the Southern sun: a place where anyone could prosper, where ambition and hard work, not skin color, determined one's chances for success or failure.

"Durham! The very name has become a synonymous term for energy, pluck and business ability," declared the *Durham Negro Observer* in 1906.

> When you shout Durham! the gloomy and befogged financial atmosphere becomes clear and there is a mad rush and scramble for her bonds. When you say Durham! the wheels begin to turn, the smoke rolls in massive clouds from every stack and the sweet assuring music of busy machinery is heard. Durham! and as if by magic, everything springs into new life, the veins and

arteries of business throw off their stagnation and the bright sun
of prosperity sends its radiant beams out upon the world . . .

This gushing adoration cannot be dismissed merely as local
boosterism; black newspapers across the South described the
town in much the same terms. "There is more grace, grit, and
greenback among the Negroes in Durham and more harmony
between the races than in any city in America," said the *Atlanta
Independent* in 1921—quite an endorsement coming from a
city with its own jealous black elite. A black weekly in Richmond, Virginia, sang Durham's praises even more fervently:

> Go to Durham . . . you need the inspiration. Go to Durham
> and see the industrious Negro at his best. Go to Durham and
> see the cooperative spirit among Negroes at its best. Go to
> Durham and see Negro business with an aggregate capital of
> millions. . . . Among your New Year's resolves, resolve to go to
> Durham!

Such was Durham's universal appeal to turn-of-the-century
blacks that even W. E. B. Du Bois and Booker T. Washington, the
preeminent black leaders of this era (opinionated men who
agreed on little when it came to politics, economics, and race
relations), agreed that Durham was a model for the rest of the
nation. After visiting the city in 1903, Washington declared
that "this was the city of cities to look for prosperity of the
Negroes and the greatest amount of friendly feeling between the
two races of the South." Although less given to hyperbole than
Washington, Du Bois saw Durham in essentially the same positive light after visiting there less than a decade later. The
accomplishments of the town's black population were, he wrote,
"more striking than that of any similar group in the nation."

Blacks prospered largely because Durham was home to the
first great black-owned business in America, the North Carolina Mutual Insurance Company—"the largest Negro insurance company in the world," wrote Washington, "with assets
amounting to $100,000, owning its building, a large three-
story structure, and being operated with nothing but Negro
clerks and agents." Started on a shoestring in 1898 by a former
slave, the life insurance company grew vigorously, spinning off

a black-owned bank and a fire insurance company. Its leaders founded a black college—which became the first publicly supported liberal arts college for blacks in the United States. It provided home mortgages for hundreds of black families, people of dependable but modest means who could not have otherwise bought their own homes. And the Mutual served as the nucleus for virtually all other black enterprises in Durham. By the time of Du Bois' 1912 visit, the company had an income of more than a quarter of a million dollars and a decade later the Mutual moved its headquarters into a new six-story brick-and-marble building it had constructed on Durham's prestigious Parrish Street.

For all its importance as a source of capital and jobs for a people who lacked both, the Mutual was even more significant as an emblem of racial pride. The company symbolized the potential for "Negro Progress." It subverted the belief held by most whites, and even by many blacks, that the race brought over from Africa in chains could prosper outside of slavery only as laborers. But the Mutual thrived, and because it did, it allowed all African-Americans—even the illiterate and the poor, the former slave and the children of slaves—to point to something tangible and say, "This is what *we* did; this is what we *can* do." In the black search for the good life in America, wrote one journalist, "all roads lead to . . . the North Carolina Mutual." In part, that was because the Mutual, operating in the vacuum of the segregated and underdeveloped South, quickly assumed a range of functions and responsibilities far beyond those of a mere insurance company. A black woman in New Jersey, trying to locate relatives down South, wrote the Mutual for information. A cash-strapped congregation in rural Alabama solicited the Mutual for a donation to build a new roof. The unemployed asked for jobs; the childless, for help in finding a baby to adopt; the oppressed, for justice. Of course, the Mutual could not help everyone in all situations, but its leaders recognized the company's unique role in black life. In many respects, the Mutual was the closest thing to a government that the nation of black Americans had at that time.

The founder of the company was John Merrick, born a slave

in 1859 to a black mother and a white father. Working as a barber in Raleigh in 1880, Merrick was persuaded to move to Durham and open a barbershop there by Julian S. Carr, a leading white industrialist tired of making the trip to Raleigh for a decent haircut. An ambitious businessman in his own right, Merrick soon owned six barbershops in Durham (three for whites and three for blacks) and ran a real estate business on the side. On an October evening in 1898, Merrick and six other leading black men of Durham met in the office of Durham's only black physician, Aaron McDuffie Moore, each agreeing to put up $50 to acquire a small insurance business from the Royal Knights of King David—one of many Negro mutual aid associations in that era, with roots going back to the Free Africa Society of the eighteenth century. Merrick had been secretary of the Royal Knights since 1883 and insurance seemed like a good business opportunity for several reasons, most importantly because there was no white competition. White insurance companies didn't consider blacks a good business risk. Merrick and his group had made a wise decision. After a few lean years, the Mutual took off.

If the Mutual resembled a government for African-Americans in the new century, then C. C. Spaulding served as its head of state. Charles Clinton Spaulding left his family's farm in southeastern North Carolina in 1894 for Durham, where his uncle, the town's black doctor, Aaron Moore, lived. The twenty-year-old Spaulding worked at a variety of "Negro jobs"—dishwasher, bellhop, waiter, butler—before managing a black cooperative grocery. Eventually, Moore offered his nephew a chance to run the new insurance business, which was floundering. Spaulding proved more than equal to the task; his business sense rivaled that of Buck Duke. A white Durham judge saw in Spaulding a new type of black man, restless and ambitious. Merrick, said the judge, represented "the old-fashioned, contented Southern darkey," portly, affable, and ingratiating to whites. By contrast, the younger man, said the judge, was "lean, Cassius-like, and copper-colored, he seldom smiled. . . . All he asked of life was an open field and a fair chance. He was strictly business."

Like Buck Duke, Spaulding invested heavily in advertising, playing on the very real fears of poor blacks that their deaths would cause financial hardship for their families. "Death is pursuing you this moment," reminded one such ad. "Don't let your departing words be: 'Good-bye darling. I bequeath you my troubles and debts. Give me a decent burial.' " Premiums were only a few pennies each week, with death benefits furnishing little more than a coffin and a burial. At first, Spaulding spent his time convincing blacks that a black-run business was dependable. When given the choice between identical products offered by black and white firms, many African-Americans favored the white product. This was due, in part, to the influence of white propaganda, but black consumers also saw that Negro businesses often failed. The reason was that black firms were generally undercapitalized and managed by individuals who lacked a formal education and who had no business network to back them up. Still, Spaulding was infuriated by the bias. "Colored folks," he once complained bitterly, "think the white man's ice is cooler." Always the pragmatist, however, Spaulding developed a strategy to win blacks over. When a policyholder died, Spaulding placed advertisements trumpeting the delivery of the Mutual check as if the person had won the lottery. Not until the company's reputation was firmly established did Spaulding end the ghoulish practice.

As the business grew, so did Spaulding's influence in national Negro affairs. He served as secretary-treasurer of Booker T. Washington's National Negro Business League, on the boards of many black companies, as a trustee for black colleges, and in a leadership position in dozens of social, charitable, and service organizations. After the Depression, which the Mutual weathered with little damage, Spaulding was hailed as the "undisputed leader of the black business world." His endorsement of the New Deal was sought after and given, providing black Americans with new influence in Washington. When the Roosevelt administration looked for qualified blacks to name to high positions, it turned first to Spaulding for advice.

White Durham was proud of the Mutual's record, and, per-haps, even prouder of its own pride in it. By not slapping down the symbol of black prosperity—by aiding it in many ways, in fact—Durham had earned its reputation as a progressive Southern city. A history of Durham written in 1925 (by a white author) credits the progress of Durham's blacks first to "the character of the Negroes themselves . . ." But a second factor, says the author, "has been the policy of white people, a policy of tolerance and helpfulness."

> That fine spiritual fruit of honest toil, well expressed in the adage, "Live and let live," has characterized the attitude of the leading white men toward the colored race. This means that the Negro has been allowed to stand on his own merit; he has not been patronized as a dependent, neither has he met enmity and persecution because of his success or failure.

W. E. B. Du Bois confirmed this claim when, writing of Durham, he observed that "a Southern community is thus seen to have in its power to choose its Negro inhabitants. If it is afraid of ambition and enterprise on the part of black folks . . . then it will get the shiftless happy-go-lucky semi-criminal black man and the ambitious and enterprising ones will either sink or migrate." And Durham's reputation as a model for race relations was solidified in 1925 when the eminent black soci-ologist E. Franklin Frazier declared the city the "Capital of the Black Middle Class," writing, "Have the men of the white South recognized these brothers under the skin? Yes. They show respect for their achievements. They have been friendly to their enterprises."

In the city's everyday life, in nearly all venues, there was lit-tle of the racial tensions that marred society throughout the rest of the South. Race relations in Durham, declared a jour-nalist who lived there for several years, were "distinguished by mutual politeness" and by "little public friction between the races." In 1921, students from white Trinity College paid their annual visit to black Wall Street Church. A Trinity student spoke for the entire assemblage when he stood up and expressed the hope that there would soon be "complete understanding between white and colored races of the South." In Durham the sentiment did not sound hopelessly naive.

Forty years later, it appeared to some that the promise of racial understanding had been realized in Durham. The U.S. State Department regularly brought African dignitaries to the city, to show the world that the stories in the sensationalist press about race problems in America were exaggerated or exceptions to the rule of racial comity. The African diplomats were taken on tours of the North Carolina Mutual offices, where they were shown row after row of black workers in starched white collars. Over dinner at Schrafft's restaurant (with blacks and whites seated at the same table), they heard from the mayor that, at least in Durham, cooperation and tolerance were the order of the day. The Africans completed their tour—a final round of handshakes, the last hearty expressions of goodwill, a concluding blaze of smiles—while high above them, unnoticed in the flickering twilight, swallows rose and fell in a region of blue sky and great wandering shadows.

CHAPTER TWO

We had virtually no contact whatever with
Negroes . . . the only time I really saw them was
when we would go downtown in Durham on
occasion late in the day. The tobacco factories
would be having a change of shift. Pouring out of
the factories like black smoke from a furnace
came the thousands of Negroes who worked there.
They walked down one side of the street and we
were on the other. . . . No one really seemed to
think of them as individuals. They were just a
mass of people living their life as a race
completely apart from the rest of us.

          —RICHARD NIXON, Duke Law School student

SPRING 1953

She had been dozing lightly for the past hour, lulled by the
rhythmic swaying of the bus and the hot, still air, so that when
the driver called out sharply, "Durham!" she turned to glance
out the soot-streaked window and thought she must have
heard wrong.

This wasn't Durham.

Ann Wilson was seated in the colored section of the nearly
empty Trailways bus with two-year-old Lydia sprawled asleep
across her lap. Her anxiety increased with every tumbledown
shack that passed as the bus rumbled through "Hayti," the
black section of town. Where was the prosperity everyone back
home talked about? Where were the Negro factory workers who
rode around in shiny new cars, dressed in fancy clothes? She
knew that the stories about Durham's streets being paved with

gold were just foolish talk, but many of these streets weren't paved *at all*.

She had not wanted to leave her father's house in the first place. Her mother had died when Ann was only six years old, and now, just eighteen, she would have preferred to remain in the home William Randolph George had built with his own hands outside tiny Hallsboro, North Carolina. But she had been given no choice. Her husband, French Wilson, had found a job at the Central Leaf Tobacco factory and had sent for her and the baby, enclosing a one-way bus ticket along with his letter. Her father was a church deacon and he believed the injunction "till death do you part" to be as inviolable as "Thou shalt not murder." Ignoring her tears, he put the young mother on the bus bound for Durham, handed her a plate of cold chicken and a jug of ice water for the journey north (the bus made a meal stop but the restaurant did not serve blacks), and told her to be a good wife to French.

It wasn't that Ann didn't love her husband; far from it. She had never been happier than on her wedding day, dressed in a mended but still beautiful navy blue dress. French had never looked finer to her, even though she knew from her family's faces that he appeared silly to them. He wore a borrowed patch-pocket suit that hung so large on his slight frame that he looked like a child playing dress-up. Ann didn't care. Even the fact that it was a shotgun wedding didn't spoil the day for her. A few years before, Ann had taken to slipping out of the house with a wild group that included French—wild by the standards of rural North Carolina in the 1950s, anyway. When Ann started losing her breakfast in the mornings and sleeping all afternoon, her father fretted about the mysterious illness that had swept over his youngest child. The puzzle was cleared up when a group of older church women took their deacon aside and delicately explained matters to him—naming French as the father. With his shotgun waiting in reserve at home if he needed it, William George marched over to French's house. Sitting on the sofa, the stern father fixed his eyes on the boy and asked, "What are you gonna do?" The couple were married a week later.

French disappeared a month later, taking all their money with him. Only fourteen and pregnant at the time, Ann nearly killed herself with grief. She retreated to her room, refusing to come out for meals or even talk to anyone through the door. Her family had little sympathy for what they considered merely the histrionics of a spoiled child. Still, someone had enough compassion for her to leave Ritz crackers and orange juice beside her door each day. She left her room only at night when everyone was asleep, and then she drifted ghostlike through the house to empty her slop jar out the back door and floated back silently to her room. This continued for several months before her father's congregation once again took matters into their own hands. They crowded into her darkened room, throwing open the windows, singing hymns and praying over the grieving woman-child, exorcising the demon of grief and calling Ann back to the world in Jesus' name. Unable to resist the community's resolve, Ann emerged from her room. French reappeared shortly before the baby was born, but the months of worrying had weakened the developing fetus; Ann lost the child soon after the birth.

The couple remained together and two years later Ann gave birth to a healthy baby. They named her Lydia. Soon her husband left to take the job in the tobacco factory and, before long, summoned her to Durham.

As the bus shuddered to a stop at the terminal building, Ann searched through the blue haze of diesel exhaust for her husband among the knot of people meeting friends and relations. He wasn't there. Maybe he was inside the terminal, she hoped. She woke Lydia, tied the girl's white high-top shoes to her pudgy feet, and straightened the white ribbon in her hair. French would be happy to see his daughter, Ann thought, noting with satisfaction how cute the child looked in her green-and-white dress.

With the toddler in tow, Ann climbed off the bus and walked hesitantly into the terminal. She searched the dingy room but didn't see her husband, so she sat down on a hard wooden bench in the colored section and waited, gripping her daughter's arm so thieves wouldn't run off with her. Each minute

Ann waited, a snake of worry twisted inside her. What would she do? French had sent no phone number. She considered her situation: she and her baby were penniless in the city, where she knew no one but her husband. And he was . . . where? She had his address—311 Canal Street—but it could have been 10 Downing Street for all it meant to her. Besides, how would she hire a cab or board a bus without money? Desperate, Ann forced herself to ask the white man at the ticket window what she should do. He waved her over to a policeman who stood just outside the door of the bus station.

Ann had never talked to a policeman before, certainly not a white one, but now in tears she did as she was told. After listening to her story, the policeman whistled to a Yellow Cab idling at the curb. He gave the taxi driver French's address with instructions to take her there, but to return her to the bus station if her husband couldn't be found. The policeman said he'd pay for her bus ticket back home.

Ann's luggage—a small footlocker and a shopping bag filled with Lydia's things—fit easily into the cab's trunk. She and Lydia climbed into the backseat of the car and they drove off.

French was not at 311 Canal Street. A grim-faced woman who lived there said that yes, he rented a room in the house. The older woman stared at Ann suspiciously. Then she noticed the young child cradled in Ann's arms and smiled. "Why, you must be French's wife," she said. Her name was Minnie. She was the "landlady" of the house; she also worked at a hotel laundry and (Ann learned later) made extra money reselling bootleg alcohol.

After putting the "luggage" inside, Minnie led the young mother to her husband. Ann heard the house before she saw it. Music from a jukebox blared from the windows; men in stained overalls, factory workers, and women in frayed dresses were sitting on the crumbling front steps. Everyone had a drink in one hand and a cigarette in the other. "There's French," Minnie said, pointing through the screen door to a tangle of people inside the house. It took Ann a moment to spot him. Light-skinned, with close-cropped hair and a mustache, French peered out the door, and when he saw his wife and

34

child guilt swept across his face, but a grin replaced it as he came out to welcome them. He embraced Ann and tickled his daughter, and steered them to a nearby ice-cream parlor. Sitting beside him at last, feeling his warmth as they ate ice cream together and laughed at Lydia's efforts with a cone, Ann believed that maybe things would work out for them after all. The snake inside her was lulled to sleep.

That night, however, Ann had another surprise in store. Not only didn't they have a house to themselves, the couple and their baby had to share their small bedroom with another man who slept in one bed while Ann, French, and Lydia crowded into another. Ann went to bed first each night, before the stranger came in, and got up last each morning. It was an unbearable arrangement for her. Eventually, she and the baby moved into the dining room, sleeping on a sagging foldout bed.

It wasn't long before things soured further. What little money French earned at the tobacco factory he spent on Minnie's homemade liquor. He often disappeared for a day or two, arriving at home sullen and exhausted. Ann was forced to go to work as a domestic for a white woman. When the woman asked how much she charged, Ann quoted her the going rate back home—thirty cents an hour or three dollars for a ten-hour day. Ann didn't know that domestics got five dollars a day in Durham, and her new employer saw no reason to tell her, so she struggled to support her daughter and herself on far less than the little made by other domestics.

Among Ann's few comforts were her visits to a local church, the Jesus House of Prayer. It reminded her of worshiping back home, offering a small continuity in her life. She went only at night, however, when few people were there, because she didn't have any clothes she considered appropriate for services. When she arrived home one night after attending church, she found French furiously pacing the floor. From his shouted questions, Ann understood that Minnie had told him his wife was acting too friendly with the men who bought liquor at the house.

"Someone talks to me, I'm going to answer them," she said defiantly.

Without warning, French slapped Ann hard across the face,

knocking her into the wall. She picked up a small ax kept by the woodstove and struck French with its blunt end, catching him off guard and hurling him into and through the front door. Broken glass skittered across the floor. Without looking back, she ran out of the house and down the street to the courthouse, where she collapsed in a doorway.

The next day Ann had French arrested for beating her, but she allowed him to talk her into withdrawing the charges with expressions of contrition and promises of a new beginning. Released from jail, French immediately reverted to his old ways. This cycle continued for some time, until Ann couldn't bear his treatment anymore and moved out, eventually sharing a house with a single woman. She and French later reconciled and they had another baby, a daughter, Marilyn, but their life together remained chaotic and dismal, living in broken-down houses, working long hours for little pay. Finally, French disappeared. He sent Ann a letter three weeks later from Richmond, Virginia, where, he said, he had found a better job, and wanted Ann and the children to join him.

"I couldn't take it in Durham," he wrote. "I brought my family there, but couldn't do nothing for you." She replied with a short letter: "I already followed you to Durham," she reminded him. "I'm not following you any further."

If she was to have any sort of life at all, Ann would have to build it herself, she realized—and not wait for a husband who could not or would not support her and the children. After obtaining a divorce, Ann dropped her husband's last name and took the name of a man she dated for a time: Atwater. She continued working as a domestic, and also tended other people's children. She moved into a small house on Fowler Avenue in the Hayti area, full of rotting floorboards and holes in the walls big enough to allow birds in. The bathtub had fallen partially through the floor, listing at an angle like a ship about to sink. The spigot in the tub was broken and the water sprayed into the air. The children called it Niagara Falls. The bathroom was off the porch, and the latch to its door was broken, so that sometimes the wind would pull the door open, exposing the person sitting on the toilet. Once a month, the black landlord rode around Hayti in his new car with the windows rolled up against the dust it kicked up, collecting rents and leaving behind waves of impotent rage.

Over the years of hard work and little reward, Ann was filled with what she would later describe as a "meanness"—a shapeless and explosive anger that lay just beneath the surface and soon became as familiar and all-pervasive as the scent of tobacco that hung over the neighborhoods. Her anger was directed at more than just the landlord—the little man in a smart suit who smiled while telling her that he couldn't afford to repair her house and then scurried back into the leather-upholstered Buick and drove off. How could such a small target account for such a vast anger?

In attempting to explain her rage, Ann would say, haltingly, feeling her way as if through a darkened room, "You want your children to . . . to have things—things others have. You want . . . ice cream on the weekend. It takes something out of you. How come others can have it but you can't?"

There was nothing unique about Ann's life of struggle and pain in Durham. By 1950, most employed blacks in Durham (those lucky enough to find work) toiled as unskilled laborers. Each weekday morning Durham's white neighborhoods were invaded by an army of black women—all dressed in identical gray-and-white maid's uniforms. For all the stories hailing Durham as the home of the New Negro, blacks there lived a life not much different from that of blacks in other Southern cities. While the town's economy had stagnated following World War II, time alone doesn't account for the vast difference between the Durham praised so passionately by Booker T. Washington and the dead-end town awaiting Ann at the end of her long bus ride in 1953.

Washington's description of Hayti as a city of "neat cottages" and "well cared for children in clean yards . . . many of which were adorned with flower beds" rings false when read alongside the description of the same area—from roughly the same period—by Durham resident Pauli Murray:

> It was as if the town had swallowed more than it could hold and had regurgitated, for the Bottoms was an odorous con-

glomeration of trash piles, garbage dumps, cow stalls, pigpens and crowded humanity. You could tell it . . . [by] the smell of putrification, pig swill, cow dung and frying foods. Even if you lived on a hill just above the Bottoms, it seemed lower and danker than the meanest hut on a graded street.

In fact, all but a few blacks living in Durham were consigned to slum life. Most lived in substandard housing, lacking indoor plumbing. Without proper sanitation, disease swept through Durham's slums like an armed invader, carrying off the young, the old, and the weak. One of every three babies born to a black mother in Durham died within the first year, and surviving to adulthood was no guarantee of a long life. A majority of African-Americans in the "City of Opportunity" were dead before the age of forty.

While blacks were crowding into disease-ridden slums near downtown, whites were building mansions outside of Durham and enjoying the new luxuries bought with the tremendous profits they earned from cheap labor, black and white. The newly wealthy businessmen established sporting clubs— among others, the Quail Roost Shooting Club and the Durham Country Club (with a nine-hole golf course). Writer Ernest Seeman accurately portrayed the Durham of his youth when he described this neighborhood of "large houses and well-groomed lawns, where several of its richest and most righteous rajputs and masters of machinery lived."

Edward Parrish was typical of these Durham nouveaux riches. Given to wearing white suits and a neatly clipped white goatee, Parrish would often parade through town in his brougham carriage, his wife seated beside him, her delicate skin shielded from the sun by a lace parasol. As the tycoon outfitted his country estate, he demanded that every touch be just so, down to the selection of the family dog. "Now, I do not want a fair dog," he informed the breeder imperiously. "I want the best dog."

How is one to reconcile the terrible reality of slum life—and death—with Durham's reputation among African-Americans as the "Capital of the Black Middle Class" and as a national model for race relations? First, it is worth noting that not everyone joined in the general celebration of Durham. The *Baltimore Afro-American* warned its readers that "many things that have been said about Durham are false . . . ," and added that the city "has been advertised to death." In the same year that Booker T. Washington credited Durham with having "the greatest amount of friendly feeling between the two races of the South," a professor at local Trinity College wrote that "there is today more hatred of whites for blacks and blacks for whites than ever before." The *Cleveland Call and Post* doubted that "interracial conditions in the city are . . . better than they are elsewhere in the South."

These few voices of doubt and dissent were drowned out by the larger chorus of black leaders, both locally and nationally, who sang ceaseless hosannas to Durham, praising it as the Promised Land—despite overwhelming evidence to the contrary. The reason for this contradiction is found in the overlapping spheres of politics and that last American taboo: class. The place to begin untangling these contradictions is the North Carolina Mutual Insurance Company—symbol of "Negro Progress."

For a variety of reasons, both blacks and whites distorted the nature of this black success story and its significance to other African-Americans. The Mutual presented itself as merely the most visible face of a vibrant and economically maturing black community, but it quickly became a vehicle of and for the black bourgeoisie in Durham, separated from the bulk of the black population. In her novel *Song of Solomon*, Toni Morrison captures this distant relationship between the black working class and the Mutual. Like the faceless (and nearly nameless: "Robert Smith") insurance agent who opens the novel by leaping from a hospital roof, the Mutual was, and at the same time was not, part of the black community:

> [Smith] never had a woman that any of them knew about and said nothing in church but an occasional "Amen." He never beat anybody up and he wasn't seen after dark, so they thought he was probably a nice man.

Where many whites saw black America as a monolithic, undifferentiated mass, the African-American community has since slave days been organized along a hierarchy based in large part on skin color and assimilation into the white world. These distinctions were invisible to whites not so much because blacks tried to hide them—although they certainly had no reason to broadcast intraracial divisions to a hostile white world—as because whites simply did not care to look. Light-skinned mulattoes, often fathered by the slave owner, were favored by them and were sometimes given small privileges—an extra mouthful of food, less difficult work—in exchange for information about the activities of other, darker slaves. As Pauli Murray points out in her book of family history, *Proud Shoes:* "Even slavery had its bitter rivalries for meager advantage . . ." After slavery, she continues, color persisted as the most obvious and so the most important criterion for establishing a social hierarchy in black society.

> Among mixed bloods, one never made the mistake of calling an octoroon a quadroon or a quadroon a mulatto, although all mixed bloods were loosely called mulattoes. When people had the same parents and the proportion of white blood was not a factor, gradations of color and features determined prestige within the family. Of these, complexion had the greatest single value. Seldom was there a greater struggle for supremacy than among sisters and brothers who knew all the subtleties of caste. The wider the variations among them the more bitter the struggle . . . A mere feature which cast doubt—an off-shade coloring, bulge of nostril, fullness of lip or crinkle of hair, even the color of the gums or soles of the feet—could upset the precarious balance in a household . . .

The Mutual is a case study of this color-caste system at work. Among the company's founding triumvirate, John Merrick was the son of a black mother and a white father, and C. C. Spaulding and his uncle Dr. Aaron McDuffie Moore proudly traced their roots to a long line of mixed-race freemen. The pattern also extended into the ranks of the "Mutual family," where officials were almost always light-skinned, had "good" hair, or, at the very least, were descended from blacks who had been released from slavery long before the Civil War. The company hired young blacks with college degrees—nearly always the children of an already elite class. Over time, through intermarriage and social affiliations, a black nobility emerged in Durham, with few links to working people like Ann Atwater. The Mutual's influence in other areas—banking, real estate, education—guaranteed a nearly seamless, insular Negro ruling class. A rare working-class student at the city's premier educational institution for blacks, North Carolina College, complained that even into the 1960s the faculty there thought that "light-skinned students were more intelligent" and charged that the children "of the professional class . . . used to toss their heads and flaunt themselves around the students whose parents were black working class."

The Mutual also forged links with religious leaders in Durham that allowed them to control the most powerful of all black institutions: the church. According to historian Walter Weare, "[Spaulding] saw to it that photographs of black bishops appeared on company calendars, that every Negro minister in Durham received a Christmas gift from the Mutual, often including a crisp five-dollar bill from the president himself . . ." A visitor once marveled at the conservative influence the "Parrish Street Gang" exerted over Durham churches, singling out powerful White Rock Baptist Church, "the home church of Spaulding, Shepard, Kennedy and the town moguls."

> In this church you meet capitalism undressed and undiluted. In this church capital dominates and I don't mean chicken feed. It is an inter-locking directorate . . . When you rise to preach, you look into the faces of people . . . who are connected either by family or business with [Mutual executives] Shepard, Kennedy, or Spaulding. All of them are officials of the church. . . . Now go there and preach a red hot sermon about the proletariat.

And, indeed, when a young Adam Clayton Powell, Jr., showed up at White Rock in 1932 looking for a preaching post and outfitted in cream-colored trousers and a sharp jacket, the future firebrand was turned away. "That boy is too sporty for White Rock," snapped an elderly congregant. Eventually, the interference of the Parrish Street Gang in religious affairs led one

White Rock minister to protest attempts to "Mutualize" his church.

The Mutual, held up as an example of "what Negroes can do," was more the exception that proved the rule of black limitations in a white-dominated society, and worked to enrich only a limited number of elite blacks. That didn't prevent the company from using the race issue on occasion, urging poor blacks to hand over their nickels and dimes each week to the "Mutual man" in the name of racial solidarity—even when it meant paying rates higher than those charged by white-owned companies. "[M]any advantages which accrue to our race," said a defensive Spaulding, "more than offset this slight difference in rates."

And, of course, in convincing laboring blacks that "we're all in this together," the Mutual was assisted by a largely unfriendly white world that *did* lump all African-Americans into a single group. Despite his position as head of the largest black-owned business on the continent, C. C. Spaulding could be brutally beaten by a soda jerk at a Raleigh, North Carolina, soda fountain in 1931 for drinking a Coca-Cola in the whites-only section. News of the event not only outraged Durham blacks but bound them together—rich and poor, light-skinned and dark.

The town's inflated reputation didn't come just from the boasts of the local black bourgeoisie, however. Durham the city—a complicated jumble of prosperity and poverty, success and failure, struggle and conformity—was replaced by Durham the "Symbol of Negro Progress," in an often acrimonious debate that raged in the black community during the early decades of this century. A battle raged between two titans: the professor Booker T. Washington and the brilliant, mercurial, and quarrelsome W. E. B. Du Bois. The two fought for the hearts and minds of black America—and, at least for Washington, for the blessings of white society. At issue was nothing less than the path black Americans should take in their search for dignity, equality, and prosperity. After surviving more than three centuries of subjugation in the New World, black America stood at the crossroads. Washington pointed in one direction, Du Bois in another.

Booker Taliaferro Washington was born a slave on a small Virginia plantation in 1856—the same year that James "Buck" Duke entered the world, and less than a hundred miles away. Like Duke, Washington was above all a pragmatist who preached a gospel of industrial progress. To this doctrine Washington added the racial message that blacks should cease striving for political and social equality and depend entirely on economic advancement to lift the race—a philosophy that became known as the Tuskegee Idea (for the school in Alabama where Washington transformed his ideas into action). "The opportunity to earn a dollar in a factory just now," he declared, "is worth infinitely more than the opportunity to spend a dollar in an opera house."

Washington also advised blacks to spurn higher education, ridiculing degrees in Greek, Latin, and law as "ornamental gewgaws" and stressing the sufficiency of industrial education for his people. He explained: "We are trying to instil into the Negro mind that if education does not make the Negro humble, simple, and of service to the community, then it will not be encouraged." Southern whites nodded in vigorous agreement, thrilled to hear a black man restating the old Southern dictum "Education spoils a nigger."

In fact, all of Washington's conservative message was immensely popular with whites, and not by coincidence, for his every public utterance was carefully crafted to appeal to two audiences. To blacks he promised happier days ahead; to whites he spoke soothingly of limited incremental changes, of the need for racial harmony and the maintenance of "social standards."

"In all things that are purely social we can be as separate as the fingers, yet one as the hand in all things essential to mutual progress," Washington assured his white listeners in a speech delivered at the 1895 Cotton States Exposition in Atlanta, Georgia, an address that rocketed him to national attention. Washington's triumph was due in part to timing. Frederick Douglass, the outspoken leader of the African-American community for several decades, had died only months before the Atlanta speech, leaving a vacuum that the ambitious Washington quickly filled. Timing was also important to his appeal with whites, for Washington was well aware of the xenophobia then rising in America as immigrants poured into the country, and he exploited these emotions to the benefit of native-born blacks. Washington sympathized with whites who recoiled at "the incoming of those of foreign birth and strange tongue and habits . . ." Rather than hiring these strangers, he suggested that whites turn to

> the eight millions of Negroes whose habits you know, whose fidelity and love you have tested . . . people who have, without strikes and labour wars, tilled your fields, cleared your forests, builded your railroads . . . [W]e shall stand by you with a devotion that no foreigner can approach, ready to lay down our lives, if need be, in defense of yours . . .

Whites, particularly Northern industrialists, were only too happy to support this "moderate Negro," funding his projects and lavishing praise and honors upon him. He was a favorite on the speaking circuit of white college and business organizations, national magazines ran flattering profiles of him, and he was the first black man to dine in the White House, a guest of President Theodore Roosevelt. Durham, with its thriving insurance business, was the best proof possible that Washington's accommodationist program delivered the goods. Blacks would prosper if they just kept their noses to the grindstone and stayed out of trouble—that is, politics. The "City of Negro Enterprises," he dubbed Durham, blithely ignoring the fact that the prosperity he saw there didn't extend much beyond Parrish Street.

Using today's standards, it is easy to conclude that Washington had simply sold out to white society. Others have dismissed his campaign to court white approval as the tactics of a "favorite slave" and houseboy—both of which Washington was. While these factors may explain Washington's motivations and style, they do not help modern-day Americans understand why so many of his black contemporaries—in Durham and throughout the country—worshiped the man and supported his agenda of modest change. It is critical to note that Washington's crusade took place against a backdrop of terror and intimidation in which the genocide of black people in

America appeared a very real possibility. To understand him, and his appeal to so many blacks, it is necessary to recall their society, and the one they had only recently escaped.

The first black slaves on the North American continent arrived in North Carolina via the West Indies in 1526, on the ship of a Spanish explorer–slave trader. During the following 337 years before the Emancipation Proclamation ended slavery in 1863, an institution of enormous brutality was fashioned, its cumbersome legal underpinnings growing over the centuries. From the beginning, the cornerstone was the guarantee of white supremacy. It was enshrined in Carolina's Fundamental Constitution of 1669, which declared: "Every freeman of Carolina, shall have absolute power and authority over his negro slaves . . . ," and restated many times over the decades, including in 1829 when Thomas Ruffin, Chief Justice of the state Supreme Court, wrote: "The power of the master must be absolute, to render the submission of the slave perfect."

It is impossible for contemporary Americans to fully comprehend what it meant to live under a system in which some individuals had absolute power over others. As Stephen Williams, a survivor of that system, told an interviewer: "Man, man, folks what didn't go through slavery ain't got no idea what it was." Perhaps only those who endured the twentieth century's death camps—Hitler's, Stalin's, or Pol Pot's—can imagine the nightmare of slavery as it existed in the nineteenth-century South. While conditions varied from plantation to plantation, the majority of slaves lived a twilight existence in which no area of human relations or personal dignity was sacred. They were property—things—and so had no rights.

Codifying the treatment and rights of "free Negroes" within a slave society was always a troublesome task for lawmakers, for the mere presence of nonslave blacks threatened the established order. Uppermost in whites' minds was the fear that free blacks might start a general slave revolt. To prevent this, white lawmakers enacted a measure in 1765 banning groups of three or more blacks from gathering for any reason. Twenty years later, the General Assembly passed a law prefiguring the Nazi requirement that Jews wear yellow Stars of David. Free

Negroes were to be identified by a "badge of cloth . . . to be fixed on the left shoulder, and to have thereon wrought in legible capital letters the word FREE." (The absurdity of the law—someone required to wear the word FREE clearly wasn't— apparently didn't register with the lawmakers.)

After the Civil War, survivors of slavery in North Carolina formed Equal Rights leagues to lobby for political changes. In 1865, while white legislators gathered in Raleigh to revise the state constitution, 117 black delegates representing half of all the state's counties met across town. They drafted a message to the white delegates, calling it a "moral appeal to the hearts and consciences of the people of our State." In respectful, even friendly language, the black delegates asked "to have the disabilities under which we formerly labored removed, and to have all the oppressive laws which make unjust discriminations on account of race or color wiped from the statutes of the State." White reaction was swift and stern: white legislators sent back a message instructing blacks to end "the assertion of impractical claims for social and political rights." In the end, black North Carolinians were granted only those very limited rights enjoyed by free blacks before the war.

While blacks did win the right to vote when the Republican Party came to power three years later, and even served in various offices, the interregnum lasted less than a decade. In 1876, as part of a deal that put Republican Rutherford B. Hayes into the White House, Southern blacks were abandoned by the North. Federal troops were withdrawn from the region and former slaves left to the tender mercies of Dixie whites. There followed a period of political repression and outright physical violence against blacks only slightly less dire than slavery, which historian John Hope Franklin has termed "one of the most merciless, terror-driven assaults in the annals of modern history." Roving groups of armed white men (called Red Shirts) waged a reign of terror against blacks and Republicans. One of the worst incidents of political violence took place in the town of Wilmington, North Carolina, on November 10, 1898, when 400 armed and mounted Democrats stormed through the black section of town, burning the offices of a Negro newspaper and assassinating black officeholders. Thirty blacks were massacred that day.

White leaders—former planters—were clearly fighting to regain their antebellum positions of political and economic privilege. Since they couldn't get the support of a majority of Southern whites for that agenda, they buried the issue of class altogether and instead spoke of reestablishing white supremacy, a popular theme with all members of the race. "North Carolina is a white man's state," cried the leader of the state Democratic Party to a cheering crowd, "and white men will rule it"—as if there was any danger of blacks seizing control of the government.

The Democrats' most effective method for generating support was to play on the white fear of imposed "social equality." What they were really talking about was the need to protect Southern women from the depravity of black men, who—whites all knew—were sexual brutes craving white female flesh. That message was always subtly present in Democratic appeals to white voters—and sometimes not so subtly. Once, the Durham White Supremacy Club sponsored a parade float with sixteen young women dressed in virginal white and sporting banners with the slogan "Protect us with your vote." This combination of sexual fears and political power was an enormously potent and dangerous mix. Frantic to escape the new violence caused by it, blacks, called Exodusters, streamed out of North Carolina heading for Western states.

The Democrats first created whites-only primaries to keep blacks from office. Then, as the white elite increased its power, they used literacy tests and property requirements to strip blacks of the vote. (To maintain race unity, poor, uneducated whites were exempted through "grandfather" and "good character" clauses.) Where blacks had been able to serve on juries and share public accommodations with whites, Jim Crow laws were passed denying them these rights. By the turn of the century, white supremacy had been reestablished.

"Two snakes full of poison" is how Patsy Mitchner, a former slave, summed up her experience before and after the war. "Their names was slavery and freedom."

This was the world blacks faced when Washington preached

accommodation, a society in which the call for the most elementary human rights, framed in the least objectionable manner possible, might be viewed as treachery, in which a wrong word or mistaken gesture often led to violent death. Washington offered dispirited blacks a path that, though slow, at least led toward progress, and that did so without incurring the deadly wrath of whites, who controlled nearly all institutions—the courts, the legislatures, the schools, the press, the police. Given these circumstances, it's not surprising that so many blacks agreed with Washington. What is more remarkable is the fact that, despite the dangers and odds against them, a significant number of African-Americans pushed for full and immediate equality as promised in the Constitution, spurning Washington's safe path for the high and perilous road blazed by William Edward Burghardt Du Bois.

The first great black American leader born outside the South, the Harvard-educated Du Bois dared to confront not just the white elite but also the black elite—Washington and his followers—*and* the inchoate culture of materialism that was then beginning to remake America. As a young professor at Wilberforce College in Ohio, Du Bois had initially praised Washington's 1895 speech, telegraphing his congratulations "upon your phenomenal success at Atlanta—it was a word fitly spoken." That sentiment would soon change. In his 1903 book, *The Souls of Black Folk*, Du Bois began by admitting Washington's genius in "grasp[ing] the spirit of the age . . . triumphant commercialism," calling him "the most distinguished Southerner since Jefferson Davis . . ." (a wholly sarcastic compliment, as Du Bois biographer David Levering Lewis has pointed out, and a harbinger of what lay ahead). Then Du Bois tore into Washington for the older man's lack of a spiritual counterbalance to "the evils of Get and Grab." And in racial issues, wrote Du Bois, "Mr. Washington's programme practically accepts the alleged inferiority of the Negro races." It was fine that Washington's views about race were fostering a spirit of reconciliation between the North and the South, he continued,

> but if that reconciliation is to be marked by the industrial slavery and civic death of . . . black men, with permanent legislation

into a position of inferiority, then those black men, if they are really men, are called upon to oppose such a course by all civilized methods, even though such opposition involves disagreement with Mr. Booker T. Washington. We have no right to sit silently by while the inevitable seeds are sown for a harvest of disaster to our children, black and white.

Du Bois didn't completely reject the economic path set out by Washington—but he insisted that commerce alone wouldn't achieve the ultimate ends both he and Washington wanted: the full liberation of their people. Like Washington, Du Bois found much to praise in Durham, singling out the town's "new 'group economy' that characterizes the rise of the Negro American"—a segregated economy in which blacks traded primarily with one another and so established a full range of enterprises that paralleled the white community: banks, schools, manufacturers, doctors.

But it wasn't enough, declared Du Bois.

Washington, he said, was wrong in telling whites that blacks didn't want or need political and social equality or higher education. "Negroes," wrote Du Bois, "must insist continually, in season and out of season, that voting is necessary to modern manhood, that color discrimination is barbarism, and that black boys need education as well as white boys."

Du Bois attacked Washington and his followers not only for abandoning politics but also for repeating demeaning stereotypes about blacks. Washington incorporated "darky" jokes into speeches before white audiences and ridiculed blacks who preferred loud suits to more conservative clothes. John Merrick, the ambitious barber who founded the Mutual Insurance Company, also played along with racist stereotypes to enhance his popularity with white business leaders in Durham. In a 1900 advertisement, the former slave boasted that the barbershop he ran for whites was sterilized, "Negro and all."

For both Merrick and Washington these were tactics used to wrest some small measure of control over their lives from a dominating white world. In public, Washington railed against court challenges to Jim Crow laws. Privately, he secretly bankrolled them. According to his peers, Merrick could with "great poise, tip his hat to the white man and at the same time call him a son-of-a-bitch under his breath." Behind the "hypocritical smile" and "feigned goodwill" was "a hatred hidden by fawning," revealed Louis Austin, publisher of Durham's influential black newspaper, the *Carolina Times*. As the twentieth century opened, however, "wearing the mask" (as the poet Paul Laurence Dunbar called this dissembling) was fading from favor—a reminder of slavery as unwelcome as the bullwhip or leg iron.

By the second decade of the twentieth century, black America had come to a fork in the road and had to choose: accommodation to white supremacy or unyielding opposition to it. Du Bois and a coalition of progressive blacks and whites formed the National Association for the Advancement of Colored People (NAACP) in 1909–10 primarily to counter Washington's influence. Beneath his gentle exterior, Washington was a ruthless and jealous man who commanded a powerful network of supporters and spies, dubbed by the opposition the "Tuskegee machine." The machine contested Du Bois at every turn, ensuring that the NAACP's magazine, *Crisis*, was banned from Negro college campuses and pulling strings in an attempt to destroy Du Bois and his movement.

Durham was a microcosm of this national black debate. After being warned by the local white establishment that "if the negro is to continue to make politics his chief aim . . . there can be but one ending," Durham's black elite lined up behind Washington. Unlike poor black workers such as Ann Atwater, wealthy and middle-class blacks saw little to gain and everything to lose from joining Du Bois. The Mutual's newspaper was quite open about the company's determination to resist Du Bois' call for an aggressive challenge to white rule. "We have turned from pursuing the phantom of political spoils," it proclaimed, "and are settling down to development along safe lines." John Merrick argued that all blacks should avoid politics, demanding, "What difference does it make to us who is elected?" In his only known speech, Merrick charged:

> Negroes have had lots of offices in this state and they have
> benefited themselves but very little . . . nothing comparing with

what they could have done along business and industrial lines had they given it the same time and talent. . . . Let us think more of our employment and what it takes to keep peace and to build us a little house and stop thinking we are the whole Republican party . . .

Dr. James Edward Shepard, one of the Mutual's founders, who quit the firm to devote himself to education, was also a Washington man. With the financial backing of Durham's white leaders, Shepard founded North Carolina College, a school based on Washington's theories of self-improvement. At the college's first commencement in 1912, Shepard applauded the white president of Southern Railways as he exhorted the newly trained black teachers to "above all . . . avoid creating in the minds of your pupils dissatisfaction with the opportunities that are open to them."

C. C. Spaulding, the proud, almost taciturn office manager of the Mutual who assumed full control of the firm in 1923, was in many ways a transitional figure, linking the past, as represented by Washington, to the future, which belonged to Du Bois and his more militant partisans. A complex man—as those caught between eras often are—Spaulding removed the grinning mask of servility, but could never quite put it aside. When white salesmen asked to see "Charlie," Spaulding's secretary was encouraged to respond, "Charlie? We don't have a Charlie here, do we, ladies?" Yet in a 1941 speech, this same man blamed blacks themselves for discrimination, citing the effects of ignorance, crime, and poor work habits. He founded a black political institution, the Durham Committee on Negro Affairs, which developed into the most dynamic organization of its kind in the nation, but he consistently refused to back a more fundamental program of reform that would have aided poor blacks. Spaulding, like the majority of the black elite in Durham—and throughout the nation—didn't challenge the system of white domination so much as attempt to work within it. The accommodationist philosophy that guided the company could not have been more obvious had the legend "Don't Rock the Boat" been chiseled in stone above the Mutual headquarters's massive doors.

While this convoluted structure of race and class profited the black elite, it would be wrong to label Spaulding, Merrick, and the rest as corrupt. Most of them were generous, self-sacrificing, and even, in their own way, courageous. In general, they were very good men caught in a very bad system, a system which had grown out of slavery, and which was in many ways an extension of that terrible institution, merely adapted to new circumstances. Under slavery, the primary route to freedom for blacks, short of running away (with its risk of recapture, physical torture, or death), was to be manumitted—legally released from slavery—by the master after "years of loyal service." While this was sometimes done while the master still lived, manumission of slaves was more commonly a feature of wills. The unwritten rule that governed this process was simple: black submission to white rule in exchange for freedom— or at least the *possibility* of freedom—someday.

Spaulding and other black accommodationists counseled blacks to continue this tradition in the age of Jim Crow. The word "loyalty" appears again and again in documents of this time, beginning with Booker T. Washington's reminder to whites that "we have proved our loyalty to you in the past, in nursing your children, watching by the sick-bed of your mothers and fathers, and often following them with tear-dimmed eyes to their graves . . ." When rumors spread that black soldiers would desert American forces in World War I, C. C. Spaulding organized a rally at which 200 blacks swore allegiance to America while the North Carolina Mutual filled the air with patriotic songs. In 1944, when Northerners were applying pressure on the South to end the most blatant forms of racial discrimination, NCC's president, James Shepard, demonstrated his loyalty to the South (if not his race) by telling a national radio audience that Dixie would solve its problems by itself and needed no advice from outsiders. Shepard, Merrick, Spaulding, and Washington had few illusions about what they were advocating: loyalty to a social system that, stripped of the flowery nostalgia about the "Southern way of life," was based on white supremacy. To the black elite, though, this was the best method of earning freedom, a technique proven under slavery, and so most likely to show results under a system not so very different from slavery. Hadn't they, in fact, prospered to an unprecedented degree under Jim Crow?

The group that gained the most from having a divided black community, of course, was the ruling class of Durham's leading white families. The Dukes, the Carrs, and the Parrishes all depended on the small number of affluent and politically conservative blacks to act as a buffer between themselves and the potentially more aggressive black masses in Hayti. Spaulding and his friends played this role for decades. When black veterans returned from overseas following World War I and demanded the democracy for which they had risked their lives, the Mutual leader counseled a "go slow" approach, arranging meetings between black and white groups to defuse a dangerous situation. He helped avert the race riots that convulsed more than a score of other cities, killing many blacks, but his efforts also shielded the established (and white-dominated) social, economic, and political order in Durham. In 1933, Spaulding derailed the first attempt by the NAACP to integrate higher education in America. In March of that year, the NAACP and a small group of local blacks led by newspaper publisher Louis Austin encouraged Thomas Hocutt, a graduate of the all-black North Carolina College, to file a petition in Superior Court seeking enrollment at the University of North Carolina, Chapel Hill, School of Pharmacy. For Durham's black elite, pressing for desegregation was still too radical an idea—and one which, if implemented, would threaten their own economic well-being. Spaulding summoned the participants to Mutual headquarters, where he denounced them as "rabble-rousers" whose thoughtless actions would spark violence.

"If my actions will cause a race riot, you had better grease up your muskets," replied the independent Austin, "for I am going back Monday to pursue this cause." Spaulding prevailed, however, through his close friend at NCC, James Shepard, who refused to send Hocutt's transcript to Chapel Hill.

A few years later, the white power structure called on Spaulding again, this time to halt a riot already in progress. In June 1937, black Durhamites ran into the streets, celebrating

Joe Louis' victory in the ring over a white man. Pent-up black rage soon turned cheering to stone throwing, aimed at whites driving through Hayti. Durham's police chief told Spaulding to get "your people" off the street—which the president of the Mutual quickly did.

In the black slums of Hayti, where people like Ann Atwater worked hard but saw little hope of ever getting ahead, feelings about Spaulding and the other "Big Negroes" were complex. On the one hand, there was an undeniable and widespread sense of pride, even of collective achievement, in the successes of Spaulding and the Mutual. Novelist Gwendolyn Parker accurately portrays this admiration for the "Federated," her stand-in for the Mutual:

> The gleaming building of the Federated, as large as anything the white man might build, may have been founded by these men, but it grew and prospered from all of the dimes that were spent on its insurance policies, and as a result, all the colored people regarded the Federated as their own. . . . The individual triumphs were the triumphs of colored men everywhere, and . the individual successes heralded all the triumphs to come.

But admiration was often tinged with resentment for these unelected black "leaders" who, after achieving a level of comfort and even luxury for themselves and their families, preached patience to those still living and dying in squalor. "Negro masses," wrote newspaperman Austin, "are suspicious of all Negro leaders who are so smart they never ruffle the feathers of the oppressors." When these same leaders were quoted as saying that Durham had "good" race relations, a black tobacco worker retorted, "I guess things are pretty good for them."

In 1943, a strike at the R. J. Reynolds factory in nearby Winston-Salem brought the always present but rarely discussed class divisions within that black community to the surface. Jobs there, as in the Durham factories, were segregated by race, with whites operating machinery (and earning higher wages) and blacks toiling in "preparation"—stemming, cleaning, and conditioning tobacco—under appalling conditions for low pay. When a union organized to represent black workers there, local black professional men sought to prevent the move, which they said would hurt race and labor relations. A group of these white-collar men sent a letter to the editor of a local newspaper, urging black workers to vote against the union. Once again playing the role of the race-and-class buffer, they advised workers to forget about collective bargaining and to pursue instead the old Washingtonian agenda of "good will, friendly understanding, and mutual respect and co-operation between the races."

This time the black workers refused to defer to the black aristocracy. To everyone's surprise, the workers, half of whom were women, fired back their own letters to the editor, stressing the class division between them and those blacks who criticized the union movement. "Our leaders always look clean and refreshed at the end of the hottest day, because they work in very pleasant environments," charged Reynolds worker Mabel Jessup. "All I ask of our leaders is that they obtain a job in one of the factories as a laborer and work two weeks. Then write what they think." Another employee wrote that these leaders "have always told us what the white people want, but somehow or other are particularly silent on what we want." An independent group of workers put the issue even more simply: "We feel we are the leaders instead of you."

Winston-Salem's Local 22 of the Food, Tobacco, Agricultural, and Allied Workers was a unique organization, with the union hall functioning as the center of a rich cultural and political community. Members staged plays, sponsored sports teams and sewing circles, and taught courses in black history and current events. The local city library's collection of African-American books was limited to a few dog-eared copies of Booker T. Washington's *Up from Slavery* and a few other equally innocuous works. "They didn't have books by Aptheker, Du Bois, or Frederick Douglass," recalled a member of Local 22, and added proudly, "But we had them at *our* library." The union championed other progressive groups as well. After it sponsored a membership drive for the foundering local branch of the NAACP, the civil rights organization grew from 11 to nearly 2,000 members, making it the largest affiliate in the state.

Uncowed by either white employers or the black elite, Local 22 might have ignited the first stirrings of a unique mass movement in the American South: a grassroots labor organization composed of roughly equal numbers of men and women, demanding better working conditions, increased worker democracy, *and* civil rights. For one brief moment all eyes were on Winston-Salem. A visiting reporter from the *Pittsburgh Courier* found "a growing solidarity and intelligent mass action that will mean the dawn of a New Day in the South. One cannot visit Winston-Salem and mingle with the thousands of workers without sensing a revolution in thought and action. If there is a 'New' Negro, he is to be found in the ranks of the labor movement."

But the New Day in the South had not yet arrived. Instead, the Cold War became an excuse to crush scores of progressive American movements, and Local 22—already years ahead of its time in challenging racism and worker exploitation and with a leadership that included Communists—was easy prey for an industrialist "anti-Red" campaign. The trade union movement as a whole buckled under fierce right-wing attacks and quickly abandoned black workers. The incipient movement in North Carolina collapsed. It was, in the words of historians Robert Korstad and Nelson Lichtenstein, a heartbreaking "opportunity found and lost."

That storm weathered, life went back to normal. On the surface—where the elites of both races attempted to live their lives—all was serene. Black leaders continued to nudge white society for small concessions while at the same time attempting to stifle the more urgent demands of a frustrated black poor. Even C. C. Spaulding, heir to Booker T. Washington, could feel the tremors coursing beneath placid Durham. "There is a growing feeling on the part of Negroes," he informed whites, "that the white people . . . are not treating them right. . . . The younger element of Negroes in North Carolina do not believe in the leadership of the older Negroes. They think that the older Negroes represent the servile type and that a more aggressive leadership is needed . . ."

White leaders had heard this rhetoric before, however, and

chose to ignore it. They told themselves that what Spaulding sensed was nothing more than the usual "grumblings" of a few "bad" Negroes. They told themselves that Durham was still the Magic City, the home of Duke and Carr, of Merrick and Moore. They repeated to one another all the clichés about racial harmony that they had been mouthing for the last half century, about the long but steady climb of progress, about Durham being "different" from the rest of the South. And in the end they managed to convince themselves so completely that when the quake finally came, when Ann Atwater and hundreds of other poor black residents of Durham's slums poured into the streets demanding the reconcilement of myth and history, of dream and reality, the white families who had ruled Durham like monarchs fabricated a credible display of shock, indignation, and even betrayal.

CHAPTER THREE

It is a great mistake to assume . . . that there is a
conflict in interest between different classes of
citizens—certainly if comparative wealth is the basis
of the classification.

—JAMES "BUCK" DUKE, 1915

SPRING 1939

The whoops and shouts of children at play rose from the
schoolyard into the humid air, mingling with the languorous
scent of tobacco that drifted over from the warehouses on Pettigrew Street. At the bottom of a stairwell leading to the school
basement, a boy crouched, furtively eating his lunch. Although
he was a short twelve-year-old, knots of muscles already
spread beneath his worn and patched shirt. His eyes were the
color of pecan shells and his long, stringy hair was just a shade
darker. To the boy, the sounds were alarm bells ringing off the
bricks of the school building, making his stomach ache as he
forced down his lunch of a browned biscuit smeared with lard.
Poor folks' food.

"Hey, C.P."

The voice came from above, but the boy did not look up.

"I said, 'Hey, C.P.'"

He heard a second child join the first. He knew that they
were smiling, nudging each other as they stared down at him.

"Whatcha eating, C.P.? Whatcha got for lunch?"

"Yeah. Sure smells good, C.P."

He still said nothing, only continued chewing the greasy
dough. Just then the school bell clanged recess to an end and
C.P. heard the two boys at the top of the stairs give a final

snicker before tearing off. He waited another minute until the playground fell silent. Then he dropped the last piece of biscuit to the ground, wiped his hands on his pants, and trudged up the stairs, across the yard, and into school.

Claiborne Paul Ellis, known to everyone as C.P., lived just a weed patch north of the railroad tracks separating white Durham from black. The houses were surprisingly alike on either side of this crucial dividing line: small, dark, and cramped. They had front porches in identical states of disrepair, tin roofs warped and rusted to a similar dull red hue, and flyblown outhouses in each dirt backyard. At night these houses glowed with the flickering yellow light of kerosene lanterns that lent the district an aura considered quaint—by those who didn't have to live there. This was East Durham, an area of run-down houses built around the turn of the century by the textile manufacturers for their workers. C.P.'s father, Paul Ellis, had gone to work as a mill hand when he dropped out of school in the fourth grade. He had moved his young family to Durham in 1927, when C.P. was only a few months old, from a small town nearby when the mill there had closed.

African-Americans have always occupied the lowest level of the Southland's great social pyramid, but as the new century progressed the region seemed unable to decide who it despised more: blacks or poor whites. Within the ranks of the poor whites, another division became blurred during this period, the one separating the unemployed "white trash" from the working poor, primarily mill hands like Paul Ellis. In truth, very little separated the experiences of these two groups. Mill employees labored at dangerous jobs under miserable conditions—and for poverty wages—breathing in cotton dust until their lungs were brown with the stuff and they suffocated. At first, there was at least the possibility for advancement in the mill, but over time Southern businessmen began sending their sons to Northern colleges where they learned all the latest management techniques. An army of efficiency experts returned to the South, stopwatches in hand, to assume their duties as supervisors, wringing every last ounce of productivity from the workers while blocking their rise in the new corporate world. Before long, workers were simply born into mill life and very few escaped it. And although it was their underpaid labor that transformed Durham into the Jewel of the New South, their presence in the "better areas" of town was not welcome. On the rare occasions that they ventured out of their neighborhoods, mill hands were immediately recognizable by their deathly white pallor. Passing them on the street, businessmen might smile to one another and exchange a single sharp-edged word: "linthead."

Of course, the owners held a far more positive view of mill life and of their own role in the world of their making. James "Buck" Duke could praise Durham's classless society, oblivious to the fact that at around the same time he was paying $1,250 for a season's use of a private box at the Metropolitan Opera House in New York City, the highest-paid mill hands back in Durham were receiving only $320 for a year of hard labor.

The paternalism that governed relations between white planters and slaves in the Old South was extended in the New South to include poor white factory workers. In the early days, mill owners greeted workers by their first name each morning, inquiring about the health of children, who might also be known by name. If a worker fell ill, the mill boss would often pay the doctor's bill. One owner hired a full-time nurse to care for workers and their families. When a smattering of education was considered a good thing for workers, some mills offered classes at night at no charge. Like a stern but caring "daddy," William Erwin, the tall, bespectacled president of the Erwin Cotton Mills, pedaled his bicycle around the mill village in West Durham in the evenings, enforcing a 10 P.M. "lights-out" rule. For the workers he referred to as "my people," Erwin built a huge auditorium where they attended concerts and plays, movies and flower shows. Later, he added a swimming pool, tennis courts, and even a small zoo.

Erwin's beneficence, however, did not silence the rising critics of a system that traded informal "favors" for complete submission to the owner's authority. "His mill villages are better than most other companies," admitted one union leader, "but he preaches baths, swimming pools, and that kind of thing and then won't pay a wage that is anything near even a living wage."

In fact, most of the improvements dribbled out by mill owners over the years were really meant to prevent unions from taking hold in the South. Mill owner Julian Carr went so far as to implement at his Durham Hosiery Mills a system of "industrial democracy" based on the U.S. federal government. Employees elected a "house of representatives" and Carr appointed foremen to the "senate." The only thing this scheme lacked was democracy, for ultimately power resided exclusively in the "executive branch," which could veto any measures passed by the "legislature." Only Carr family members served in this branch of "government."

Where workers couldn't be enticed into rejecting unions, owners simply mobilized to crush the movement. They were usually successful. When the first tobacco union was organized in Durham in 1918, the Sovereign Cigarette Company responded by firing the union activist they considered the "ringleader." Workers formed a committee to complain to management about the firing and they, too, were immediately dismissed. The few strikes these weak unions dared to attempt won no concessions, and usually resulted in the dismissal of strikers and their nonstriking family members. Firing meant not only the loss of a job but the loss of housing, too, since most workers lived in mill villages. Given the power of the mill owners, it is not surprising that unionization efforts were, in the words of one knowledgeable commentator, "mere foam before passing gusts."

The Durham industrialists were quick to silence any opposition to their policies, whether it came from inside or outside of the mills. A newspaper editor learned this lesson when he dared to criticize the Dukes' harsh treatment of workers—including the practice of whipping children in the mill. His printing business mysteriously dropped off and then a creditor, "backed, as I learn, by the Dukes," called in a loan. "[U]nless matters improve," he wrote union friends, "[I] will be compelled to sell my office at a great sacrifice and leave the city." Even the powerful president of the University of North Carolina in neighboring Chapel Hill was not immune from these attacks. When he attempted to host a forum on industry and race relations, a mill owner (and member of the university board of trustees) pulled strings behind the scenes in a futile attempt to oust the president.

Organizationally unable and psychologically unprepared to challenge the rule of the Big Men, as the business leaders were known, the mill hands simply endured their lot. They were raised on an ethic that extolled the power of the individual to shape his or her life, and then forced into a world where they were treated like cogs in a vast machine. Many drank to mask the absurdity of their lives. Others turned to extreme religious movements, including snake handling. Crowded into one-room church buildings, the faithful clutched live rattlers, copperheads, and cottonmouths to their bosoms or draped the snakes around their necks while they prayed in a spiraling frenzy of religious passion. It was a perfect metaphor for their lives.

"So it's bizarre," observed one Southern intellectual. "So? Their *world* is bizarre."

One of these little men, Paul Ellis was descended from yeomen farmers forced into tenancy and then off the land altogether when tobacco prices plummeted, thrusting him and thousands like him into the new industrial society that was transforming the South. C.P.'s mother, Maude, was an emotionally distant figure, already defeated by hard work and poverty by the time C.P. was born. Paul Ellis toiled on the night shift at the mill and painted houses during the day in a vain effort to raise his family a notch or two. The family did not prosper, however, and, in fact, struggled merely to stay in place. Faced with such daunting circumstances, Paul Ellis drank himself into oblivion every weekend, often turning violent when intoxicated. Years later, C.P. was still haunted by the memory of his father, drunk and wielding an ice pick on the porch of their house, while he huddled inside with his mother behind the locked door.

C.P. and his one sister were raised in chaos and poverty, as their parents had been, and the future held for them nothing more than it had for those who had gone before: a few years of schooling and then the mills. If they didn't die there, amidst the chattering machinery and cotton dust, they could look forward to a brief and exhausted "retirement" before returning to the red Piedmont soil, their lives having slipped away, trivial and unnoticed.

This being the South, however, another element defined their world: race. W. E. B. Du Bois writes movingly about the moment he discovered he was black, as a young child in school. The class, which had both blacks and whites in it, exchanged visiting cards. "The exchange was merry," he recalled, "till one [white] girl, a tall newcomer, refused my card,—refused it peremptorily, with a glance. Then it dawned upon me with a certain suddenness that I was different from the others; or like, mayhap, in heart and life and longing, but shut out from their world by a vast veil."

C. P. Ellis experienced a similar moment of awakening, when he first realized that he was white. Of course, he had always known that his skin was white, just as Du Bois was never under any illusions about the color of *his* skin. But race in America has always been a matter more of ideology than of genetics, and during this era there was usually one moment for most Southerners (of either color) when race became life's fulcrum. For C.P., it occurred when he was eight years old, playing football in a weedy field with a group of black children who lived just over the railroad tracks. It was, of course, whites against blacks. After the black team had won and the game was breaking up, one of C.P.'s teammates, miffed by the loss, yelled at the departing opponents, "You niggers get back across the track."

Probably the boy meant nothing much by it. Certainly the black children did not take the insult too seriously, for the games between the two groups continued on the following Sunday, but for C.P. the world had changed instantly. In that moment he understood that blacks were not simply black, they were niggers. More than that, he realized (and thrilled to the recognition) that he, a white boy, poor as he was, was not a nigger—could never be a nigger.

"Yeah," C.P. called out then, his voice deepened with new authority, "you *niggers* need to get back home."

The word had an electric crackle to it; saying it aloud produced the same feeling you got when you grabbed a snake in your bare hands. Shouting it out to the backs of black boys already disappearing into the bushes that flanked the railroad tracks, C.P. felt a tingle coursing through his body.

It was a new sensation for the boy: the feeling of power.

As mothers appeared on porches one by one throughout the mill village, calling their children's names, C.P. reluctantly wandered home, dusk descending, the pale yellow lamplights sputtering on in houses as he passed. Over the family's meager supper, he and his father talked about the Durham Bulls' latest victory and C.P. managed to wheedle a promise from his father to take him to the next ball game. The Bulls had won the Piedmont League pennant a few years back, and while they hadn't yet repeated that feat, several promising new players had been recruited that year.

As he climbed into bed that night, C.P.'s thoughts lingered on the upcoming game at the newly built ballpark, with its unique round tower that reminded the boy of a castle. Images formed and dissolved before his closed eyes. He saw men, resplendent in white uniforms, running effortlessly backward against a field of deep green. Fly balls fell from the sky and smacked into leather gloves. There were hot dogs and peanuts, and surrounding him was the scent of tobacco and whiskey. As he drifted into sleep, the images tumbling into one another, that word still clung to his lips like crumbs of bread: *nigger, nigger, nigger.*

It was not always so in the South. Four decades earlier, a white Southerner—the son of slave owners—paced across a platform before a packed audience of poor farmers and workers, both white and black, imploring them not to head down the road of racial politics. "You are made to hate each other," he told the crowd. "You are deceived and blinded that you may not see how this race antagonism perpetuates a monetary system which beggars you both . . . The colored tenant . . . is in the same boat with the white tenant, the colored laborer with the white laborer . . ."

The speaker was Tom Watson, a charismatic leader of the Populist Party, the political arm of an agrarian economic crusade that, for a brief moment, looked as if it might topple the emerging New South oligarchy. The mass movement of discontented farmers burst out of Texas in the mid-1880s like a flood-swollen river over its banks, and swept across the country, spawning member-owned mills and warehouses, steamboat lines, banks, insurance companies, and newspapers. The original organization, the Farmers' Alliance, was for whites only, but an affiliated Colored Farm Alliance was soon started and quickly attracted more than one million members. With the rise of the Populist Party in 1892, farmers and laborers formed the first mass multiracial coalition in the country's history. There has never been a third-party movement to match it, not in the number of electoral victories it won, nor in the feeling of class unity across racial lines it engendered. Populist candidates, black and white, campaigned together throughout the South, speaking from the same podium. If that doesn't sound revolutionary today, consider that as recently as 1959 the television networks refused to broadcast speeches by blacks to the Republican and Democratic national conventions, cutting to commercials rather than offending white viewers in the South. And yet, more than a half century earlier, crowds of destitute Southerners, black and white, stood shoulder to shoulder cheering Tom Watson when he promised to "wipe out the color line and put every man on his citizenship irrespective of color."

But the movement eventually failed. The power of the oligarchy, fueled by trusts and giant holding companies, was too great, and appeals to racial solidarity were ultimately irresistible to white Southerners. One of the great tragedies of Southern history is that many of the most progressive politicians—who backed low interest rates, tax and educational reforms, and policies favoring small farmers—were most willing to play the race card to win elections. Tom Watson himself, who had spoken with passion and idealism about wiping out the color line, became one of white supremacy's greatest supporters. He joined the fight to disfranchise blacks and ended his life as a United States senator railing against not only blacks but Jews and Catholics as well, and was admired and supported by the Ku Klux Klan.

The Big Men of Durham learned an important lesson from the Populist affair: the best way to preserve the status quo was to keep blacks and whites fighting each other. It was clear that if workers of the two races ever united they could challenge the industrialists' rule. Partly by design, then, and partly by custom, blacks and whites were kept apart in the tobacco factories, working on different floors and even in separate buildings. Whites received the higher (though still inadequate) wages and better jobs, operating machinery and supervising other workers. Blacks were relegated to the "dirty" jobs of stemming and sorting, where they earned low wages.

Predictably, black employees resented their white counterparts: "You're over here doing all the nasty dirty work," recalled a black female tobacco worker. "And over there on the cigarette side white women over there wore white uniforms." Where black women cleaned manure from tobacco leaves, the stench was so bad that the women stuck orange slices in their mouths to keep from vomiting. "They did not treat us black folks right. They worked us like dogs," lamented one worker, concluding (in words that would have made even stolid old Buck Duke smile), "Them white women think they something working doing the lighter jobs."

Even a man as perceptive as W. E. B. Du Bois for years viewed the world exclusively through the lens of race. "I was bitter at lynching," he confessed, "but not moved by the treatment of white miners in Colorado or Montana. I never sang the songs of Joe Hill, and the terrible strike at Lawrence, Massachusetts, did not stir me, because I knew that factory strikers like these would not let a Negro work beside them or live in the same town." A different system was used at the textile mills, which, with few exceptions, hired only whites. There, the mere threat of hiring blacks was usually enough to keep mill hands in line.

Soon, a pecking order was developed in Durham (as elsewhere) in which the fiercest battles raged between the bottom-most groups. The white workers saw the black population of Hayti as a dark and threatening cloud always hovering nearby, ready to roll in with the next wind, taking jobs, food from their tables, and (given how close to the edge mill hands lived) life itself. Toss in the old sexual fears of black men ravishing white women and the result was not so much a color line or even a color wall as a virtual color fortress. As a final insult, Durham's Big Men now derided the "vulgar" racism of their white employees. It was often remarked throughout the South that the "better class of people" were far more relaxed, even friendly, in their relations with blacks. At least, it was remarked upon by this same "better class." Of course, they could easily afford that cordiality—toward blacks of "the right sort," a tiny circle that included the heads of the North Carolina Mutual, the Mechanics and Farmers Bank, and a few others.

For the inhabitants of East Durham, racism flourished, a part of the environment, as natural and as unquestioned as rain in the spring or hunger pangs at night. When there wasn't money to take C.P. to a ball game, Paul Ellis would mutter that it was the fault of the niggers. When he was laid off during hard times in the 1930s, the niggers were blamed. Any setback, disappointment, or reversal was easily and perfunctorily blamed on those dark-skinned residents living just beyond the railroad tracks. The process was so ingrained that it required no thought. In fact, it depended upon just this absence, for logic would have quickly pointed to the obvious, that the residents of squalid Hayti were just trying to get by and were in no position to oppress anyone.

When he had been drinking, Paul Ellis would sometimes sit with his son on their porch telling the boy stories about the glory days before the Civil War. C.P. relished the tales about Jefferson Davis, Jeb Stuart, Stonewall Jackson, and all the other warriors who had fought to preserve the "Southern way of life" and who, said his father, had been defeated by outsiders and traitorous blacks. But the Lost Cause was not lost forever. Paul Ellis told his son that there was a secret society of Southern men who would rise up someday and restore Dixie to her former greatness. During one of these drunken sessions, Paul Ellis whispered to the boy that years ago he himself had been a member of this group. Did he sense a glimmer of doubt in his son's eyes? Perhaps. Who was Paul Ellis after all but a nearly illiterate linthead who barely provided for his own family and who drank himself to sleep nearly every weekend night.

Ellis, though, had proof. He climbed unsteadily to his feet and went inside, returning a minute later with a memento of his more illustrious past. In his outstretched hands, he held the white robes and conical hat of the Ku Klux Klan. "Only the Klan looks out for the white man," Paul Ellis told his son, with the profound solemnity of inebriation. "You just watch. The Klan'll save this country."

C.P.'s father died a few years later, at the age of forty-eight—not an unusually early death by mill standards. The doctor wrote "heart attack" on the certificate, but this was before the disease called brown lung was discovered, and it was likely the years of breathing cotton dust that had killed him.

By this time, C.P. had started a family of his own. At seventeen, he had married a sixteen-year-old girl, a neighbor, Mary Dixon, the daughter of a tobacco factory worker. They met at the local soda fountain, where she worked after school and on weekends. The newlyweds moved into what Mary called a "run-down, shacky house," and when Paul Ellis died C.P.'s mother and sister moved in with them. A poor student, C.P. had quit school in the eighth grade and had gone to work at a service station, washing and greasing cars. Soon there were babies, and C.P. worked one job after another, earning just enough to keep the family together. Then their third child, Larry, was born blind and profoundly retarded. After that, no matter how hard C.P. worked, there was never enough money. The lights were often cut off because they hadn't paid the power bill. On many nights, their little house was lit by kerosene lanterns, just like during the bad old days of C.P.'s youth. The children went to school in patched, ill-fitting clothes, just as C.P. had, and they were just as quickly labeled poor white trash and written off by teachers. C.P. looked on in horror, powerless to change the course of events as another generation of Ellises suffocated in poverty. He began to drink, at first just on weekends like his father, and then on weeknights, too, and then sometimes during the day.

"Do right, support the police, salute the flag," C.P. remembered his father once telling him, "and good things will happen to you."

But it wasn't working out like that.

CHAPTER FOUR

> We are fundamentally opposed to the principle and
> practice of compulsory segregation in our
> American society, whether of races or classes or
> creeds.
>
> —The Durham Statement, 1942

> The principle of segregation of races as to housing,
> schools, churches, and similar public activities is on
> the whole accepted by both races as being sound and
> sensible.
>
> —North Carolina governor
> J. MELVILLE BROUGHTON, 1943

By late 1955, two years after arriving in the city, Ann had secured a position that was as good as a black woman of her class could hope for: she worked as a domestic in the home of a wealthy white family. Better still, the family was from up North, from Philadelphia, and treated Ann better than most Durham whites, driving her to and from her job each day and even allowing her to rest on their bed when she felt ill during the day. She needed to lie down more and more often as time passed. The high blood pressure that accompanied her obesity—she weighed over 300 pounds by this time—caused her to grow light-headed with exertion.

On a morning in December 1955, word reached Durham that blacks in Montgomery, Alabama, were boycotting the city's segregated bus system. The news delighted Ann. She didn't think of herself as a reformer, but her religious beliefs led her to conclude that all people were equal. Didn't the Bible say that God created man in His own divine image? And hadn't

God led His people out of slavery for a purpose—to be free and live in equality? No, her God did not approve of segregation and neither, then, did she. Although she supported the distant boycott, the fact that Durham's own public transportation was segregated didn't concern her too much since her employer drove her to and from work. Ann was content to praise the Lord for developments down in Montgomery and, in her heart, to wish them the best of luck.

It took some time for the ripples caused by the bus boycott in Montgomery to generate a similar reaction in Durham, and by then Ann was working for a different white family. They, too, were generous, providing her with cast-off furniture, clothing, and, most important, food. A couple of times each year the family bought a side of butchered beef and stored it in a large freezer in their basement. These were always happy occasions for Ann and her children because they were given the old—but still wholesome—meat when her employers cleaned out the freezer to make room for the new beef. She received more than just meat from the family. When Ann had trouble nursing her younger baby, Marilyn, the family provided her with a case of milk. And they gave her leftovers and excess vegetables that might otherwise have gone bad in their huge pantry. It was like living in a cornucopia; for weeks at a time Ann didn't see the inside of a grocery store.

This generosity was not, however, a sign of liberalism in racial affairs. Like most wealthy white Southerners, her employers no doubt felt genuine affection for Ann and her children, and, if asked, they probably would have termed their relationship "close." But, like mill owner William Erwin, who provided "his" white workers with everything but a decent wage and some control over their lives, Ann's employers used "favors" and "kindness" as a way to preserve their superior position over their black help. If questioned about Ann's low wages (five dollars for a full day's work), they would have pointed, with rising indignation, to the food, clothing, and furniture they provided her. Surely, such generosity *more* than compensated for the low pay. The real beauty of the arrangement was that it allowed whites to maintain their dominant social and economic position without feeling guilty. The white family believed they were doing the right thing for Ann. After all, what would an uneducated black woman do with the extra cash? Spend it unwisely, most likely, perhaps even disastrously on drink or worse. No, they knew best what their help needed.

One day, Ann was folding clothes at her job while her employer was having tea with a friend in the next room. Ann barely noticed their talk until the conversation drifted to the escalating local controversy over segregated buses. "What's so special about sitting up front?" remarked her employer between sips of tea. "As long as they get a seat, that's all that matters."

For some, deep religious convictions can soften harsh human emotions. Ann Atwater was not one of these people. If anything, her devotion transformed simple anger into righteous wrath. At these times, she resembled a biblical prophet, her face clouded over, her immense body trembling with holy rage, one finger thrust like a spear straight at the sinner's heart.

The offhand comment about bus segregation had such an effect on Ann. At her employer's remark, Ann charged out of the laundry room, her eyes flashing, her stout arms pumping like pistons. From her mouth issued a torrent of words, a roiling sermon on injustice, inequality, and divine retribution worthy of the Baptist preachers of her youth. Stunned, the two white women cowered in their seats as Ann's anger rained down, their bone china teacups rattling in their saucers. Ann concluded with an expert twist of the white Southerner's tail: she observed that black cooks might be spitting in the stewpots and their white bosses would never know it.

Overcome with emotion, Ann would not recall whether she was fired or whether she simply walked out of the house that day. In any event, the result was the same. The secondhand supplies she had grown to depend upon—the shoes for Lydia, the slightly worn dresser for Marilyn, and the food for them all—were gone, a true catastrophe. Ann marched home, still trembling, but now her outrage was mixed with fear and uncertainty. Alone in her tiny bedroom, she fell to her knees and prayed for guidance.

Unable to find a full-time job, Ann worked sporadically, wherever she could find a position. As money grew scarce, so did food. Like thousands of other poor people in Durham—black and white—Ann grew expert at "stretching" meals. One day's main meal might consist of cabbage and fatback. The next night, she'd use the leftover grease, add flour, and pour the resulting gravy over rice. On the third night, all the leftovers would be stirred together.

The Montgomery bus boycott that precipitated these events, like the sympathetic action it prompted in Durham, shocked most whites. Segregation was such an integral part of the Southern way of life that it was, in a sense, invisible to whites, as unremarkable as the air they breathed. They would no sooner question the color line than they would the concept of heaven and hell or the fact that man must earn his bread by the sweat of his brow. And, as with these other truths, most white Southerners considered segregation to be of divine origin. As the *Richmond* (Virginia) *Times* declared in 1900, "God almighty drew the color line and it cannot be obliterated." To impose an anachronism: *de*segregation simply did not compute. And most whites believed that blacks were just as satisfied with the arrangement as they were. This view was surprisingly common across the political spectrum, even with such "enlightened" individuals as W. T. Couch, the liberal director of the liberal University of North Carolina Press in neighboring Chapel Hill. Having invited black scholar Rayford Logan to organize a symposium on the topic of "what blacks want," in the 1930s, Couch was stunned when every contributor advocated an end to segregation. There must be some mistake, Couch informed Logan, and demanded that the contributors be allowed to revise their articles. None did, of course. The mistake was Couch's.

Yet, had whites been paying attention, they would have known that blacks had been resisting segregation since Jim Crow laws were first enacted. There was a long history of protest specifically targeting segregated public transportation, beginning in 1867 with demonstrations that ended Jim Crow streetcars in New Orleans, which were soon followed by similar victories in Richmond, Virginia, and Charleston, South Carolina. Even the terror of the post-Reconstruction era couldn't quell these protests entirely. Blacks in Atlanta waged an effective boycott of Jim Crow trolley cars in 1894, and in the next decade, boycotts spread to over a dozen Southern cities, including Houston and Mobile. In Durham, the earliest recorded protest against segregated buses occurred in 1938, when a black man named Vernon Farrington ignored the law and sat down next to a white man. Unfortunately for Farrington, his seatmate was an off-duty policeman. For violating local custom, and law, Farrington was rewarded with a beating.

In 1943—the same year that saw North Carolina's chief executive assuring citizens that both races found segregation "sound and sensible"—a sixteen-year-old black Durham high school student challenged the ordinance. Doris Lyon sat with a girlfriend in a seat just in front of the rear side door in a nearly empty bus. As the bus proceeded on its route and more passengers boarded, whites, seated from the front, filled that section. Once again, a white Durham policeman happened to be riding the bus—a detective, W. E. Gates (who also wasn't wearing a uniform). Gates told Lyon and her friend to give their seats to whites and move to the back of the bus. The friend complied, but Lyon said there was no room in the back and remained seated.

At the resulting trial, Gates testified that he told Lyon, "Girl, you'll have to move to the back," and showed her his badge. When she still refused to move, the detective grabbed her by the wrists and pulled her to the back seat. He claimed that during this tussle Lyon struck him on the head with a schoolbook. When the bus drove off, Lyon returned to her original seat, and when she refused once again to move, Gates arrested her. She was convicted of violating the Jim Crow law and fined five dollars.

More than a decade before Montgomery resident Rosa Parks refused to relinquish her bus seat, Private Booker T. Spicely, a young black soldier stationed at Camp Butner on the edge of Durham, did the same thing. On July 8, 1944, Spicely and a black woman boarded the bus in the black section of Hayti, sitting in the empty front section. As the bus filled, blacks were told to move to the back. Spicely refused. Records from this era do not report whether or not this particular black serviceman had seen action overseas. Many who had, however, returned to America feeling that they had earned the full rights of citizenship. What is known is that Spicely was serving his country and was likely to be heading overseas soon. And he was wearing his uniform on the bus that night, so there was no question that the bus driver knew that the obstinate black rider was a soldier.

The thirty-six-year-old driver, Herman Lee Council, argued with Spicely, who reacted with defiance by moving even closer to the front of the bus. At the next stop, Council again told Spicely to move back. Spicely again refused, and, according to Council's testimony, made disparaging comments about the driver's military status (or lack thereof). After an exchange of angry words, Council continued driving. At Club Boulevard and Fourth Street, Council stopped the bus and Spicely got off, using the rear door. Council testified that the black soldier yelled for the driver to step outside, saying he was going "to get" the driver, who was "no better to stop bullets than I am."

Council then exited the bus from the front. He later testified that Spicely walked toward him with one hand in his right pocket. The driver drew a .38 caliber pistol from his pocket and fired twice directly at Spicely. The first bullet hit the black soldier in the heart. The second also penetrated his chest. Council left the mortally wounded soldier lying on the sidewalk, returned to his bus, and completed his route. At the end of his shift, the white driver went to the police station and turned himself in. Spicely died at a local hospital soon after the shooting. Police later determined he had not been armed.

During Council's trial, one of his lawyers pointed out that the driver was merely upholding North Carolina's segregation law. Another claimed that Spicely had "been profane" to the white driver, and added that by defying the law the soldier had brought dishonor to his uniform, which "should be a symbol of law and order." The jury took just twenty-eight minutes to find Council not guilty of any crime.

Public transportation was just one arena in which North

Carolina blacks contested second-class status. In 1932, a group of black ministers in Raleigh ignited a scandal by boycotting the dedication of a war memorial after being told to sit in the back of the auditorium. A few years later, black students in Greensboro launched a movie theater boycott after the owners of North Carolina theaters issued a statement condemning "the appearance of colored people in scenes with whites on an equal basis." When Wally Nelson, a representative of the pioneering civil rights organization CORE (Congress of Racial Equality), visited Durham in January 1952, he encountered a black citizenry ready to defy Jim Crow laws using the innovative techniques of nonviolence.

"Durham is an interesting community in several respects," Nelson reported back to CORE headquarters, on his first stop in a multistate tour to lead a boycott of segregated theaters throughout the South. "First, there is a high degree of openly expressed concern about the practice of racism in the community. I mean by this that there is a restlessness which has a healthiness about it."

Discussing the idea of a theater boycott at a black PTA meeting and later before a huge crowd at a Baptist church, Nelson was overwhelmed by the response. "Everywhere I went," he wrote, "I was received almost as a hero." By contrast, Durham's leading white newspaper denounced the idea of a boycott, calling it "dynamite" and "a distasteful aggressive suggestion . . . quite unfair to the theaters."

These actions were part of a long history of challenges to racial oppression stretching back to slave days, a tradition that included countless acts of defiance ranging from the personal and the spontaneous—such as Private Spicely's refusal to give up his bus seat—to well-organized mass insurrections. While mass action had become less frequent after the turn of the century, individual rebellions remained common. Ann Atwater's refusal to be silent when she felt black aspirations for equality were being mocked in her employer's house fits this pattern. And, like Spicely, Ann paid a price for "insolence." The loss of a good position wasn't a death sentence, but it could be expected to cause hardship to a black woman in Ann's position. Ann continued to rebel against discrimination, however. Store clerks in downtown Durham waited on all white customers before helping any blacks—and then served light-skinned blacks first. Ann, whose skin was the color of strong black coffee, would have had to wait until everyone else in the store had been helped, if she had gone along with this game. Instead, she simply chose what she wanted and headed for the door, the article in plain view. When the clerk yelled, "Hey, you didn't pay for that!" Ann responded, "You *wait* on me and I'll *pay*." It didn't take clerks long to recognize Ann and to decide that it was easier to just wait on the large black woman as soon as she was ready. "You either drop your head or hold it up," Ann explained her actions. "And I won't drop mine."

Enumerating these challenges to Jim Crow doesn't prove that either Ann Atwater or Durham, North Carolina, was unique in this regard; they were not. Even a superficial examination of Southern cities during the pre–civil rights era reveals scores of similar protests. What was happening in Durham was part of a *nationwide* process of increasing dissatisfaction with the status quo and a growing willingness to do something about it. In order to dispel any doubts among whites about "what the Negro wants," leading black Southern thinkers gathered in Durham in October 1942 to produce a manifesto. The resulting document, which became known as the Durham Statement, acknowledged that the nation's primary task was to win the war against fascism abroad. But the Statement's authors vowed not to end their demands for justice at home during wartime. In an article published a month after the Durham conference, the far more militant founder of the Pullman porters' union, A. Philip Randolph (who had not been invited to the meeting in Durham), demanded answers to some thorny questions raised by the war effort: "What have Negroes to fight for? What's the difference between Hitler and that 'cracker' Talmadge of Georgia? Why has a man got to be Jim-Crowed to die for democracy? If you haven't got democracy yourself, how can you carry it to somebody else?"

White Southerners could ignore the groundswell of discontent, but, especially following World War II, blacks were simply not going to tolerate a life separate from and unequal to the American mainstream. Martin Luther King, Jr., was referring to this reality when, asked what motivated Rosa Parks that afternoon in Montgomery, he replied, "She had been tracked down by the zeitgeist."

If most white Southerners balked at recognizing the obvious, some federal officials acknowledged the changing times. By executive order President Truman desegregated the military in 1948, raising expectations among black Americans that conditions would improve even more. Six years later the U.S. Supreme Court issued a ruling that seemed to confirm that optimism. On May 17, 1954, Chief Justice Earl Warren read the Court's unanimous decision in a collection of school segregation cases brought by the NAACP.

"Segregation of white and colored children in public schools has a detrimental effect upon colored children," ruled the Court. "It generates a feeling of inferiority as to their status in the community that may affect their hearts and minds in a way unlikely ever to be undone. . . . We conclude that in the field of public education the doctrine of 'separate but equal' has no place. Separate educational facilities are inherently unequal."

Brown v. *Board of Education* overturned eighty years of established law and centuries of custom. It is not coincidence that such a momentous decision centered on the schoolhouse. "Black people knew that education was important," wrote one historian, "because under slavery the law had rigidly denied it to them." Soon after the Civil War, the Freedmen's Bureau established schools for blacks, a task also undertaken by many churches and missionary societies. As public education expanded in the South, North Carolina legislators proved adept at giving blacks equal educational opportunities on paper while funneling most state resources to white students. An 1875 amendment to the state constitution provided for "separate but equal" schools for whites, blacks, and Indians, laying the foundation for discrimination. Since funding for schools came from counties and local communities, blacks and Indians, who had been economically disadvantaged, could not offer the quality of education to their children that whites could. And wherever housing patterns loosened slightly, officials gerrymandered school districts to keep them racially homogeneous. As a result, by 1880, when 76 percent of North Carolina's white children could read and write, only 45 percent of black children were literate. Over the decades, this pattern of discrimination persisted. Whereas the state began funding white public schools in 1879, no black schools received state money for another thirty years.

In 1916, a dozen years after Booker T. Washington proclaimed Durham the "City of Negro Enterprises," the county's black schools were so impoverished that even a white school inspector was outraged. "In no other county did I find the school houses upon the whole in such an inferior condition as I find them in this county for the colored school children," he reported. Some whites attempted to mollify critics (and, perhaps, their own consciences) by urging patience, claiming that it was only a matter of time until black students caught up with their white counterparts. However, educational conditions did not improve as the century progressed. In 1930, a far smaller percentage of black children attended school than did white children, and those blacks lucky enough to see the inside of a schoolhouse endured overcrowded classrooms taught by severely underpaid teachers. The going rate for black teachers was just half the wage paid white teachers. In Durham, where blacks comprised roughly one-third the population, the county provided $155,000 for the education of its white children and only $21,000 for blacks. Forced to operate on a shoestring, one black school in Durham squeezed 51 students into a single classroom. The school, which served 300 students, had four toilets, one drinking fountain, and no cafeteria.

In 1938, Nathan Newbold, a white educator who served as North Carolina's top official for black schools, circulated a prophetic warning, which, like all other such alarms, was ignored by the white populace. "It is natural and logical," wrote Newbold, "for intelligent Negroes to exhibit a feeling of unrest, whether wisely or unwisely, over conditions which to them seem to mean there is no hope for equality of educational opportunity for them in a great state like North Carolina." Blacks pressed for better schools whenever they could. Even Durham's nervous black elites, loath to push the white power structure too far, were willing to expend considerable political capital over education. In 1936, a delegation headed by the Parrish Street Gang petitioned the city for a twelfth grade at all-black Hillside Park High School. It took a year for a senior class to be added to the school, and even then officials deliberately limited classes to vocational training, and not precollege education. Still, the addition was a rare and precious victory.

At the same time, blacks were also knocking on the doors of North Carolina's universities and colleges—as whites scurried to lock and bolt them. Thanks to white obstructionism, and bolstered by the black upper classes jealously guarding their segregated domains, North Carolina preserved its lily-white campuses until 1951, when UNC finally admitted five black graduate students. In the end, maintaining a system of "separate but equal" colleges proved too expensive for impoverished Southern states. Perhaps a few moralists were disappointed that it was economics and not ethics that triumphed over racist ideology, but clearly economic pressure achieved better results than black appeals to white morality. A North Carolina College (NCC) student would later put it this way: "Not Jesus Christ, not morals, not what's right, not nothing's going to make the white man stop segregation but hurting his cash register." For whatever reason, the immediate goal had been accomplished: after decades of struggle, black students had finally gained a toehold in the most cherished white institutions of power and prestige.

Despite earlier battles, few whites in Durham—or anywhere else in the South—were prepared for the sweeping nature of *Brown* v. *Board*, which seemed to deal a fatal blow to "separate but equal" schools. Certainly, the white power structure in the South had resisted before what they had perceived as federal intrusion into regional life. When the newly created Federal Commission on Higher Education had called for desegregation in 1946, the South had simply ignored its recommendations. A similarly stony reception had greeted President

Truman's Committee on Civil Rights' report, *To Secure These Rights,* also issued in 1946, calling for the "elimination of seg- regation, based on race, color, creed, or national origin, from American life."

But *Brown* v. *Board* represented the law of the land and not merely the abstract recommendations of a federal commis- sion. Many Southerners at first appeared ready to go along with, if not embrace, the new system. But within a year and a half, unyielding defiance of federal authority had become the norm. The national government itself was in part to blame for this reversal after it showed it was divided on the issue. That ambivalence was most clearly embodied by the President of the United States, Dwight Eisenhower. The Eisenhower administration had officially supported the NAACP's position on *Brown,* and just one day after the Court's decision was handed down, the President suggested that Washington, D.C., serve as a role model for the nation and desegregate its schools ASAP. So saying, he declined to speak publicly on school desegregation for the next three years—just when his backing was most crucial. And after its initial unanimous decision, the Supreme Court also sent mixed signals. The Court's enforce- ment decree, issued a full year after *Brown,* seemed concilia- tory to segregationists, imposing no deadline for achieving racially mixed schools and calling merely for "good faith implementation." The Supreme Court also ruled it was the job of federal district courts to determine what constituted "good faith"—to the delight of segregationists such as Georgia lieu- tenant governor Ernest Vandiver, who observed that those judges were "steeped in the same traditions that I am. . . . A 'reasonable time' can be construed as one year or two hun- dred. . . . Thank God we've got good Federal judges."

With its hopes of preserving the Southern way of life buoyed, Dixie mobilized to oppose the federal government's latest intrusion. Several governors who had earlier preached a "go along" attitude now dug in their heels. Nearly the entire Southern congressional delegation signed a "Southern Mani- festo" pledging resistance to forced school integration.

North Carolina's reaction was typical of much of the upper

South. A majority of its white population initially appeared ready to accept desegregation, albeit unhappily. Reflecting this fact, and also wanting to preserve its image as a Southern liberal oasis—a fiction carefully crafted to attract Northern manufacturers—the state legislature declined to join its more radical Southern neighbors in passing a bill of "interposition." (This principle claimed the right of states to interpose their will when they believed Supreme Court rulings violated the U.S. Constitution.) Instead, the legislature contented itself with passing a symbolic "resolution of protest" against *Brown*.

Within the state's political leadership, however, acceptance of desegregation was short-lived. In the waning days of 1954, five months *before* the Supreme Court handed down its muddled implementation order, a committee appointed by the governor of North Carolina concluded that "the mixing of the races forthwith in the public schools throughout the state cannot be accomplished and should not be attempted." Still, North Carolina's white population would likely have accepted integrated schools if the state's new governor had used his position to push for such a path. Instead, he played the race card for his own political gain, setting back by years, if not decades, black aspirations for equality.

When Lieutenant Governor Luther Hodges, Sr., became Governor Hodges in the fall of 1954 (after the death of Governor William Umstead), few North Carolinians knew much about him aside from the fact that he had been a successful businessman and an administrator of the Marshall Plan in Germany. But Hodges quickly proved to be a consummate politician of the Southern progressive type, using words like "compromise" and "understanding" while adroitly undermining any real change in the status quo. Hodges embodied the sentiment expressed by another white North Carolinian: "We're just like Georgia and Alabama except that we do it in a tuxedo and they wear suspenders." To be precise, Hodges did it in a gray flannel suit, for he was a pragmatist, dubbed the "Businessman's Governor," a believer in method and technique over ideology and manifesto. A man born to bureaucracy, Hodges would never stand in the schoolhouse doorway, shaking his fist and proclaiming, "Segregation forever!" Rather, he would quietly appoint a committee to deliberate for eternity over exactly which door, and of what dimensions, would best facilitate the ingress and egress of all students. The style of a Hodges was different from that of a Wallace, but the result was the same.

When the Supreme Court issued its implementation decree for *Brown* v. *Board* in 1955, it left a good deal of "wiggle room," and Hodges used every bit of it, in an effort to head off political attacks from his right. The legislature approved his plan shifting responsibility for desegregation from the state to local school boards. If black parents or the NAACP wanted to challenge school segregation legally, they would now have to sue each of the state's school boards (and there were scores of them) individually.

Hodges' chief political foe at this time was an outspoken segregationist named I. Beverly Lake, an assistant state attorney general, who, it was rumored, planned to oppose Hodges in the 1956 gubernatorial race. Lake took a public stand against any sort of compromise, saying that the state should close its public schools rather than desegregate. When Lake supported using state money to fund private white schools, Hodges, who had earlier opposed the idea, crab-walked quickly to the right. On August 8, 1955, only a few weeks after Lake had gone on the offensive, Hodges unveiled his new school program in a statewide address carried live by sixty radio and ten television stations. Remarkably, he called for blacks to submit to a path of "voluntary segregation." If they did not agree to this "compromise," he cautioned, he would be forced to close the state's public schools entirely.

Blacks weren't fooled by this tack. They understood that the governor's scheme was just a way for North Carolina to say "maybe" and "someday" when it really meant "no" and "never." Louis Austin, editor of Durham's influential black weekly, the *Carolina Times*, called Hodges' address "a cheap dime store political speech . . . [that] did more to sell the National Association for the Advancement of Colored People to the Negro man in the street than all the literature, newspaper articles and speeches that have ever been written or uttered in its behalf . . ."

Austin reflected and helped forge the uncompromising position of most black North Carolinians toward Hodges' plan: "The Negroes of this state will not be stampeded into such an unholy scheme," he wrote. "We will not be rash, we will not be boastful, we will be polite and considerate but before eternal God we will never again turn back the clock to the time when we must grin and bear without protest the insults and humiliations that go with segregation."

But Hodges' speech had not been directed so much at blacks as at whites; he had avoided being "out-seged" by Lake, while still giving the impression of "moderation." The governor won over all but the most rabid segregationists, who (with witty accuracy) ridiculed his plan as a "Hodge-Podge." The governor's crowning achievement or lowest point was the enactment of a "compromise" plan at a special session of the state legislature in July 1956. The measure, known as the Pearsall Plan (for the head of the governor's committee that drafted it), allowed local boards to close schools rather than integrate them and provided state funds to send white children to private segregated schools. The plan amounted to a bureaucratic end run around *Brown*.

Governor Hodges applauded the Pearsall Plan for "its faith in the people, and its trust in the Democratic process"—an odd characterization for a measure designed solely to cheat one-quarter of the state's population out of its right to a decent education. Once again, though, Louis Austin exposed Hodges' duplicity, using the blunt language that marked all of Austin's writings: "If history fifty years from now does not record him as the governor of this state who had the greatest opportunity for progressive leadership, but made the greatest failure at it, it will record him as the most stupid . . ." About the Pearsall Plan itself, Austin was just as unsparing: "It capitulates to intolerance, to hatred and proceeds to hammer out a way through which intolerance can be nourished. . . . [It] says to the citizens of the state, go ahead, indulge your hatred at the state's behest. The Plan would put a premium on hatred. It would pay . . . for racial hatred."

In the matter of school desegregation, Durham's reputation for tolerance, racial harmony, and liberal politics once again proved sadly overrated. Compared even with other Piedmont cities, Durham's reaction to *Brown* was unremarkable, neither as openly hostile as that of Henderson (where community leaders expressed "shock and dismay" at the ruling) nor as congenial as Greensboro's, where, on the night following the announcement of the Supreme Court decision, the school board passed a resolution pledging to desegregate community schools. As a member of the city's school board put it, Durham would not directly oppose the court order, but neither would it "rush out and do everything the next week in terms of compliance." That proved an understatement. City officials threw up one stumbling block after another to delay implementation of the Court's intent. Writing a decade after *Brown*, one observer noted that the Durham school board "had to be dragged inch by inch, courtsuit by courtsuit, into contemporary society."

Perhaps following the lead of the state's chief executive, Durham first used the bureaucratic device that could be called "Death by Committee." Rather than attempt to quash the idea outright (something it hadn't the power to do), the board first attempted to study the issue to death. The task force formed to investigate the city's options was called, ominously, the "Segregation Committee" and included two of the board's most ardent segregationists. When pushed to act, the board pointed out that it had a committee looking into the issue, intimating by its tone that only revolutionaries (possibly Communist dupes) would advocate rushing on a matter of such sensitivity.

And there matters rested for three years, while schools in progressive Durham remained as segregated as those in reactionary Birmingham.

The concept of the "turning point" was created by historians to impose a pleasing narrative structure upon history—which is generally too messy and complicated for easy storytelling. We learn that things were one way, something happened, and then things were another way: On Monday peasants toiled in the mud for feudal kings. On Tuesday, surrounded by cud-chewing cows on the fields of Runnymede, King John signed the Magna Carta. On Wednesday, *mirabile dictu:* Democracy. True turning points exist, but they are nearly always the visible tip of a vast and highly complex social process.

Such was the case of the civil rights movement of the 1960s. It was built on a foundation laid for centuries, stone upon bloody stone. Individual black men and women protested their enslavement in every way imaginable—running away, stealing, killing themselves rather than living in bondage. They appealed, nearly always in vain, to white morality. "Sir," begins a petition by slaves to the Massachusetts colonial government in 1773:

> The efforts made by the legislative of this province in their last sessions to free themselves from slavery, gave us, who are in that deplorable state, a high degree of satisfaction. We expect great things from men who have made such a noble stand against the designs of their *fellow-men* to enslave them. We cannot but wish and hope Sir, that you will have the same grand object . . . in view in your next session.

They pursued that glimmering American phantasm called Justice by attacking legalized discrimination in voting, in public accommodations, and in schools. In truth, the movement began the moment the first black men and women were led ashore in chains.

An important strand of the national story runs through Durham and it involves two men who had a profound effect on the movement: Douglas E. Moore and Floyd B. McKissick.

Born the grandson of a preacher in Hickory, North Carolina, in 1928, Douglas Moore decided to follow his grandfather into the Methodist ministry and in 1951 he enrolled as a divinity student at Boston University. The postwar years were full of political turmoil and excitement, and Moore joined with a small group of similarly radical students organizing for change in "spiritual cell movements" (as befitting leftist divinity students) and holding demonstrations protesting various social evils. For a short time, Moore also attended meetings of the Dialectical Society, a student group that gathered each week for a potluck supper and discussion. But the talks proved too abstract and bloodless, and far too disengaged from the social and political issues of the day. Moore didn't think much of the student leader of the society either. "Just another Baptist preacher" was how he sized up Martin Luther King, Jr. For his part, King, who was cultivating an image as a genteel intellectual at that time, seemed a bit intimidated by the radical student and showed little interest in joining Moore's activist group.

After graduation, the two students left Boston to shepherd congregations in the South. In 1955, Moore was surprised to learn that his former timid classmate from BU was leading a bus boycott in Montgomery. He wrote King expressing support and urging him to turn the action into a national nonviolent protest movement. "I have maintained for years," Moore wrote, "that one hundred well-disciplined persons could break the backbone of segregated travel in North Carolina in less than a year." But King's vision remained narrower than Moore's. The Montgomery preacher's only response was a polite thank-you note signed by his secretary.

Meanwhile, Moore combined pastoral duties with social activism. After serving as minister for two small-town Methodist churches, he became the pastor of Durham's Asbury Temple Methodist Church in 1956. Despite the city's reputation for good race relations, Moore quickly sized up Durham's white power structure as being the "same as any other place: They wouldn't give up nothing." At least not without a fight. On the hot and humid evening of June 23, 1957, Moore led a group of six other blacks (three women and three men) into the segregated Royal Ice Cream Parlor and, without fanfare, sat down in the white section and asked to be served. Speaking later to a reporter, Moore disingenuously explained, "We just decided we wanted to cool off, to get some ice cream or milk shakes." When the group refused to move, they were arrested and eventually convicted of trespassing, in a case that went all the way to the U.S. Supreme Court. It was the first organized sit-in in North Carolina history. That action, and a related suit against the ice cream parlor brought by Moore, sparked a six-year bat-

THE BEST OF ENEMIES

tle to integrate the parlor. Durham's black Ministerial Alliance initially opposed Moore's "radical" efforts, as did the powerful citywide political organization the Durham Committee on Negro Affairs (DCNA). Confrontation through direct action was just not the Durham way. For anyone who questioned that reality, Private Booker T. Spicely's fate at the hands of a Durham bus driver served as a cautionary tale. Besides, the black elite had always wrung concessions from the white power structure—slowly but surely—through back-channel meetings, arguing their case in a dignified, rational, and, above all, civil manner. They had desegregated Durham's tennis courts in this manner a few months earlier. After some black youths had attempted to use the courts (which, like most park facilities, were reserved for whites only), a small group of black community leaders had met quietly with town officials and had reached a compromise. Blacks could use city parks as long as they went in small groups. That was how it was done: graciously and slowly, so you didn't arouse the lightly slumbering redneck dragon over in the poor white neighborhoods. Over the years, the pattern became so well established that a visitor to these negotiations might have concluded that both parties were reading their lines from a script: "Of course," the white town fathers would say, "*we* don't mind (sitting at a table with you . . . sending our children to school with yours . . .), but you know how *they* are," nodding toward the collection of sad houses with their sagging porches and dusty yards where the white laborers lived.

"Oh, yes," the black leaders would respond, smiling ruefully and shaking their heads in commiseration, "we *appreciate* your delicate position. However, we have our positions to consider, too . . ."

And that was how things got done in Durham. Moore's actions, however, threatened to upset this delicate balance. The minister was not alone in his fight: he had a powerful ally in newspaperman Louis Austin. Though Austin was known for speaking his mind, one week before the Royal Ice Cream sit-in he ran an editorial that was outspoken, even for him. Preparing the reader for what lay ahead, Austin began with a lengthy excerpt from Thomas Paine's *The American Crisis*, starting with the famous line "These are the times that try men's souls." Then Austin continued:

> [T]his newspaper senses a stagnation that is beginning to creep over the Durham Committee on Negro Affairs which, if allowed to continue, is certain to spell its doom. . . . [The DCNA] is becoming too high-brow, too soft and too compromising. . . . [T]he Durham Ministerial Alliance . . . is dragging its feet on these same vital issues. . . . The old guard of the Alliance appears to have smothered efforts of the younger and progressive members to push the segregation question to the front. Thus the two most influential organizations among Negroes of the city have become practically "dead ducks" on the all-important question of civil rights.
>
> There comes a time in the life of an organization when it needs new blood, new faces and some new ideas. There comes a time when those who have been in control too long become satisfied to rest on their oars and boast of their past achievements. That is the darkest hour of any organization and in that hour a major operation may be the only hope for its salvation. Certainly, this is no hour to be at ease but an hour for positive action. The struggle for freedom and human dignity for all must go on. It must not be sacrificed on the altar of greed and power merely to obtain a few crumbs for the few. What we do now will determine the destiny of thousands who come after us. God forbid that we falter or recoil from performing our solemn duty.

Austin's statement is extraordinary not simply because he was confronting Durham's most powerful black institutions—a risky venture for a paper that depended on the advertising revenues doled out by the leaders of those same groups—but because the conservatism he denounced existed throughout the South. The newspaperman was daring the black bourgeoisie in Durham and across the nation to join in a new and more aggressive struggle. The NAACP itself was an example of the trend toward ossification. For all its important work on behalf of black people, the NAACP was primarily an organization of lawyers whose idea of a good fight was a courtroom battle. This was already apparent when, in 1956, Martin Luther King, Jr., offered his opinion that perhaps the lessons learned from the Montgomery bus boycott could help in the fight over school desegregation. When told of King's suggestion, the NAACP's Thurgood Marshall allegedly snapped, "I don't approve of using children to do men's work." A year later, Marshall went even further, dismissing King as a "first-rate rabble-rouser."

Austin was quite consciously shining a spotlight into the gap that had always existed between the black masses and the Big Negroes as symbolized by the NAACP, a chasm that had been ignored in favor of racial unity. While most blacks were genuinely pleased by the NAACP's work for school integration, there was, wrote one black journalist, "a widespread doubt that a nationally directed battle of attrition that took so long and cost so much to bring so little to so few would ever get to the heart of the issue."

If the civil rights movement of the 1960s was a second American Revolution, as some have called it, then Louis Austin was, especially in the crucible of North Carolina, its Thomas Paine, his stirring rhetoric pointing the way toward freedom at a crucial moment. By supporting Moore, and, more importantly, by endorsing his new tactic of direct action, Austin would soon have an impact far beyond Durham or even the borders of North Carolina.

In pursuing his suit against Royal Ice Cream, Moore turned to a young Durham lawyer named Floyd McKissick. The two were well matched. McKissick, just five years older than Moore, not only believed in developing new strategies for achieving racial justice; he was an activist in his own right. A World War II veteran who had served in Europe, McKissick, like so many other black soldiers, returned home with increased expectations for equality only to run headfirst into continued discrimination. McKissick's first chance to join in a collective direct action against segregation came in 1947 while he was attending law school at North Carolina College in Durham. The still-new civil rights organization CORE traveled through Durham on its "Journey of Reconciliation," an interracial bus trip throughout the South organized to test compliance with a recent Supreme Court decision banning segregation on interstate buses. McKissick joined the riders for a short time and was inspired by the Gandhian tactics used by CORE. He would later refer to the experience as "my baptism in nonviolence." In 1951, McKissick applied to the law school at the University of North Carolina in Chapel Hill and was rejected because of his race. With the legal aid of Thurgood Marshall (who became a family friend), McKissick was enrolled, and later became the first black to graduate from that school.

Besides representing Moore in his lawsuit against the ice cream parlor, McKissick helped the minister organize many other sit-ins around Durham over the next few years, sometimes accompanied by the black Boy Scout troop which McKissick headed. The young lawyer was on civil, if not close, terms with Durham's older black leaders, but he labored under no illusions about their willingness to take bold action. McKissick understood that future battles would require the involvement of younger, less conservative blacks, and so he formed and led NAACP youth chapters at several of Durham's black colleges and trade schools, as well as one for high school students.

Through his law practice, McKissick also emerged as the leader of the fight to desegregate Durham's public schools, guiding black parents through the maze of requirements devised by the school board to delay integration. In the fall of 1959, after a long legal campaign, his eldest child, Joycelyn, became the first black student to enroll at formerly all-white Durham High School. Like all such racial pioneers, Joycelyn understood that she would have to pay a price for being first. Her father and mother prepared her for the verbal insults she would endure from other students. They warned her about the physical abuse she would surely receive. And they explained that she would have to respond with strength and dignity to the barely concealed hostility emanating from her teachers and school administrators.

"You've got to be a warrior," her father told her. "There are certain things you might have to do, for the sake of all black people. And no matter what you do as an individual, you're reflecting your group and your family. So make sure you're correct."

Even with all the warnings, the reality of being the only black student in a white school was worse than she had expected. On the first day of classes, Joycelyn's parents escorted her to school through a gauntlet of angry whites screaming "Coons, go home" and "I. Beverly Lake for governor" (a reference to the segregationist politician) and of course "Nigger, Nigger, Nigger." Someone had distributed handbills that read: "Remember Little Rock. The people there at least had the guts to fight. Does Durham have less courage?"

Opening day was just the beginning of her troubles. White students taunted Joycelyn in the hallway as she walked between classes. She was often kicked and once was beaten up. A group of girls shoved her head into the toilet. But Joycelyn lost her self-control only once—after a white girl kicked her from behind as she was putting a book into her locker. The force slammed her into the metal locker, cutting her head. In pain and overcome by anger, Joycelyn jabbed her fingers into the other girl's eyes. The white girl never bothered her again, but Joycelyn would always consider the incident a personal defeat, saying, "I felt I should have been stronger; I should have been above that." With that one exception, Joycelyn ignored the taunts and punches during her senior year at Durham High School.

Despite her personal strength, Joycelyn relied on her whole community, including Louis Austin, a close friend of her father's. Austin gave Joycelyn her first job, sweeping the floor at the *Carolina Times*. She later wrote a column for the paper. She drew strength from the older man's steadfast support and intellectual nourishment from his commanding intelligence, which grappled with a wide range of issues, from anticolonial movements in Africa to presidential politics here at home. The church played the largest role in helping Joycelyn and the other students during that first year of token integration. Each afternoon, the black students who had been inserted into white schools throughout Durham assembled at Union Baptist Church or St. Joseph's AME Church to pray and to sing together with members of the community, sharing their stories of harassment and finding in one another's company the courage to forge ahead just like Daniel into the lion's den.

By 1959, the era of student activism had begun in Durham, under the leadership of Floyd McKissick, Douglas Moore, and Louis Austin, and backed by the black churches—particularly the black church women. College students and some still in high school gathered regularly to plan sit-ins and other protests against Jim Crow, refusing to place all their hopes in the quiet diplomacy practiced by a few older and affluent blacks. Neither would they limit themselves to the slow and equally uncertain process of seeking justice within the courts. Whatever the risks, they were determined to push ahead in a nonviolent direct assault on white privilege. As youth advisor to the state NAACP, McKissick spread the gospel of direct action among North Carolina's black students. That mission was supported by McKissick's neighbor and colleague the Reverend Douglas Moore, now a board member of Martin Luther King, Jr.'s, influential Southern Christian Leadership Conference.

An editorial appeared in the NCC *Campus Echo* that year: "Traditions are not changed by laws, court orders, or the moderate attitude on the part of some benevolent persons," it read, "they are changed by more concrete action." In retrospect, that statement seems prescient, but it merely reflected the mood already widespread among the young in Durham's black community as America stood poised on the cusp of a new and turbulent decade.

CHAPTER FIVE

I'd like a cup of coffee, please.

—Ezell Blair, Jr.
  Woolworth's, Greensboro, N.C.
  February 1, 1960

It was a time of great fears, and some hope. An Air Force general blessed with the surname of Power warned a shaken Senate committee that the Russians could render this country defenseless with a missile strike lasting only thirty minutes. Speaking in similarly grave tones, the Secretary of the Army pointed to another Red menace, China, calling it "a crouched tiger ready to spring on any prey that is weak and wounded." And while Americans were still digesting these worrisome assessments, out of the Middle East came the first sketchy reports of Egyptian troops massing on the Israeli border. Was this the harbinger of a new war, one that would draw in the United States?

Despite the fear spawned by a Cold War that threatened to turn hot, there was encouraging news as well. The upcoming race for the White House already appeared interesting. Rumors flew around Washington that the handsome young millionaire from Massachusetts, Senator John Kennedy, might try out the waters in the Indiana primary. Closer to home, the tobacco industry—and so the Piedmont region—would benefit from a bill wending its way through Congress, legislation designed to keep tobacco support payments steady and high. Durham was gearing up for its annual Boy Scout Week. Caterers rushed to place extra orders for chicken to supply the many "Blue and Gold" banquets to be held around town the following week, while young boys spent their afternoons building displays of Scout craft in the windows of downtown businesses.

Across the railroad tracks on that afternoon of February 1, blacks discussed all of these events and others not mentioned by whites. They welcomed the news that North Carolina representative Graham Barden would not seek reelection in the fall, since this meant that Adam Clayton Powell, Jr., the flamboyant black representative from New York, would inherit the job of chairman of the House Education and Labor Committee. Black Durhamites laughed about the many powerful whites who would be stewing in their own juices over the prospect of an "uppity" black man controlling the purse strings for federal education programs. Hayti was also abuzz over Negro History Week, due to commence on the following Sunday. People anticipated lectures, films, and plays. The best part, however, would be the choruses—groups of young children, scrubbed clean and dressed in their best knee-pant suits and ruffled dresses, arranged on church pulpits in rows from tallest to the smallest, reciting the poetry of Langston Hughes, Gwendolyn Brooks, and Claude McKay. The children would gamely stammer through their recitation, leaving out a word here and adding one there until each child would be at a different point and the poem would fade off into an unintelligible murmur— to the delight of gathered relatives. On the North Carolina College campus in the southeastern part of Durham, where the spring semester was just underway, students compared class assignments and reading lists. And they worried over early quizzes and passed whispered information about who was seeing whom—and who was no longer seeing whom—after the long holiday break.

On that same mid-winter afternoon, some sixty miles to the west on the modern campus of North Carolina A&T University, Ezell Blair, Jr., an eighteen-year-old freshman, sat trembling in his dorm room, anticipating the dangerous journey he and three friends were about to undertake. In a few minutes, they would leave the college campus and walk the few blocks down Market Street to downtown Greensboro. Turning right onto South Elm Street, they would continue for another block until reaching a two-story red-brick building bearing a commonplace red-and-gold sign: F. W. WOOLWORTH. After buying a few items at the five-and-dime store—a comb, toothpaste, note-paper—the four young black men would head for the lunch counter at the rear of the store, sit down, and order coffee. That was the extent of their plan.

In the North, such a diversion from studies was unremarkable, but in the Jim Crow South, this was an act of revolution, an assault on the fundamental structure of Southern society. For the Woolworth's lunch counter, like similar restaurants throughout the South, was reserved for whites only. There could be terrible consequences for the students. They might be thrown out of school, their careers ended before they began. They would certainly be subject to arrest, and for black men and women in the South this carried with it the possibility of a savage jailhouse beating.

An observer in his dorm room that afternoon would not have considered Blair a revolutionary. Short and thin, with a boyish face and a distracted air, Blair was majoring in science to please his parents, but he was inclined more to poetry, music, and art—and to none of them in a rigorous fashion. Revolutions need dreamers, too, however, and this quality had led him to the task nearly at hand. As a child, Blair had spent long hours imagining life in a truly just society. At Sunday School, he had demanded to know why a just God would allow Negroes to suffer persecution. And when the state of Israel was established in 1948, the six-year-old Blair told his friends he would someday drink out of Woolworth's whites-only water fountain. Surely, if the Jews had found freedom after thousands of years, then one day Negroes, too, would enter *their* Promised Land.

During Blair's first semester of college, the subject of confronting Jim Crow laws often arose in late-night discussions with friends, but such extreme actions always remained in the fuzzy and safe category of things to do "someday." And then, on January 31, 1960, a friend named Joseph McNeil stormed into Blair's dorm room and slammed the door. Blair looked up. Uh-oh, he thought, here comes trouble.

"All right," said McNeil tersely, "tomorrow we're going down."

"Going where?" asked Blair.

"We're going to sit in at Woolworth's."

"Oh, no, man," protested Blair. "I've got an exam."

McNeil would not be put off. For years a white businessman named Ralph Johns had tried to convince A&T students to defy the color line in Greensboro. McNeil often shopped at Johns's small clothing store and there the white radical had bent his ear, with the usual results: maybe, someday. But when McNeil returned to Greensboro after spending Christmas with relatives in Wilmington, North Carolina, the waiter at the lunch counter in the bus station had refused to serve him. It was one rejection too many; he had had enough of Jim Crow.

Besides Blair and McNeil, there were two other students in the room that evening: Franklin McCain and David Richmond. McNeil turned first to the six-foot-four-inch McCain.

"Are you chicken?" he asked.

"No, man, I'm not chicken," McCain replied.

McNeil asked the other two students if they were chicken, and they, of course, said no. The matter was put to a vote and the reluctant Blair lost, three to one. Now the diminutive freshman waited nervously in his dorm room, dressed in his best suit and preparing to risk everything for the right to order a cup of coffee at a five-and-dime lunch counter.

There were only about a dozen people sitting quietly at Woolworth's L-shaped lunch counter when the four black students sat down and Blair ordered a cup of coffee.

"I'm sorry," replied the white waitress. "We don't serve Negroes here."

Blair, who was known on the A&T campus as "the Mouth," didn't hesitate.

"I beg to disagree with you," he informed her, using his best freshman English. "You just finished serving me at a counter only two feet away from here." Ignoring the waitress's growing anger, Blair continued to press for service, arguing, with a logic that only infuriated the woman, that if Woolworth's didn't want to serve the public perhaps they should sell membership cards. "If you do that," he concluded, "then I'll understand that this is a private concern."

The waitress stalked off, and a black kitchen worker stomped over.

"You're acting stupid, ignorant!" she hissed at them. "That's why we can't get anywhere today."

Disappointed, they waited in their seats, doubts flitting inside of them. Soon an elderly white woman approached the four. They were prepared for anything: verbal abuse, physical violence. The well-dressed woman was "the epitome of what we were fighting," McCain recalls thinking: white, middle-class, old, and probably set in her ways. She regarded the four black students for a moment and then told them how proud she was of them.

There were no arrests made that day. The store manager hoped that by ignoring the students they would eventually grow bored and leave. The students, however, remained seated quietly but resolutely on the lunch-counter stools until the store closed. Then Blair and his friends filed out of the store, promising to return the next day.

Callis Brown first heard of the lunch-counter protest that evening while watching the nightly news at his parents' home in Durham. His reaction was immediate: "We ought to do that here." A junior at North Carolina College, Brown telephoned a few of his college friends and asked what they thought. The universal response was: "Let's do it." The next morning he went to see the man he had long considered his mentor, Louis Austin. Should NCC students take up the sit-in? The publisher smiled at Brown and nodded.

When Floyd McKissick learned about the sit-in over in Greensboro, he cried, "Oh my God, these kids have jumped the gun!" He and Douglas Moore had always intended to enlarge their direct-action protests to include other cities and states, but neither of them had set an official starting date. They had, however, already decided to launch the nationwide sit-in movement in Durham. "It was felt that it would be easier to integrate stores in Durham," Moore explained, "because the merchants would not want the publicity attendant to a long boycott." The city was trying to attract businesses to its new Research Triangle

Park and the civil rights pioneers figured that local stores, wanting to avoid any bad publicity, would be "pushovers."

The sit-in was planned to achieve the maximum national effect and paced to build a powerful and sustainable movement capable of destroying Jim Crow. By their spontaneous action, the Greensboro students had forced the Durham leaders to scrap their plans for cool deliberation. Moore, McKissick, and Austin realized immediately that the moment was upon them: the revolution had begun. They could only hope to steer it in the right direction. Invited by the head of the Greensboro NAACP, Moore and McKissick drove up that first night to meet with the A&T students, to instruct them in nonviolent direct action, and to coordinate plans to spread the sit-in. Back in Durham, NCC student leaders contacted their counterparts at Shaw University in Raleigh and urged them to orchestrate their own sit-in and to pass the word along to other black schools. From the pulpit of the influential *Carolina Times*'s editorial page Louis Austin preached the gospel of the sit-in that Saturday:

> The sitdown strike . . . is the most encouraging incident that has occurred within the past five years. . . . The students taking part in the sitdown strike have probably caused a patch of goose pimples to appear on the backs of all the Uncle Toms in Greensboro and elsewhere in the state. . . . The sitdown strike of the A&T students, we hope, will serve to awaken members of the race, in North Carolina, if not the entire South, to the vicious practice of which they are the victims.

On the following afternoon, a plane arrived at the Raleigh-Durham airport from New York City bearing a young white man, serious-looking behind thick-lensed glasses. He was whisked by car through the dense pine forests surrounding the airport to an address on Durham's North Side. Only a few people knew of his presence in Floyd McKissick's house, where Callis Brown and other NCC students were finalizing plans for a sit-in at a Durham lunch counter. Without delay, McKissick introduced the visitor, Gordon Carey, to the students. Many of them already knew of Carey from his role as field secretary of the nation's oldest and preeminent direct-action civil rights group: the Congress of Racial Equality, or CORE. A CORE activist since 1951, Carey had helped arrange a march to protest school segregation in Richmond, Virginia, in January 1959, and had even initiated an ill-fated lunch-counter sit-in in Miami in April of that same year. The assistance of CORE, with its national network of activists and long experience with direct-action campaigns, would be vital in transforming the Greensboro sit-in from an isolated "incident" into a true movement. At least for the moment, it was also important that this aid remain behind the scenes. The organizers didn't want to hand the white establishment ammunition for its perennial allegation that any racial unrest in the South was incited by outside agitators.

At ten o'clock Monday morning, February 8—a week to the day after the Greensboro sit-in had erupted—the lunch-counter incident was transformed into a true movement. Some fifty NCC students, joined by four white students from Duke, walked into the Woolworth's store on Main Street and filled up the seats at the lunch counter. After ignoring the students for two hours, the manager closed Woolworth's, citing a telephoned bomb threat. With military discipline, the students marched down the block to the Kress building, an Art Deco structure which was, coincidentally, one of the most beautiful commercial buildings in Durham. It was a strange sight: a phalanx of well-dressed black college students filed in silently and walked through the ornate main floor (a stylized version of an ancient Egyptian temple), passing clusters of plaster lotus blossoms while the white shoppers stood immobile and frowning in the aisles, confused about what they were witnessing. When the students reached the lunch counter at the back of the store, they sat down at the empty stools and waited. The counter was closed almost immediately.

As the group headed across the street to the Walgreen's segregated lunch counter, the manager there decided not to wait for trouble. He closed off the serving area before the students even entered the store. In a little over two hours, the protesters had shut down three lunch counters.

True to form, the Durham police focused on the protest's white participants, assuming them to be the ringleaders, and arrested Carl Hickey, a twenty-one-year-old Duke Divinity School student, and Gordon Carey. According to a police captain, Hickey was placed under "protective custody" and Carey, who held a New York driver's license, had refused to reveal his occupation. He was, however, carrying business cards identifying him as field secretary of CORE. The angry policeman told a reporter, "We are not going to tolerate this agitation from outsiders—anyone who deliberately comes in here and tries to stir up trouble is going to be taken in custody until we can find out more about him." Now that CORE's presence was revealed, the protesters felt free to make the most of these links, emphasizing the national dimensions of the movement. McKissick told reporters that the sit-in was actually sponsored by several national and local civil rights and religious organizations.

Conspicuously absent from this list was the NAACP, the country's dominant civil rights organization since 1909, but still dedicated to the slower tactic of filing legal challenges to segregation. In fact, the NAACP had snubbed initial requests by the Greensboro students for legal counsel in their battle against segregated lunch counters, reopening the split within the black community that had been exposed during the Montgomery bus boycott. This time, however, the older, more accommodating generation represented by the NAACP could not paper over the division or simply use its greater institutional clout to force renegades into line. As the movement escalated, it became clear that a sea change was occurring not just in America but within black America itself. Journalist Louis Lomax was one of the first to understand the dimensions of this shift and to describe its significance. In an insightful piece written for *Harper's* magazine in June 1960, Lomax predicted that "this revolt, swelling under ground for the past two decades, means the end of the traditional Negro leadership class."

> [T]here is a twinkle in the southern Negro's eye. One gets the feeling that he is proud, now that he has come to full stature and has struck out with one blow against both segregation and

the stifling control of Negro leaders. In all truth, the Negro masses have never been flattered by the presence of these leaders, many of whom—justifiably or not—they suspected were Judas goats. The Negro masses will name leaders and will give them power and responsibility. But there will never again be another class of white-oriented leaders such as the one that has prevailed since 1900.

The controversial civil rights leader Bayard Rustin put it even more bluntly: the sit-ins "have broken the back of professional Uncle Tomism."

The movement continued to surge with no signs of abating. Even before the Durham sit-in, hundreds of A&T students had joined the four original protesters crowding into several segregated lunch counters in downtown Greensboro. The day after the Durham protests began, 150 well-disciplined students in Charlotte closed down eight lunch counters. And while protests persisted in all these cities, the student movement continued to mushroom throughout the state to Raleigh, Winston-Salem, and High Point, and then beyond the borders of North Carolina to Chattanooga and Nashville, Tennessee, and Richmond, Virginia.

Unlike the NAACP, Martin Luther King, Jr., quickly understood the significance of the lunch-counter protests. On the second week of the sit-ins, the Reverend Fred Shuttlesworth, a colleague of King's, was visiting North Carolina and saw for himself the students' energy and dedication. He immediately called King's new home office, the headquarters of the Southern Christian Leadership Conference in Atlanta. The student protests could "shake up the world," Shuttlesworth reported excitedly. "You must tell Martin that we must get with this."

After nearly a decade of prodding by Douglas Moore and others, King was at last prepared to endorse a national nonviolent direct-action campaign aimed at ending Jim Crow. Although slow to warm to the idea, King would embrace the cause so completely that it would seem his own. To repay a debt to the more radical preacher, King accepted Moore's invitation to come to Durham to put his blessing on the lunch-counter movement. From the pulpit of White Rock Baptist

Church, King joined the student crusade on the evening of February 16. The move had two important effects. First, it solidified King's standing—in the eyes of both blacks and whites—as *the* leader of the black protest movement in America. At least as important, King morally and politically legitimized a youth-led agenda of confrontational social change that would define one of the most crucial decades of the American Century. Together, King and the lunch-counter movement were much more powerful than either one was alone.

The crowd that gathered at White Rock in the heart of Durham's black Hayti section on that chilly February night seemed to sense the event's importance. The church auditorium was packed, people standing shoulder to shoulder in the aisles and around the edges of the hall, the overflow filling adjoining rooms and spilling outside onto the dew-soaked church lawn. First, there was a rousing warm-up speech by King's associate and successor in Montgomery, the Reverend Ralph Abernathy. Then Louis Austin introduced King to the adoring crowd. King praised the students who had, as he put it, "fashioned . . . a creative protest that is destined to be one of the glowing epics of our time. . . ."

King went on to promise the students the "full weight" of support of the SCLC, and exhorted them to keep on fighting until the war on segregation was won. If anyone still had doubts that this was a national movement, King dispelled them that night. The protest, he declared, was important to all Americans.

With symbolism befitting the evolution of the black struggle for freedom in America, King, speaking at the church that until recently had embodied accommodationist aspirations in America, endorsed civil disobedience as the fundamental organizing tactic for black progress, exhorting the students to risk arrest if need be. After that night, wrote Taylor Branch, "Fill up the jails" was King's new battle cry. It also quickly became the battle cry of a new generation.

Speaking to reporters outside the church after the rally, an equally combative Ralph Abernathy met head-on the charge of being an outside agitator. "Write this down, and get it straight," he thundered. "I'm no outside agitator; America is my home."

Inspired by King's soaring rhetoric, the Durham students continued the sit-ins at the three targeted stores every business day for the next six months, with protesters drawn not just from NCC, with its traditionally middle-class student population, but from black trade schools, including Durham Business College, Bull City Barber College, DeShazor's Beauty School, and even Hillside High School. (The high school students played a crucial role in keeping the sit-ins and picket lines going when college students were busy with exams or out of town on vacations.)

The lunch-counter sit-ins signaled a new consensus for change among black Durhamites of all classes. Thanks largely to the groundwork laid by Douglas Moore, Floyd McKissick, and Louis Austin, the town's black elite was willing to promote confrontation over quiet persuasion. Three years earlier, the black Ministerial Alliance had turned its back on Moore's antisegregation protests, but now its leaders issued a statement, imbued with religious significance: "The Pagan Authorities paid the early Christians an ambiguous compliment when they charged that they had 'turned the world upsidedown.' Those who would continue to deny the Negro his constitutional rights will also charge us with disturbing the peace and tranquility of our Town. Peace without justice and equal opportunity is no Peace."

In a sense, it is not surprising that the leadership of Durham's black churches should have come to the aid of the student demonstrators. After all, King himself was speaking, first and foremost, as a preacher, fulfilling an emerging mission of religion: preaching the social gospel of justice and equality. Nonreligious white liberals have typically downplayed the role of religion in the civil rights movement, but historian Aldon Morris is correct in asserting that the lunch-counter protests were not primarily a college phenomenon. "Sit-ins," he points out, "were largely organized at the movement churches rather than on the campuses"—certainly the case in Durham, where students, under the guidance of Reverend

Moore, generally met in movement churches. Meetings were opened and closed with prayer and the singing of freedom songs—often hymns and spirituals. The spirit of religious mission was so pervasive that one student described the movement as being "very much like a church inside." It is no exaggeration to say that without the church, there would have been no movement.

More surprising was the conversion of the black business and intellectual classes in Durham, best exemplified by the Durham Committee on Negro Affairs. From its inception in 1935 at a country club for those of Durham's black elite, the DCNA had always been a creature of the so-called Big Negroes, most of whom were connected to that cornerstone of Washingtonian black enterprise, the North Carolina Mutual. C. C. Spaulding, head of the Mutual, was elected the DCNA's first president. However, pushed by the radical triumvirate of Austin, Moore, and McKissick, the DCNA was already becoming more energetic by the end of the 1950s. The organization opposed black candidates for public office whom they deemed too accommodationist and its members walked alongside the pioneering black students integrating Durham's public schools. When the college students began sitting in at the Durham lunch counters, the DCNA leapt into the fray—this time on the side of the protesters. They circulated a statement announcing their position:

> [C]ertain public officials and other highly placed persons within the state have called upon the responsible Negro leadership (including college presidents) to use its influence to halt activities of Negro students and their white counterparts who have joined the movement. It is our opinion that instead of expressing disapproval, we have an obligation to support any peaceful movement which seeks to remove from the customs of our beloved southland, those unfair practices based upon race and color which have for so long a time been recognized as a stigma on our way of life and a stumbling block to moral and economic progress of the region. . . . In conclusion, we commend these students . . .

106

Officials of state-supported black colleges had to be more circumspect since they depended upon the funding provided by the all-white state legislature. NCC president Alfonso Elder labored behind the scenes to aid students participating in the sit-ins. He passed the word along the student grapevine that freshmen and sophomores who left campus during usually restricted hours would not be punished, and he overlooked the fact that the dining hall was staying open late to feed protesters returning from duty on the picket lines.

White America reacted to the lunch-counter sit-ins with equal parts alarm and confusion. Reprising his role as the innocent-on-the-sidelines, President Eisenhower answered a reporter's question about the lunch-counter movement by saying he would have to "reserve judgment on the sit-down disorders" since he was "one of those persons that believes there is too much interference in the private affairs, and, you might say, personal lives already." Former president Harry Truman, idealized by many blacks for integrating the military, may have been more decisive than his successor, but his stand on the lunch-counter protests didn't please blacks. "If anyone came into my store and tried to stop business," said Truman, "I'd throw him out. The Negro should behave himself and show he's a good citizen." Louis Austin ridiculed Truman's statements as "positive proof that however great a man becomes there is a time in his life, if he lives long enough, when he needs a nurse." The powers-that-were in North Carolina attempted to crush the student movement from the outset, with Governor Luther Hodges declaring his contempt for those "who deliberately engage in activities which any reasonable person can see will result in a breakdown of law and order." State solicitor W. H. Murdock advised store owners to order demonstrators to leave, and when they didn't, have them arrested for trespassing, invoking the Royal Ice Cream case as a precedent.

White Durham's reaction to the lunch-counter movement was sadly predictable. While couching their views in the honeyed language of Southern progressivism, the men who ruled Durham were as opposed to integration as their less cultured counterparts throughout the state. The self-declared "friends of the race" expressed disappointment in the students' radical approach to solving whatever problems might still exist in the Magic City. The *Durham Sun* opined: "[I]t is doubtful if the closings have advanced any cause of the Negroes, have contributed anything constructive to racial relations in North Carolina, have inspired any interracial friendship or have done anything to bring whites and Negroes into any area of greater understanding. From the community standpoint, whatever may be said for the militant approach, it is unlikely that civic unity is being served." The *Durham Morning Herald* weighed in with a stern editorial, ruefully observing that "race relations in Durham reached a dangerous low in the sit-down protest" and advising the misguided students that "difficult as is the assignment, racial issues ought to be resolved in good will . . ."

As the protest movement reached into other segregated public facilities, such as theaters and motels, white resistance hardened. Demonstrators had eggs thrown at them and coffee and hot soup spilled in their laps; a white woman spat a mouthful of chewing tobacco into a protester's face; a seventeen-year-old student demonstrator was knocked unconscious by a group of white hoodlums at Walgreen's; a white motorist tried to run down a group of picketers. Far from protecting demonstrators, the Durham police often initiated the violence. Joycelyn McKissick, a leader of Durham's lunch-counter movement, was brutally beaten by three policemen in the lobby of the Holiday Inn at a peaceful demonstration. "The cops just started hitting," she says. "They didn't even bother to ask why we were there, or turn us away. They just started hitting us with billy clubs. And kicking. I somehow hit the floor and these three cops just stomped me in the stomach." The savage beating left McKissick permanently disabled.

Despite the brutality, the students were committed to nonviolence and for the most part bore the insults and indignities without striking back. Outnumbered and outgunned, they realized physical confrontation was foolhardy. "Before Martin Luther King got involved we were ready for fights," recalls

Callis Brown. "It was: 'You want to take a swing at me? Go ahead, we'll get it on right now.' But King made us see that nonviolence was the way to go. After all, who's got the bullets?"

For most of the student demonstrators, however, nonviolence wasn't simply another strategy such as picketing or sitting in; it was an act of faith. They traced their philosophy to Thoreau and Gandhi, debating the great works of civil disobedience at Floyd McKissick's office on Main Street in study and prayer sessions that often lasted all night. And, of course, there were references to the examples of Christ and the early martyrs. "Let them curse, you bless," advised Louis Austin, "let them call names; let them spit on you. You must walk on and sit down with dignity and as ladies and gentlemen in a spirit of love, humility and forgiveness. . . . You are on a mission of destiny."

It never occurred to Ann Atwater to join the lunch-counter protests, although she believed in them completely. If she was arrested, who would take care of her two children? And what would become of her job as a domestic? How would she provide for her family if she was fired? And there was an even more serious problem, one filled with a bitter irony that exposed the class divide in black America. Suppose Ann sat in at a lunch counter and, however unlikely, was served. What would she do when the check came? Like most domestics and other black laborers, Ann couldn't afford a meal out, even at a dime-store lunch counter. While Ann backed the lunch-counter protests in theory, a victory there would make no difference in her daily battle to raise her family and improve their lives.

King himself would recognize and decry this fundamental flaw in the early civil rights movement. In 1968, he would write "that the integration of public facilities was meaningless if blacks didn't have the wherewithal to pay for goods and services."

But in 1960, only a few "radicals" spoke about the problems facing blacks in terms of class. King may have embraced direct action, but in the early 1960s he was still very much the product of his black middle-class upbringing, and he would occasionally lash out against stereotyped lower-class behaviors. At these times, he sounded more fussbudget than rebel, as when he scolded blacks that "they may not be able to buy perfume in Paris, but they could all afford a nickel bar of soap."

The movement was defined—by blacks and whites alike— using the narrow and simplistic language of race. Raising the issue of class was likely to get you tagged as a Communist, a designation which killed your political effectiveness, not to mention your ability to put food on the family table. This dynamic had defeated the striking black tobacco workers in Winston-Salem in the 1940s. The lesson wasn't lost on the civil rights workers two decades later. *Steer clear of class; focus exclusively on race* was the unwritten rule during this era dominated by Cold War politics. By following this principle, the movement would achieve its short-term goal of integrating lunch counters, theaters, buses, and motels. One after another, these institutions would cave in to protesters' demands and admit blacks—as long as they could pay for the services. The same principle would also prolong the harsh realities of life for poor blacks like Ann Atwater, let alone for the equally poor, and increasingly threatened, whites like C. P. Ellis.

CHAPTER SIX

Racists need devils, or they need gods, and often they need both.

—JOEL WILLIAMSON

C. P. Ellis sat behind the wheel of his rusty Buick, parked on the shoulder of Chapel Hill Road, surveying the scene. A faint flush of anger crept up his neck and spread across his hard-set face.

First they wanted to eat at the lunch counters, he thought. Then they had to sit in the white section at the movie theaters. Now here they were by the hundreds on the front lawn of Howard Johnson's, demanding the right to eat at a regular sit-down restaurant. C.P. shook his head in disbelief. Now it seemed he couldn't turn around in Durham without running into a group of demonstrators, marching up and down in front of some business carrying picket signs declaring DEMOCRACY LIES BURIED HERE and THIS GENERATION WILL NOT TOLERATE SEGREGATION, and daring the police to do something about it.

He watched as a lone white man walked out of the restaurant and stood before the crowd, raising his hands for quiet. "I'm Clarence Daniels," the man yelled. "I suppose you know that I am the manager and I'm ordering you to leave." No one moved. A few snickers rose from the crowd. Then a tall black man turned his back to Daniels and started singing. The entire assemblage joined in and soon the air was filled with a hymn-like freedom song. C.P. had heard this one often enough so that, against his will and much to his dismay, he anticipated each line before the lyrics were actually sung.

We shall not, we shall not be moved.
Just like a tree

Planted by the water,
We shall not be moved.

And then the part C.P. hated most:

Black and white together,
We shall walk together.
We shall not be moved.

Black and white together, repeated C.P. with disgust, that's what this was really all about. Everyone knew it. A few years before, during the first school integration battles, the counsel to the Governor's Commission on Integration declared that "the eventual goal of this movement to integrate public schools is racial intermarriage and disappearance of the Negro race by fusing into the white." C.P. had forgotten the exact words, but he remembered the substance of the man's charges. The theory was common knowledge. The lawyer's unguarded remarks about race were still the exception among "quality people," however. Most of the time the Southern gentry spoke in code about such things. Still, C.P. and everybody else knew exactly what was meant when a politician was quoted in the paper saying that he favored "states' rights" (to keep blacks in their place) and opposed "bloc-voting" (political organization by blacks).

Now C.P. scanned the crowd until he found what he was looking for: whites and blacks, "standing together" all right, some even holding hands. The sight of a white woman allowing a black man to caress her hand made C.P. almost ill. It was unnatural. It was wrong. He started up his car and swung it back out onto the highway, leaving behind a blue-black cloud of smoke that drifted over the protesters. The outrage that the demonstration stirred in C.P. stayed with him as he drove back across town to the small gas station he had recently bought.

He had acquired the station through chance. C.P. had been driving a truck for a Raleigh bakery for a few years, delivering cookies to small neighborhood stores, most of them located in the black sections of Durham, when he was notified that the business was about to close. C.P. was anxious about finding another job, but during a conversation with the owner of one of the stores on his route, he learned that a nearby service station was for sale. The man suggested that C.P. buy it. C.P. just snorted. "Where would I get that kind of money?" he asked. He had nothing in the bank, and possessed no collateral, unless you counted the tiny trailer he and his family crowded into. "Shoot, C.P.," said the man, "I'll co-sign the note with you." And he did. After a lifetime of working for others, C.P. was suddenly a small-business owner.

C.P. arose each day possessed by a strange sensation: optimism. He arrived at the station punctually just as the sun was filtering through the pine trees that still grew in thick groves in the white working-class neighborhoods south and east of Durham proper. He was free to set his own hours, to earn what he could. In fact, he was working harder than ever before, and far longer hours, but he told himself that this was different; this was how all small businesses began. Look at "Wash" Duke. *He* started with fifty cents and had built an empire. Hard work would eventually be rewarded.

C.P. could fix anything mechanical, but he was no businessman. He had foundered in school after teachers told him he had no head for figures. Only the exceptionally bright student from the poor neighborhoods was encouraged and nurtured, like a rare orchid found growing in a patch of crabgrass. The average and slower students were patted on the head and passed over, and if they didn't cause trouble they were allowed to mark time in the classroom until, frustrated and bored, they withdrew to take their rightful place as the muscle and bone of industry. No one saw anything wrong with this system. After all, it didn't take much education to haul tobacco or push a few buttons on a machine in the textile mills.

After making the monthly payment on his loan, paying his few employees, and sending off the tax money to the government, there was no more to live on than before. C.P.'s enthusiasm turned to frustration and ultimately to despair, and the morning sunlight that slanted through the pine groves around the station now seemed to mock his ambitions, illuminating the huge chasm between C.P.'s dreams and what the world really offered him.

Even the Negroes were doing better than he was. They drove around Durham in cars that were bigger and newer than his, and they sat in their offices high up in the North Carolina Mutual building over on Parrish Street while he was busting his knuckles greasing and repairing cars in a dingy little gas station. And it was not lost on C.P. that the demonstrators around the Howard Johnson's that day in August were wearing clothes better than anything he or his family owned. What kind of man is outdone by niggers? C.P. asked himself sometimes late at night, exhausted after a day at the station and an evening of drinking liquor. And the answer always came back, like the hollow, clattering echo of a stone tossed down a dry well: Not much of a man at all.

Not long after the demonstration at the Howard Johnson's, C.P. stumbled onto another answer, one that promised him a chance for redemption.

He was complaining about the demonstrations to a customer at his service station and the man said that if he felt that way, he should drop by the Klan rally that was being held that evening just northwest of town. The suggestion triggered memories of his father's love for that group. The idea grew as he worked that day and in the early evening he closed down the station and drove over to the area the man had indicated. As he approached his turnoff, he saw several highway patrolmen directing traffic. Slowing down for the bottleneck, he noticed that the men in uniform were waving over vehicles with large flashlights. He was surprised to see they were not state patrolmen at all. They were outfitted in a uniform C.P. didn't recognize: white helmets, heavy black boots, light blue shirts, and dark blue pants with what appeared to be webbed Army belts, some of which held holstered guns. He followed the stream of cars and pickup trucks down a dirt lane that wound through pine woods and emerged into a large open pasture. C.P. parked his car and got out. In the fading twilight, a thousand people, perhaps more, milled around talking and laughing. Makeshift booths sold barbecue and iced tea. Musicians performed on a stage set up at one end of the pasture while families sprawled on blankets. Some men and women were dressed in the traditional white Klan robes like the ones C.P.'s father had kept in the attic. A few men wore robes made of satinlike material; some were red, others a brilliant purple. But most of the people gathered in the meadow wore everyday clothes: faded work shirts or T-shirts and chinos, floral-print dresses that could be found on the discount racks of any department store. They were working people, C.P. noted with satisfaction.

When the musicians wound up their number, a small man in a suit stepped up to the microphone and welcomed everyone to the meeting of the Invisible Empire, Knights of the United Klans of America. Then he delivered an opening prayer, giving thanks to God for the gathering as the crowd stood quietly in head-lowered reverence. There followed a series of robed speakers, each talking for no more than fifteen or twenty minutes. The messages of racial hatred and religious bigotry were familiar to C.P. from far back into his childhood, and yet as he stood in the meadow, lost in the large crowd as the sky darkened, these speakers' words had the force of secrets newly revealed. One man, a minister, shouted that God himself had created segregation back in Genesis when He made night and day. "Hadn't God separated the black from the white?" he cried, and the crowd yelled back, "Yes! Yes!" "Wasn't God, then, the first segregationist?" he roared, waving his right hand above his head, one finger extended toward heaven. The crowd hooted and nodded fervently. He paced up and down the platform now, sweat glistening on his brow. Nimrod was the first nigger, he continued, and he defied God, and niggers had been defying God ever since. *We*, the Klan, were following God's laws, he said. Therefore, the Klan's work was God's work. The crowd cheered its agreement.

The last speaker walked slowly to the microphone, his bright green robes shimmering, his hands raised for quiet. Thin and wiry, with sharp features and eyes so deep-set that they looked as if they belonged to an animal staring out from a cave, this man was Robert Shelton, national leader of the

United Klans of America, and his deep, gravelly voice res-
onated with all the pain and suffering the South had known.
His message pierced C.P.'s heart. The white man, said Shelton,
was being dominated by niggers and Jew-Communists bent on
destroying the white race through economic oppression and
intermarriage. In his mesmerizing voice, Shelton laid out the
awful plot against the white race and its pinnacle of nobility,
Southerners. The primary target was the embodiment of
motherhood and purity, the Southern white woman. Jew-
Communists goaded black beasts to rape and brutally deflower
the wives, sisters, daughters, and mothers of the South in
order to dilute and destroy the white race. It was war, racial
war, the same war that Robert E. Lee and Stonewall Jackson
had fought. The Southern men there that night could save the
South, said Shelton. They could win the Lost Cause.

Shelton did not yell and gesticulate wildly like the minister
who had spoken earlier, but his dreadful seriousness inspired
C.P. all the more, transporting him and the rest of the crowd to
a higher plane, one of nobility and chivalry, where sober men
performed courageous deeds. It was a reminder of a better
time, before the disaster of the Civil War and the ignominy of
Reconstruction. Neither C.P. nor anyone else standing in the
field that night grasped that the very plantation culture which
they now viewed through magnolia-colored glasses was the
source of their present discontent, that a system based on slavery consigned white laborers and their descendants to peonage.

Finally, the giant wooden cross, wrapped in oil-soaked
burlap and sunk into the ground at one end of the pasture, was
set ablaze. When a robed Klansman strolled by gathering
names of those who wanted to join the group, C.P. didn't hesitate. He added his name and address to the long list. Many of
the addresses were local, some were from the nearby cities of
Raleigh and Greensboro, but many others were from small
towns across the state: Mollie, Waxhaw, Piney Creek, Trotville.
The Klan was clearly bigger than C.P. had imagined.

Sitting in his car later, waiting in the long line of vehicles
creeping back through the dense woods and out to the highway, C.P. looked over the stack of flyers and leaflets that had

been pushed into his hands at the rally. As he held them up in the glare of headlights from the vehicle behind him, one in particular drew his attention: a single page bearing a striking, almost pornographic drawing of two figures. One was a half-naked black man. His bulging eyes, wild hair, enormous dark belly, and animal-fang necklace made the barefoot figure more beast than human. The other figure was that of a woman—a white woman, young and pretty with long, wavy hair and a small, delicate nose—running to escape the black brute's out-stretched arms. In her hurry, the woman's thigh had poked through a tear in her gown. Her exposed thigh—like her breasts, which threatened to spill out of the top of the dress—was full, well rounded, flawlessly white, and heartbreaking in its vulnerability. A cartoonlike label was caught in the dress folds. It read: "Southern Womanhood." Another tag trailed the figure of the black man. On it was a single word: "Integration." Above this tragic tableau were the words "CONQUER and BREED." At the bottom of the page, C.P. read what struck him now as a kind of battle cry: "The South Must Fight or Perish."

Apparently, the Klan was better at organizing rallies than at keeping records. C.P. waited for weeks to hear back from them about his application. He considered that perhaps they were just checking him out, making sure he wasn't an FBI infiltra-tor, but as the weeks went by, C.P. ached with disappointment. He had been ready to sacrifice everything to protect his beloved South, to keep the beautiful white woman in the flyer safe from the black man's lustful rage. But he had no way of getting in touch with the Klan. There was nothing he could do but go to the station each day to continue the never-ending fight to sustain his family and drink himself to sleep each night to blunt the recognition that he wasn't doing a good job.

Now, however, he knew why. The Communists and the Jews were against him. They didn't want him to prosper, because he was a God-fearing white Christian man. They secretly helped blacks run businesses to compete with his. Now that he knew what to look for, he saw irrefutable signs of this plot every-where. Most of the media, which C.P. had learned at the rally was controlled by the Jews, concealed the conspiracy. One

journalist, though, wasn't afraid to expose the truth, a commentator for Raleigh television station WRAL named Jesse
Helms. While others spoke of the need for "understanding"
and "tolerance" during these troubled times, the proud reactionary blasted the civil rights movement as nothing more
than "anarchy" led by "professional agitators, opportunistic
charlatans, and political phonies." Even Helms didn't speak
openly about race mixing, but instead warned about threats to
the Southern way of life. C.P. rushed home from the gas station
each night to catch Helms's editorial at the end of the six
o'clock news. From Helms, C.P. learned that socialized medi-
cine was a Trojan horse for the Communists, the United
Nations was a forum for advancing Red ambitions, and Martin
Luther King, Jr., and his followers "can be labeled and proved
as Communists and sex perverts."

Helms deftly wove "Christian values" with private property
rights, linked racial themes with attacks on government
"intrusions" into business, and preached the sanctity of the
free market system so convincingly and with such scriptural
authority that his viewers believed that the Sermon on the
Mount had been a defense of laissez-faire capitalism. If Helms
at times sounded more like the voice of the country-club set
than of the good ol' boys like C.P. who struggled daily to get by,
there was good reason for that. C.P. didn't know that before
Helms took over as news director at WRAL, he had served for
years as editor of the house organ of the state's financial community, *The Tarheel Banker.* Had C.P. known, however, he
would likely not have cared. For C.P., as for tens of thousands
of other poor whites in North Carolina and beyond, Jesse
Helms was simply a steady beacon of truth in uncertain times.
A political biography of Helms (written much later, after he
had become a powerful force in the U.S. Senate) termed this
ability to reach out to "common" people like C.P. "Helms's
genius." By calling upon stock Southern themes of independence, a glorious past betrayed, and, of course, undergirding it
all, racial paranoia, Helms "persuaded working people that
their needs were the same as those of men whose economic
desires were in fact wholly the opposite." While the TV com-

mentator may have sounded like the voice of the Klan to C.P., in reality he spoke for the white men of wealth, power, and prestige who governed the state. But he used the language of the white dispossessed, of the impoverished tobacco farmers and the factory hands who lived in shotgun shacks on the fringes of the great Tarheel cities, and they loved him for it and claimed him as their own.

C.P. sat at night before the television in his battered trailer, his clothes and face still stained with grease and sweat, listening to Jesse Helms tear into the civil rights movement and the Communists who led it. "What the Russians are counting on," explained Helms, "is an *internal breakdown* in this country." These editorials linked C.P. to the world of racial politics and gave him hope that the battle for the soul of the South—and for his own soul—was not yet lost. Listening to Jesse Helms was the next-best thing to serving in the Klan.

He didn't notice when the men arrived. On this slow Monday evening at the gas station, C.P. was inside working on a car hoisted up on the lift while country music played softly from a radio on the workbench. Occasionally, someone would pull up to the gas pump outside and honk. C.P. would curse and lay down his tools, and attempt to wipe off his hands on the filthy rag he stuffed in his back pocket. During one of these interruptions, he saw them standing on the concrete apron out front smoking and talking and swigging bottles of Coca-Cola. There was nothing remarkable about the small group; they looked like everyone else in the run-down working-class neighborhoods of East Durham. After gassing up the car, C.P. returned to his repair work.

When the same group appeared on the following Monday night, C.P. grew curious. A week later he approached them and asked who they were. No one answered immediately, and in the awkward pause C.P. wondered if he had barged in on a group of criminals. Finally, after surveying C.P. with a steely eye, one of the men said, "We're members of the Klan. We meet nearby." C.P. could feel the men studying his face.

His only reaction was astonishment at his good luck. He

asked where they met, but the man who had first answered
C.P. said he couldn't reveal the exact location. Was C.P. interested in joining? he asked. C.P. nodded. The man pulled out a
piece of paper, an application, from a buttoned shirt pocket
and handed it to C.P., who retrieved a pencil from the office
and filled out the form. The group took his application with
them, promising to get back to him when their investigation
was completed.

C.P. closed up early and rushed home to tell his wife about the
visitors. Imagine, he told her, a Klan meeting hall somewhere
within walking distance of the gas station and he had never
known it. Mary wasn't enthusiastic about the Klan, but that
didn't dismay him. He had a hard time sleeping that night,
and the next day he rushed out to greet every car that pulled up
to his pumps, half expecting a group of robed Klansmen to drive
up with an invitation to follow them to their mysterious meeting
place. Nearly a week after his encounter with the Klansmen, C.P.
received a phone call from a man who told him to be ready the
following night, that someone would pick him up at his home.
C.P. nearly dropped the phone in his excitement.

He was waiting outside his trailer the next evening when a
car full of men pulled up. He was disappointed to see that they
wore ordinary clothes. Then he realized how foolish he had
been to think that secretive Klansmen would ride around
Durham dressed in their robes. He opened the door and
climbed in. There was little talking and C.P. was simultaneously nervous and excited about what would happen. Before
long, they parked in front of a nondescript one-story building
about a quarter of a mile from his service station, and everyone got out. C.P. was told to wait in a small room just inside the
front door while the men disappeared through another door,
which led into the building. After an uncomfortable few minutes, the inner door opened again and four robed Klansmen
walked in. One of them asked C.P. a series of questions while
the others stood around him. Was he native-born? White? Gen-
tile? Christian? Loyal to the United States? Willing to "faith-
fully strive for the eternal maintenance of white supremacy"?
When C.P. had answered yes to all of these, he was ordered to

stand up and follow them. They escorted him through another small room and finally to the threshold of another doorway, where the procession halted. One of the men turned to C.P. and said in a loud voice, "Sir: The portal of the Invisible Empire is being opened for you! Your righteous prayer has been answered and you have found favor in the sight of the Exalted Cyclops and his Klansmen assembled. Follow me and be prudent!"

Before they entered, a disembodied voice boomed out from somewhere inside the room:

> God give us men! The Invisible Empire demands strong
> Minds, great hearts, true faith and ready hands.
> Men whom the lust of office does not kill;
> Men whom the spoils of office cannot buy;
> Men who possess opinions and a will;
> Men who have honor; men who will not lie;
> Men who can stand before a demagogue
> And damn his treacherous flatteries without winking!
> Tall men, sun-crowned, who live above the fog
> In public duty and in private thinking;
> For while the rabble, with their thumb-worn creeds,
> Their large professions and their little deeds,
> Mingle in selfish strife, Lo! freedom weeps;
> Wrong rules the land, and waiting justice sleeps.
> God give us men!
> Men who serve not for selfish booty.
> But real men, courageous, who flinch not at duty;
> Men of dependable character; men of sterling worth;
> Then wrongs will be redressed, and right will rule the earth;
> God give us men!

C.P. trembled uncontrollably. The invocation, coupled with the slow journey through the dim rooms, aroused in him a sense of foreboding. Was he really one of those men described in the oath? Of course not, he thought. He wasn't noble or unselfish or courageous. He suddenly realized that he couldn't go through with this—they'd discover how deeply flawed he was—but before C.P. could turn to leave, he beheld an awesome sight: row after row of robed Klansmen, hundreds of them, standing silently in a cavernous hall, illuminated only by a large red fluorescent cross at an altar in the center of the room. All eyes followed C.P. as he marched a counter-clockwise circuit through the hall, pausing before small altars where the men leading him exchanged passwords with other Klansmen before continuing on their way. At a signal, the Klansmen formed a double line and C.P. was guided down this human corridor until, at last, he stood before a short, pinch-faced man dressed in a blood-red robe, the Exalted Cyclops, head of the Klan group.

"Sir," the man said to C.P., "is the motive prompting your presence here serious and unselfish?"

"Yes, sir," C.P. stammered.

"It is indeed refreshing to meet face to face with a man like you, who, actuated by manly motives, aspires to all things noble for yourself and humanity. The luster of the holy light of chivalry has lost its former glory and is sadly dimmed by the choking dust of selfish, sordid gain. Pass on!"

The ceremony continued for some time, with more perambulations and exchanges of secret passwords and hand signs, more invocations and singing, until C.P. found himself at last standing before the large central altar. Next to a giant red cross was a small wooden table and on it were a folded Confederate flag, a Bible, a glass bottle, and an unsheathed sword. C.P. was ordered to kneel on his right knee.

The Exalted Cyclops lifted the bottle high above C.P.

"Sir," the man intoned, "'neath the uplifted Fiery Cross, which by its holy light looks down upon you to bless with its sacred traditions of the past, Claiborne Paul Ellis, I dedicate you in body, in mind, in spirit, and in life to the holy service of our country, our Klan, our homes, each other, and humanity."

He sprinkled a few drops of liquid from the container onto C.P.'s back.

"In body," said the Exalted Cyclops.

C.P. felt a few more cold drops fall on his bowed head.

"In mind."

The Exalted Cyclops then poured some water into his own

hand and tossed it into the air, saying, "In spirit." With the same hand, he traced a circle over C.P.'s head and declared, "And in life."

C.P. was told to rise.

The Exalted Cyclops looked directly into C.P.'s eyes and with great warmth told him, "You are no longer a stranger or an alien *among* us, but are a citizen *with* us. I welcome you to citizenship in the empire of chivalry, honor, industry, and love. By authority vested in me by our Imperial Wizard, I now declare and proclaim you a citizen of the Invisible Empire, United Klans of America, Knights of the Ku Klux Klan, and invest you with the title of Klansman, the most honorable title among men."

As he turned around, the several hundred Klansman gathered there filled the hall with thunderous applause. C.P. was overcome by the moment. His shoulders heaved with emotion, tears trickled down his face. As he looked out at the rows of men welcoming him, he felt the old shame of poverty, failure, and purposelessness melt away. A lifetime of being an outsider was over. He felt blissfully submerged into a new and yet familiar community. The Klansmen were the descendants of failed farmers and broken mill hands just like himself. C.P. knew that each one had his own story of struggle and disillusionment, and in that moment he felt for them that deepest of all bonds, the bond of shared suffering. He knew that the outside world ridiculed them all as "Kluxers," fools dressed in bedsheets, but why should he care? That same world had always ridiculed their kind—in or out of Klan robes. They were the butt of a thousand jokes, sneered at as rednecks and crackers, lintheads and white trash.

Well, thought C.P., we'll see who laughs now.

CHAPTER SEVEN

> We tell the government that . . . it must crush out
> the Ku Klux and those who aid them, or hell will
> be a place of rest and peace compared to the
> South.
>
> —North Carolina governor
> WILLIAM HOLDEN, 1870

The Ku Klux Klan was born in the summer of 1866, in the sultry postwar tedium of tiny Pulaski, Tennessee—a jolly little club of ex–Confederate soldiers who played pranks and good-natured tricks on one another. Modeled on the fraternities then springing up on college campuses, the group took its name from the Greek word *kuklos*, meaning band. Within weeks, the organization was hijacked by embittered Democrats bent on deposing the white Republicans who had replaced the old planter rule. The Democrats were only secondarily interested in terrorizing the newly freed blacks—and then mostly because the former slaves had made political alliances with the Republicans. Klan violence and intimidation quickly became routine in North Carolina as elsewhere. Scores of Tarheel Republicans were brutally beaten. The Klan burned down homes and businesses belonging to its political rivals, and frightened many others into leaving the state. In one instance, a group of Klansmen stabbed to death a prominent state senator inside his county courthouse. To keep blacks "in their place," Klan tactics ranged from stealing black farmers' horses, to threats of violence, to floggings, to outright murder. In one particularly cruel case, Klansmen shot a black woman and her five children, finishing off one of the children by stomping him to death.

One of the group's founders was appalled by the Klan's new "political and pernicious" agenda, and said so in a letter to his local newspaper: "If it has become a regular organization, with guerilla and 'lynch-law' attributes, then better the Ku Klux had never been heard of, and the sooner such [an] organization is dissolved the better."

But the leaders of this political Klan defended their tactics by claiming that tough "law-and-order" measures would end social turmoil. Chaos *had* followed the fall of the South, just as war-ravaged societies always attract thieves and grifters. Arson, too, was a growing problem, as blacks, still unable to obtain justice in the white man's courts, torched property belonging to their victimizers. In its night-riding activities, the Klan was an extension of the prewar "paterollers," private security forces hired by plantation owners to monitor slaves. These teams were so common during slave days that they were the subject of a popular song:

> Some folks say that a nigger won't steal
> I caught two in my corn field
> One had a bushel, one had a peck
> And one had roasting ears
> Strung 'round his neck.
>
> Run, nigger, run
> Pateroller catch you
> Run, nigger, run
> Like you did the other day.

The Klan portrayed itself as the patriotic defender of law and morality in turbulent times, but the group actually caused much of the lawlessness and terror that gripped the region during those postbellum years. Its claims of public-spiritedness and moral rectitude obscured its essential nature as a terrorist organization seeking economic, social, and political power. To achieve those goals, Klan leaders, who were all from the higher social classes, needed the support of lower-class whites. To obtain it, they used a divide-and-conquer strategy drawn on the least subtle of lines: race. The group's leaders argued that the Ku Klux Klan "was a good thing for . . . poor men" since it could "protect [their] families from the darkies." Appeals to racial unity to prevent "Negro domination" stirred up such powerful emotions throughout the South that Klan activity focused at least as much on race as on party politics.

By the 1880s, when Reconstruction was a fading memory for the upper class, when Democrats had finally regained power through beatings, intimidation, rigged elections, arson, theft, and assassination, the Tarheel elites had no more need of the Klan. The former planters and new-money industrialists like Buck Duke controlled all the important institutions: courts, legislatures, schools, police. Jim Crow laws denied blacks access to the white world at the most basic levels. K. P. Lewis, manager of the sprawling Erwin Mills in Durham, explained his decision not to join the Klan by observing that "matters could be very much better handled . . . open and above-board." Of course, the "openness" Lewis spoke of was nothing more than the candor of a dictator who has eliminated all opposition, for matters were "aboveboard" only because oppression was now enshrined in the law. The same people who had risen to power employing extralegal violence now viewed the poor whites who continued using this strategy with distaste and contempt. Out of this hypocritical attitude sprang the stereotype of the savage "redneck." According to historian Joel Williamson, the idea that a particularly cruel racism was somehow unique to poor white farmers and laborers was an upper-class myth. The elite exploited this myth, writes Williamson, "to divorce itself from unflattering deeds no longer productive, and thus to arm itself to take the lead in peacefully putting things in a lasting order with itself at the top."

In slightly more than a generation, the Klan, an invention of the Southern upper classes, was universally regarded as a purely lower-class phenomenon, indeed a phenomenon so brutal and bigoted that it could have *only* come from that innately racist and inherently violent lower social stratum. The Southern redneck would prove to be one of the most durable inventions in American history.

Cut off from the upper classes, the KKK of Reconstruction eventually died out, but the organization was reborn in 1915 when native-born Americans watched in horror as millions of immigrants arrived on U.S. shores—most of them Catholics and Jews. Besides "suspect" religions, the immigrants brought with them a hunger for improved living standards, an animus against oppressive authority, and a history of collective action, particularly in labor unions. With these new threats to "social order," the Klan was back in business, as respectable as ever. They paraded in full costume down Durham's Main Street and gave presentations at the Academy of Music. In 1923, one such talk was introduced by Mayor John M. Manning. A good indication of the Klan's rehabilitation is the fact that between 1922 and 1927 the state's Grand Dragon (the group's top state position) was Henry A. Grady, a respected Superior Court judge. At its peak, the Tarheel Klan boasted 25,000 members and many more sympathizers. This new organization was as lawless as the old one. Lynchings were common throughout the South, including in the Durham area. The local Klan carried out or participated in several hangings, among them the 1920 lynching of Ed Roach, a black laborer who had been arrested for assaulting a fourteen-year-old white girl. The conservative *Durham Morning Herald* had only praise for the mob, which, according to the paper, "performed its task quietly and in a well organized manner." (The lynch party failed in only one regard; it was later determined that Roach had not committed the crime for which he was killed.)

This second incarnation of the Klan found a large following north of the Mason-Dixon line. The Klan thrived from California and Oregon in the West to Iowa and Illinois in the American heartland—wherever immigrants settled and competed for jobs with local inhabitants, bringing with them strange languages and "alien" religions. The Klan's growth caused South Dakota governor Ben Olcott to complain in 1922 that "we woke up one morning and found that the Klan had about gained political control of the state." Over in Indiana, the young Klan leader D. C. "Steve" Stephenson *was* the government, ruling the Hoosier State from his plush offices in Indianapolis. The Invisible Empire eventually foundered, however, after an outraged public demanded that Congress crush the group. Internal power struggles also mortally wounded the North Carolina Klan, which shattered into several warring factions. Despite these troubles, the Klan never completely disappeared, or at least not for long, from 1915 on. In many sections of North Carolina, any violation of the color line was an invitation for the Klan to pay a visit. A rural black family guilty of a small infraction of "social custom" would awaken in the middle of the night to find a cross burning in their yard. More serious infractions, or a blatant disregard of Klan warnings, resulted in beatings, whippings, and, occasionally, lynchings.

Klan activity in North Carolina rose and fell over the years in direct proportion to black agitation for change. When returning black soldiers demanded equal rights following World War II, the Klan's popularity once again increased. In the early 1950s, federal and state authorities finally cracked down on the group. Scores of Klansmen were sent to jail for their night-riding activities, but even then the Klan refused to die. As long as demagogues continued to manipulate race for political ends, the group was sure to survive. This was the case in 1954, when North Carolina governor Luther Hodges stirred up racial animosities over school desegregation. "Hodges has opened a Pandora's box," wrote *Carolina Times* publisher Louis Austin, "out of which has now sprung a revived frankenstein, the Ku Klux Klan."

The North Carolina Klan might have attracted even more members in the pre–civil rights era if racists hadn't acquired increased sophistication over the years. For those in the middle class (or with pretensions to the middle class), the white-robed figure saluting a burning cross was now considered somewhat tacky, a mark of poor-trash sensibilities. If the Klansman was still a figure of fear, he was now also the object of ridicule. What's more, racists had an alternative to the Klan in the white Citizens' Councils that had spread throughout the South following the Supreme Court's *Brown* v. *Board* decision. Louis Austin was one of the first to understand this trend's significance.

The respectable, "solid citizen" now indulges his racial and religious hatred in this fraternity. In place of the hood and the robe, he now wears a very respectable gray flannel suit. He and his brothers no longer prance the tobacco and cotton fields at night. They meet in well-lighted school buildings, churches and town halls. . . . These heirs apparent to the Klan kingdom have been permitted to occupy the field in racial issues in the South simply because of inaction, or what has become in our time "moderation."

The Citizens' Councils did not completely replace the Klan. Rather, the two complemented each other in preventing any changes in the status quo. Sometimes they coordinated their activities, but more often the division of labor was informal and unplanned, arising spontaneously out of a commonality of interest: white supremacy. They differed primarily in their techniques for achieving that end. The Klan had neither the economic clout nor the political savvy to manipulate social institutions, and so it depended on overt violence of the most basic type: the fist, the rope, or the gun.

The North Carolina Citizens' Councils, offspring of the New South, were more refined in their methods. Members were small businessmen, lawyers, and middle managers who believed in God, country, and a rising standard of living (at least for whites). They went to church on Sunday, sat on various civic committees during the week, and dispatched their wives to the monthly PTA meetings. Their increased purchasing power afforded them summer vacations to the beach or the mountains. They bought their wives dishwashers and upright vacuum cleaners. And every few years, with a regularity and rapture that approached ritual, they traded up for a new car. They loved their comfortable lives and lashed out at anything that threatened this idyllic existence.

In the late 1950s, school desegregation was the most immediate threat to white middle-class Southerners. Horrifying mental images of classrooms in which rapacious black boys sat within arm's reach of their innocent daughters flickered through their heads. The true purpose of the struggle for desegregation, charged an Alabama state senator, was "to open the bedroom door of our white women to Negro men." For the Citizens' Councils, as for the Klan, the sexual perils of desegregation were intertwined with the equally dreadful menace of Communist domination. Mississippi judge Thomas Pickens Brady, founder of the Citizens' Council movement, blasted the Supreme Court's *Brown* v. *Board* decision as "socialistic." The winning entry in a student essay competition sponsored by the organization promised that "[we] will fight until we have succeeded in maintaining segregation, our way of life, or until the Communists, with the aid of our own Supreme Court, have caused us to crumble from within and fall like Rome of old." A political cartoon in a Council tabloid depicted an embarrassed black man (representing the NAACP) with his pants down around his ankles, revealing boxer shorts covered with the Soviet hammer-and-sickle emblem. Jesse Helms constantly whipped up these fears in his television commentaries, devoting several evenings to "exposing" connections between civil rights leaders and Communists and fuming over "shocking sexual activities and general depravity" within the movement. Helms became a favorite among Citizens' Council members and his editorials on this alleged conspiracy were a staple feature in the organization's national magazine, *The Citizen.*

Once again in the South, the combination of sexual and economic dangers ignited a thunderous reaction, but members of the Citizens' Councils followed a course of action suited to the conservative nature of their class. Instead of the gun or the lynch rope, they reached for the telephone. A few calls were made, and blacks known to advocate desegregation found themselves out on the street. A word to the right person, and the sole supporter of a family was laid off at the factory. Black business owners who didn't take the "right position" had their notes called in, orders dropped, supplies of vital materials delivered late or not at all. Domestics were suddenly not needed anymore in households for which they had toiled for decades. The minimal funds the city allocated to black neighborhoods depended on the stand black leaders took on desegregation.

Standing behind the Councils in North Carolina, but aloof

from them, were the Big Men who controlled the institutions of the state—the bankers, industrialists, insurance company presidents, and real estate magnates whom historian V. O. Key referred to collectively as an "aggressive aristocracy." Their wealth and social position allowed them to hover above the fray, like the gods on Olympus, looking down disdainfully on the middle-class Citizens' Councils, which did the heavy lifting, and on the working-class Klan, which carried out the dirty work.

Far more damage was done to individual blacks and to the civil rights movement as a whole by the machinations of the Citizens' Councils—and by the even less obvious actions and inactions of the Durham elite—than by Klan violence. Despite the enormous variety of white intransigences to black demands for justice, when people thought of the "true" Southern racist, the image that came to mind most often was that of the robed Klansman, the redneck with a rifle in his pickup truck.

Which was fine with C. P. Ellis and his compatriots in Unit Nine of the United Klans of America. They embraced racism as a virtue and craved its notoriety. They saw themselves as the only true protectors of the Southern way of life—that ill-defined but beloved social order which was under attack from all sides. The parallels to the Civil War were striking. Evil forces once again endangered the Motherland from without, while homegrown traitors gnawed away at society's foundation from within. The Yankees were the foreign threat a century ago; today it was the Communists. The traitors remained the same: ungrateful blacks and their allies, now known as "liberals." Battling those forces today, as yesterday, was the Klan. As the tumultuous 1960s rolled along, the fight intensified and called for even greater activism.

To most blacks, change seemed to come with glacial slowness. To whites, social transformation was a firestorm roaring through Durham and obliterating the familiar landscape. Duke University, although a private institution, integrated its graduate schools in 1961 and accepted black undergraduates the following year. Picket lines of black high school and college students marched in front of downtown movie theaters for several years. The protesters had small tags pinned to their lapels with words printed in red: "I do not attend segregated movies. DO YOU?" At the lavish Carolina movie theater, blacks were allowed only in a balcony section so high it was called the "buzzards' roost." When students learned that the theater admitted East Indians into the "white" section, several of them put on turbans, painted a red spot on their foreheads, and lined up at the white ticket window. The nonplussed manager sold them tickets.

In 1963, the level of activity and the emotional pitch within the region ratcheted up a notch. In January, Alabama's new governor, George Wallace, was an instant hero with whites across the South when he declared in his inaugural address: "I draw the line in the dust and toss the gauntlet before the feet of tyranny and I say segregation now, segregation tomorrow, segregation forever." That same month, North Carolina's liberal governor, Terry Sanford, tried to improve race relations in his state by creating a biracial Good Neighbor Council, charged with persuading white businesses to hire more blacks. Without enforcement power, however, the council had little effect on job opportunities for blacks.

In Durham that January, NAACP-CORE leader Floyd McKissick convinced the still-conservative Durham Committee on Negro Affairs (DCNA) to endorse a boycott of downtown merchants who wouldn't hire blacks for positions other than custodial work. Although less obviously dramatic than the lunch-counter sit-ins, this was early evidence of an equally important shift in the movement. Boycotts had been used before, as far back as 1832, when a national convention of free blacks meeting in Philadelphia initiated a boycott of goods made by slave labor. The goal, not the tactic, was new: the pursuit of economic, rather than social, objectives. The movement was approaching a crisis, brought on, ironically, by its success in ending Jim Crow. The future, McKissick and a few others realized, lay not in seeking the right to spend money, but in the ability to earn it. The change was laden with irony. In the radical 1960s, the battle for black progress would come full circle to its beginnings at the turn of the century. Back when conservative Booker T. Washington clashed with W. E. B. Du Bois, the primary question was whether blacks should pursue economic development separate from white America, as Washington favored, or attempt to integrate fully into the larger American society, as Du Bois wanted. In the 1960s, the roles would be reversed. Mainstream groups would push for ever more complete integration while more militant black nationalists, tired of knocking on the doors of equality and opportunity without response, would turn instead to a vision of a wholly segregated America. As during the Royal Ice Cream battle, McKissick was once again ahead of the crowd. He argued ceaselessly for economic empowerment, carrying along in his wake less progressive blacks who were still getting used to the idea of direct action for even social goals.

A Christmas boycott of Durham stores which mistreated blacks had been attempted in 1960, part of a larger NAACP campaign that included six Southeastern states. "Negroes are not going to spend their money where they are not treated with dignity," said NAACP Southeastern regional director Ruby Hurley in announcing the boycott. That effort failed locally when the DCNA and the black Ministerial Alliance refused to sponsor the measure. By 1963, the students were better organized, distributing 8,000 leaflets and 1,000 letters about the boycott in the first week of March, and quickly setting up picket lines at sixteen downtown merchants to inform black shoppers. A sympathetic white reporter at the otherwise conservative *Durham Morning Herald* also publicized the boycott with articles about breakthroughs in the dispute (and secretly driving protesters to and from picket duty). The campaign's high visibility put pressure on the Ministerial Alliance to back the effort. Finally, in late March, black ministers from the group not only gave their blessing to the action but joined students and other activists on the picket lines. Louis Austin used the occasion to expound on a pet grievance: class divisions within the black community. He praised the ministers' group while chiding the "many grandstand onlookers in the race who are either afraid, ashamed, or not concerned about the welfare of the Negro masses . . . [T]he hour has come," wrote Austin, "when Negro leaders in all walks of life should stand up and be counted. If they can't stand up and be counted, they should be counted out."

While there was still a class divide in the black community, the cooperation among all levels reached an all-time high, but much of the interaction fermented behind the scenes where whites couldn't see it. For example, many of Durham's black business leaders donated money to support the movement, but they would never participate in a march or walk a picket line. In part, this was because the black elite considered such actions undignified. Their reluctance was also part of a long tradition of misleading whites about the nature of relationships within black society. For powerless blacks, deception was protection. Louis Austin's daughter, Vivian Edmonds, recalls that while her father and North Carolina College president Dr. James Shepard appeared to be fierce enemies, "that was for public consumption." The two men would never visit each other's offices, she adds, but often met in secret to coordinate plans. "NCC depended on the state legislature," she explains. "If it looked like [Shepard] had sided with Louis Austin, they would have cut off everything for the college. That is a game black people have always had to play in order to survive."

In late April, Durham had a visitor who made even the most liberal whites, and all but the most radical blacks, squirm— Malcolm X. The militant spokesman for the Nation of Islam was invited by Floyd McKissick to debate on the topic "The Future of the Negro in America." Trouble arose even before Malcolm arrived, as problems developed in obtaining a meeting hall. Duke University at first agreed to host the event, but then backed out. Next, the administration at NCC, dependent as always on the state legislature's good graces, decided their auditorium wasn't the proper place for the Nation of Islam minister to speak, so the debate was scheduled at a public recreation center. The afternoon before the debate, the city announced that that location was "unavailable." Although no friend of the Nation of Islam, Louis Austin objected to the city's arbitrary action, writing that "Negroes need no protection from Durham's city officials to safeguard them against one of their own though he comes in the ridiculous form of a Malcolm X, a Malcolm Y or a Malcolm Z." At the last minute, McKissick found a site for the debate, in a dilapidated second-story auditorium.

Although there was a small Nation of Islam organization in Durham, under the direction of a local man named Kenneth X, Malcolm wanted to avoid spending the night in a member's home, knowing from experience that he would be expected to "talk revolution" until dawn. When he learned of Malcolm's concern, McKissick invited the minister to stay in his home. "This is crazy," responded Malcolm. "We're supposed to be debating each other." But he accepted the invitation.

The day of the debate, McKissick's daughter Joycelyn, now a student at NCC, was incensed when she learned that the school had banned Malcolm from the campus. She quickly rounded up a half dozen other militant students and within the hour, every blackboard on campus had scrawled on it: "Malcolm to speak, 12 noon, ice-cream-shop." At a little past noon, Joycelyn pulled up to the ice-cream-store parking lot in her old blue Studebaker. The fifty or sixty students gathered there were thrilled when Malcolm X got out of the car, climbed on top of the vehicle, and gave a short talk, inviting everyone to attend the debate that night. Malcolm later joked that he should present Joycelyn with an honorary "X" for resisting the school authorities. Her actions did earn her a one-week suspension from the school, but the nineteen-year-old had endured far worse penalties in the past and had no regrets about the incident.

The debate itself was well attended, the tiny hall packed full of students, community leaders, and a sprinkling of white liberals from Duke University. Malcolm delivered his talk in his unique style of eloquent fury.

"The white man in America is on a sinking ship," he told the crowd. "His time has come to suffer for the mistreatment of the black peoples by his ancestors. All countries which have participated in colonialism have suffered except America. Now her day has come. For this reason, the Muslims desire separation of the races." The crowd may have agreed intellectually with McKissick's response—that yes, blacks had suffered terribly under whites, but that all God's children were capable of redemption—but emotionally they backed Malcolm all the way.

His appeal was enormous and complex. Malcolm was a charismatic leader, tall and lean, articulate, good-looking, possessing obvious physical courage, a warm and ready sense of humor, and immense faith in his mission. His background of poverty and petty crime gave him insight into the demons that haunted other poor blacks, and left him with some habits that were out of character for a devout Black Muslim. Sitting in a bar after the debate, sipping orange juice, Malcolm delighted one young woman by pulling out a thick roll of bills and peeling one off to pay the tab.

Malcolm's presence in Durham had a number of effects, all of which had been anticipated by the elder McKissick. First, it solidified relations between McKissick's NAACP-CORE group and the local NOI organization, a friendship not found at the national level, where the groups eyed each other suspiciously (if not with outright hatred) from a distance. It also put whites on notice that the demands of the local activists were a preferable alternative to the revolutionary aims of Malcolm X. Most important, his visit reenergized students who were feeling the battle fatigue inevitable in a fight that had racked Durham without any letup for five years.

Events outside of Durham also aroused local blacks. Martin Luther King, Jr., had been confined to a Birmingham, Alabama, jail cell since Good Friday, April 12, arrested in a fierce effort to integrate that city's lunch counters and other facilities. A dwindling bail fund made many adults reluctant to participate in demonstrations, so King, himself finally out on bail, organized a children's march on May 2. The public safety commissioner, Theophilus Eugene "Bull" Connor, whose reputation as a hard-line segregationist was well known, hauled nearly 1,000 children off to jail in school buses. The next morning, as another thousand children between the ages of six and eighteen gathered at a church to march, Connor unleashed a furious preemptive strike. Firemen turned high-pressure water hoses on the children, rolling them down the street like dolls, and throwing others against sidewalks, buildings, and parked cars. The force of the water was so great that it stripped the bark from nearby trees. Demonstrators left standing were chased off by snarling police dogs.

More protests followed, now with angry adults, and Connor provided them with the same treatment. The violence drew television crews, which beamed these powerful images to a stunned nation and beyond. Alabama governor George Wallace supported Connor's brutal methods and sent in reinforcements in the form of 500 state troopers. The violence set off sympathy demonstrations in Raleigh, North Carolina's capital, where hundreds of blacks marched on the governor's mansion demanding to speak to Terry Sanford, who was inside dining on fillet of beef, shrimp Newburg, and petits fours with the cream of North Carolina's society, at what one reporter rightly called "a glittering formal ball." The state's chief executive, dressed in black tie and tails, emerged reluctantly from the mansion to quiet the angry black crowd, while the dulcet tones of soprano Eleanor Steber singing "Un Bel Dì" ("One Bright Day") from Puccini's opera *Madam Butterfly* drifted out from the huge house. "This is neither the time nor the place" to discuss racial problems, Sanford told the crowd. When he suggested that demonstration leaders make an appointment for a meeting at his office, the crowd booed him back inside.

The situation in Durham was, if anything, even more volatile. On April 24, amid the escalating battle over school desegregation, with the city still dragging its feet nearly a decade after *Brown* v. *Board*, an arsonist had kindled a blaze that destroyed half of the all-black East End Elementary School. Black parents were offended by the city's decision to run classes at the devastated school on a split-shift system, rather than move the affected students into nearby white elementary schools, which had plenty of room for them. In protest, some 400 parents initiated a school boycott, on the day before the first Birmingham children's march. The action, sniffed the conservative *Morning Herald*, betrayed "an unbecoming and uncooperative spirit."

Also in April, Durham's longtime mayor, Emanuel J. Evans (who had held the office since 1951), announced that he would not run for reelection in May, precipitating a short but intense campaign between Watts Carr, Jr., a member of one of Durham's first families, and city councilman R. Wensell "Wense" Grabarek. Neither man provoked much excitement in Hayti. However, Grabarek, while not specifically promising to do anything to help blacks, did ask for the black vote in advertisements in the *Carolina Times*, a courtesy Carr did not extend. The DCNA ultimately endorsed Grabarek, hoping that he would at least "have an open mind and an open heart."

The leaders of the NAACP youth chapter at NCC decided that simply hoping that the new mayor would respond to the black community's needs wasn't good enough. They wanted to serve notice that no matter which white man was elected, he would have to answer to black demands for progress. To emphasize that point, the students scheduled a march and demonstration for election day, Saturday, May 18. Leaders of the DCNA were alarmed when they learned of the plan. A black candidate was running for the city council, and the DCNA feared that a show of black militancy on election day would alienate white voters. Despite a request from the DCNA to cancel their plans, the students—deciding that "democracy was in the streets" and not at the polls—went ahead with the demonstration.

The students gathered at the NCC campus at 2 P.M. When they were several hundred strong, the marchers headed up Fayetteville Street toward the center of downtown Durham. They sang freedom songs and carried signs that read: DURHAM: PROGRESSIVE CITY OF DISCRIMINATION and VOTE TO MAKE DEMOCRACY MORE THAN A WORD. After singing and praying in front of City Hall, the demonstrators broke up into small groups and entered several segregated downtown businesses. There were scattered incidents of violence. One hundred and thirty protesters were arrested and marched off to jail. While the demonstration was mostly peaceful, a racially charged atmosphere now gripped the city, with more and more people wondering if Durham would be "the next Birmingham." In the election, nearly reduced to a sideshow, Wense Grabarek won by 2,245 votes. Ninety percent of Durham's black voters cast their ballots for Grabarek, handing the new mayor his slim margin of victory with their 2,418 votes.

With the furor over police repression in Birmingham simmering, and the flush of excitement generated by Malcolm X's visit still lingering, the students pressed for immediate action. That night, hundreds of protesters assembled outside the courthouse and jail where their friends were held. Across the street, sullen white counterdemonstrators took up positions. Durham's police chief telephoned Mayor Evans for instructions, only to find that Evans had left town earlier that day, leaving a power vacuum at a critical time. Increasingly alarmed that the situation was escalating out of control, the chief phoned the mayor-elect, even though Grabarek would not assume office until Monday.

An accountant by profession, Grabarek did not seem up to the challenge. His sole claim to fame during a lackluster tenure on the city council was detecting a bookkeeping error that would have cost the city a million dollars. He was thin to the point of cadaverousness, and spoke in a stilted fashion that struck some as formal and others as pompous—either impression reinforced by Grabarek's habit of wearing a red carnation in his lapel at all times. But Grabarek handled his first crisis well, meeting with the students' lawyer and granting their request for food and cigarettes. The small concession placated the demonstrators outside the courthouse and they agreed to leave, defusing the situation, at least for a while.

The students were not about to squander their momentum, however, which had overnight grown greater than at any time since the lunch-counter movement had commenced over three years earlier. The day after the election, May 19, was a Sunday, and a mass meeting that had been planned for weeks was held at St. Joseph's Church. The congregation was hosting some honored guests that morning, thanks to the influence of Floyd McKissick. At the service's conclusion, Roy Wilkins, the conservative executive director of the national NAACP, came to the pulpit and delivered a restrained endorsement of the

Durham student protests. Wilkins fired up no one, but his qualified support for direct action did convince some of the older black businessmen that what the students were doing was legitimate if not necessarily advisable. Wilkins was followed by James Farmer, the more activist national director of CORE, who had traveled to Durham to coordinate the growing protests in that city and in nearby Greensboro (where nearly 1,000 protesters had been arrested in the previous week). In contrast to Wilkins, Farmer backed the students' efforts 100 percent and enjoined every man, woman, and child in St. Joseph's to participate in the direct-action campaign in any way possible. Joyous shouts of "Amen" punctuated Farmer's address.

The last speaker was Floyd McKissick. With the crowd softened up by Wilkins and aroused by Farmer, the leader of the local protest group now harnessed the enthusiasm in the church and directed it toward a specific goal. As a community, said McKissick, they would exit the church, get into their cars, and proceed in a motorcade to the Howard Johnson's restaurant on the edge of town, where they would demand service as equals, and if they were refused they would close the establishment down. While many in the crowd believed that this decision had been made on the spur of the moment, it had been planned in detail for some time. Leaders selected the hotel-restaurant to replicate the massive demonstration held there the summer before, and also because it was owned in part by Luther Hodges, the former North Carolina governor, who was now a member of President Kennedy's cabinet. Hodges' national visibility made him vulnerable to charges of discrimination. McKissick and student leaders had kept plans for the rally secret, fearing that more conservative blacks would tip off the authorities.

One thousand people left the church, heading for Howard Johnson's. By the time they converged on the restaurant, they had been joined by thousands more who had heard of the action through the grapevine and by blacks from neighboring towns whom McKissick had alerted days before. Some 4,000 defiant protesters clustered on the lawn and in the parking lot that afternoon in the largest demonstration of the civil rights era in Durham. When the police ordered the crowd to disperse, hundreds of protesters instead linked arms and sat down in the parking lot. They ignored police threats to use tear gas, continuing to sing, "We're going to eat at Howard Johnson's one of these days." It took a dozen police cars and five commandeered Trailways buses several hours to carry 700 protesters to jail. The demonstrators had fulfilled Martin Luther King's 1960 challenge to "fill up the jails."

Once again, crowds of angry whites stood across Main Street, taunting the students with renditions of "Dixie" and shouts of "Niggers!" and throwing firecrackers into the ranks of protesters. Scuffles erupted between the two groups, and the forty Durham policemen stationed outside the courthouse rushed from one hot spot to another, trying to prevent the already tense situation from turning into a full-scale race riot. McKissick and the black student leaders knew that such violence could only hurt their cause, and at 10 P.M. they persuaded the protesters to go home. Nothing, however, had been solved yet. McKissick announced that beginning the next day, the city would see thirty straight days of similar demonstrations.

At noon on the following day, Wense Grabarek was sworn in as mayor of Durham, inheriting a city described by one newspaper as "a powder keg." Within hours of his swearing-in, Grabarek sat down with a group of black student leaders to hear their concerns. The meeting between the highest local government official and militant black leaders was itself an important concession, an act of good faith on Grabarek's part that surprised the black community. The students, though, wanted more than symbols. They handed Grabarek a list of grievances on which they demanded action. The new mayor scanned the paper and immediately told the students that the first two items were impossible for him to grant. He *would not* fire a number of white employees at City Hall and replace them with blacks, and he *could not* impose a hiring quota for black clerks at a downtown store. The other items on the list, Grabarek informed the students in his stiff speech, were negotiable.

The students were exhilarated by their recent accomplishments. The day before the election, a downtown art movie theater had its first desegregated screening. Then there were the mass demonstrations at Howard Johnson's and downtown. And now the students were recognized as legitimate representatives of the black community. But there was more good news to come on that day. The U.S. Supreme Court handed down its decision in a test case that arose from a Durham lunch-counter sit-in of 1960, repudiating a North Carolina court's trespass conviction of five youths who had refused to leave the Kress lunch counter when ordered to by the manager. In a victory for the civil rights movement, Chief Justice Earl Warren wrote that states cannot use trespass laws against individuals protesting state-mandated segregation policies. The students were jubilant.

Segregationists were appalled. "States' rights are a long-gone antiquity in America," intoned an ashen-faced Jesse Helms in his evening WRAL editorial on the Court's decision. "Individual rights are slipping down the drain. The White House with its federal troops, the Supreme Court with its library of second-rate sociology books—these are the architects of chaos and disorder." Helms blasted the ruling as "tyranny," and accused the Court of "cheering on the agitators." Defying the Supreme Court, the Durham Restaurant Association met that same day and voted to maintain its policy of segregation.

That night, as darkness descended upon Durham, black citizens met once again on the campus of North Carolina College. By the time all color had ebbed from the sky, the crowd had swelled to include 3,000 protesters, and they started their slow, determined march north up Fayetteville Street. They turned west onto Main Street and continued on until reaching City Hall. They sang protest songs and listened to community leaders who assured them that after hundreds of years spent wandering in the desert of segregation and oppression, the Promised Land was at last within sight. "Our blood, our sweat, our labor are in American soil," cried the Reverend Ruben Speaks, pastor of St. Mark's AME Zion Church, standing on the steps of City Hall. "I believe we are living in a moral universe.

If we continue to demonstrate and pay the price, then we will succeed." The crowd roared and applauded.

After several speeches and more singing, the crowd splintered into dozens of small groups, which entered segregated businesses and sat down in protest. Roving bands of white toughs trailed the protesters, throwing eggs at them. Some of the white youths went further, filling cored apples with broken glass and hurling the fruit at blacks. Many of the protesters were new to the movement and had neither the training for nor the commitment to nonviolence that had characterized demonstrators since the mid-1950s. Some of these black teenagers threw rocks through the windshields of cars driven by whites. As a large contingent of whites headed toward Hayti, they came face to face with another group of blacks not traditionally aligned with the civil rights movement. Just across the railroad tracks was a phalanx of grim-faced young black men, each dressed in a starched white shirt and wearing a black beret, standing military alert and forming a human barrier to the black neighborhood. They were members of the Fruit of Islam, the security forces of the Nation of Islam. They had come, unbidden, to protect the black community and the students, as a personal gesture of support for Floyd McKissick, the one black leader in Durham who had been friendly to the Black Muslims, despite deep political and religious differences. The ragged collection of white rowdies had no idea who these unsmiling men were, but it was abundantly clear, even to them, that these were not the hymn-singing student devotees of nonviolence that they were used to. They turned around and headed quickly back downtown.

The fighting intensified as the night progressed. White teenagers cornered a black man and struck him repeatedly with bricks. A black woman had her leg shattered and a white man had his head injured in a fight at the Sears, Roebuck parking lot. The police arrested a steady stream of protesters through the night, with the last ones being processed and released just before dawn. Somehow, the night ended without an all-out race riot.

On Tuesday morning when the mayor met again with Floyd

McKissick and the student leaders he had encouraging news. He had telephoned the national headquarters of Howard Johnson's and had asked them to "encourage" the local franchise to desegregate. There was no guarantee that this would result in the restaurant's dropping its race restrictions, but it did show a good-faith effort on Grabarek's part. Two other restaurants had desegregated the night before, and others promised to follow suit within days. The city could not stand more marches and demonstrations, Grabarek argued. If he continued to get results, would the students call a temporary truce in their planned thirty days of demonstrations? After a brief discussion, the leaders agreed to give Grabarek a chance, but they also issued the mayor a warning. "Unless progress is made on a daily basis," they told him, "we cannot promise that mass demonstrations will not resume at any time."

As the meeting was breaking up, a white reporter for the *Morning Herald* asked to speak to the mayor alone. The reporter, Jake Phelps, was, in fact, a longtime advocate of civil rights, though he tried to hide his sympathies from the paper. As a freshman at the University of North Carolina at Chapel Hill in 1953, Phelps had met Floyd McKissick, then a third-year law student. The two became friends and, partly due to McKissick's influence, Phelps drafted a petition to integrate the undergraduate school. He was viewed as a friend by protest leaders and was included in many strategy meetings, where he offered advice about how white town leaders might react to black demands and actions. Phelps told the mayor that he had it on good authority that if Grabarek wanted to speak at a rally planned for that evening at St. Joseph's Church, he was welcome to come. Phelps had earlier suggested the idea to McKissick, and the black leader had said that certainly they'd listen to the mayor, but he doubted that Grabarek would take him up on the offer. To everyone's surprise, the dapper accountant agreed to attend the meeting.

The mayor showed up that evening on the steps of St. Joseph's, red carnation pinned to his lapel, only hours after a severe thunderstorm had pelted the area with hail. Like the gentleman he was, Grabarek asked permission to enter and was promptly shown in. As he walked to the front of the chapel, the significance of the moment was evident to everyone seated in the church. St. Joseph's AME Church was located in the spiritual as well as the physical heart of Hayti. The ornate church building stood on land that long ago saw services held in a rude brush arbor and led by a former slave. The present building was designed in the late nineteenth century by the same Philadelphia architect whom Washington Duke had hired to build the Main Building at Trinity College. St. Joseph's was the treasure of the black community, and boasted a soaring tower which was visible throughout Hayti, many intricate stained-glass windows (including one with the image of old Wash Duke himself), and a unique multicolored ceiling of pressed tin. In beauty, history, and communal meaning, it rivaled, if not surpassed, any church in the white community.

Although not known for his eloquence, Grabarek said all the right things that night. He told the crowd that the demonstrations had "accomplished their intended purpose" and that whites now understood "the seriousness and sincerity" of black resolve. He also thanked black leaders for delaying further marches, a decision which, he said, "proves to me that you deserve the rank of first-class citizens." The crowd greeted this concession with a standing ovation, but Grabarek understood that he had to produce real changes, and quickly. He had come prepared to prove he could get things done. He announced that three more restaurants had agreed to desegregate and he suggested that someone from St. Joseph's leave immediately to verify his claim. Several people leapt up and hurried out of the church. Grabarek continued his talk, asking for the cooperation of all people of good faith to make Durham a better city. By the time he finished, the three teams had reported back that the restaurants were indeed desegregated. The meeting concluded with a new sense of optimism, a feeling that perhaps a united black community, working in tandem with a sympathetic white mayor, would force Durham to live up to its progressive reputation.

Over the next two days, Wense Grabarek recruited members for a committee assigned the task of resolving the segregation issue. The resulting group, the Durham Interim Committee (DIC), was introduced to the public on Thursday. Grabarek's mayoral rival, Watts Carr, Jr., chaired the eleven-man body, which included two blacks. The big surprise was the inclusion on the committee of Harvey Rape, the owner of Harvey's Cafeteria, who had confronted protesters outside his business only a few nights before. Grabarek knew that Rape's presence on the committee was the key to success. If a diehard segregationist like him were to endorse a desegregation plan, others would fall into line. Grabarek twisted Rape's arm, appealing to the restaurateur's sense of civic duty, and suggesting that, without him, a far more radical plan could result. Finally, Rape told Grabarek that he needed to pray on the matter. He phoned the mayor back late that night in tears. Rape announced that the Lord had answered his prayers: he was prepared to do whatever was necessary to end segregation.

Businesses started desegregating, one after another. Over 700 white Durhamites aided the process by placing an ad in a local newspaper, pledging to patronize and support merchants "who serve the public and employ help without regard to race." By mid-June, all of the city's motels and nearly all restaurants had abandoned race restrictions, with most of the rest promising to follow suit. The city's public swimming pool had also desegregated. For most whites, the primary accomplishment was that they could go back downtown without facing marchers and picket lines. As they saw it, the city had taken a step back from the brink of catastrophe, thanks to its enlightened leaders. The national media reinforced this assessment, with print and television news reports proclaiming Durham a rare Southern example of "good sense" in racial matters—a city which had chosen the path of calm negotiations and reason, rather than that of anarchy and violence.

In fact, Durham was reacting to a host of local, national, and even international pressures that made change inevitable. When the movie theater operators agreed in June to admit four blacks per showing, it had little to do with "reason" and everything to do with the fact that just days earlier U.S. Attorney General Robert Kennedy had given Southern theater owners an ultimatum: desegregate voluntarily—now—or the federal government would do it for them. Durham businessmen were still deciding whether or not to end race restrictions when, on June 11, President John Kennedy delivered a nationally televised address on civil rights, calling on Congress to outlaw segregation in public places.

The primary factor motivating Kennedy came, surprisingly, from beyond U.S. borders, where this country and the Soviet Union were waging an intense propaganda war for allies among the African nations then emerging from centuries of colonial rule. The entanglement of the Cold War and the black struggle for rights here at home was already well understood in 1952, when the U.S. Attorney General wrote: "It is in the context of the present world struggle between freedom and tyranny that the problem of racial discrimination must be viewed. Racial discrimination furnishes grist for the Communist propaganda mills . . ." As more and more African nations achieved independence, the United States government was compelled to defend racial equality here at home. (Between 1956 and 1964 a score of nations gained independence, with eleven black African countries added to the United Nations roster in just three months in 1960.)

Progressive citizens of the Magic City patted themselves on the back for desegregating two city junior high schools in May—overlooking the fact that the action was taken one step ahead of a court order, and nearly a decade after the Supreme Court had outlawed the practice of segregation in public education. Given all of these pressures, it is clear that the choice facing Durham was not between continuing Jim Crow and dismantling the system. It was between voluntary and forced desegregation.

Even so, not all whites complied with the changes. The recently formed Durham County Citizens' Council announced its own boycott, a "selective buying" campaign targeting the recently desegregated businesses. The group sponsored a rally at the Durham County Stadium that attracted 3,500 whites, who applauded the racist rhetoric of Roy Harris, president of the national organization.

Of course, the Klan opposed any changes in the status quo, but the Durham unit engaged in no actions in this period. The Exalted Cyclops, a housepainter named Jack Murray, who had immigrated from West Germany, delivered long, wandering diatribes against the Jews, who, he claimed, had destroyed his first country and now were demolishing his second. His message was crude and obvious: hook-nosed Jewish Communists threatened to take over the country. The speeches fired up the Klansmen, but as a secret society standing outside of the mainstream, with no well-thought-out plan of action, the Klan had little influence in Durham's affairs. Some of its members had hurled bottles and rocks during the recent demonstrations, but when the marches and rallies ended, the Klansmen contented themselves with their weekly doses of ritual and vitriol. There was a flurry of excitement in the Klavern that fall when Alabama governor George Wallace came to town. C.P. attended the open-air rally and was delighted to hear the governor strike the same themes that were discussed at Klan meetings. The Supreme Court, said Wallace, was "stealing little by little as a thief in the night to destroy local government." He attacked "known Communists" within the NAACP, claiming that "Negroes are as loyal as you and I, but they have been exploited."

And night after night, Jesse Helms filled the airwaves with vague but alarming allegations of conspiracy and demanded that the authorities investigate civil rights groups. "The racial unrest that is running rampant throughout the country is now far beyond a political issue," he charged. "If it is now a spawning ground for Communism, the nation needs to know it."

"Slow and steady" is an apt characterization of Durham's progress under Grabarek's leadership in the early 1960s— especially the "slow" part. The DIC's mandate saw to that. The mayor instructed the group to "seek the highest possible level of understanding on a totally voluntary basis, acceptable to all parties concerned." The goal was "understanding," not justice, and certainly not economic empowerment. Even that modest aspiration was to be arrived at "voluntarily." Little would change under such a system, but student leaders thought this was the best deal they could get, and they were probably right. They had entered into a bargain—trading the momentum of the movement for the mayor's promise of a good-faith effort. Far from being a racist, Grabarek had begun his term of office with the best possible intentions—a decent man operating within a bad system. The problem, or at least part of it, was that blacks and whites spoke two different languages, which happened to share a single vocabulary. Both sides wanted to improve race relations. When whites, particularly white Southerners, and even more particularly affluent white Durhamites, spoke about "good race relations," they meant an absence of conflict. While this concern for social harmony was shared by some blacks (generally those few encamped at the top of the socioeconomic pyramid), when it came right down to it, most blacks did not particularly care about race relations in this sense. They cared about education, about jobs, about decent housing—about equal access to these things. They cared about having their streets paved, about having playgrounds and parks in their neighborhoods, about traffic lights being provided to make the streets safe for their children. Whites did not understand this—or at least they convinced themselves that they did not. As one unusually perceptive white journalist wrote of Durham's white community: "[Whites] don't understand what black people want because that's the easiest way to avoid giving it to them . . ."

In June, the *Durham Morning Herald* ran a full-page special report titled RACE RELATIONS: DURHAM'S STORY, complete with a chronology of recent events, several pictures, analysis, and a box at the bottom of the page with the headline APPLAUSE FROM THE NATION. This section contained excerpts of letters of praise for the mayor's and the city's "mature facing of problems of human relations." The "report" was unabashedly self-congratulatory, the kind of journalistic pat on the back that Durham had specialized in since well before the turn of the century. True, a couple of caveats were thrown in, but these were clearly meant to suggest that Durham, for all its achievements, still possessed a sense of humility. Two large photographs, arranged symmetrically above the fold, dominated the page. On the left was a picture of the recent demonstration at Howard Johnson's, with the caption "Demonstrations Began Without Warning . . ." The implication was, of course, that even after centuries of fighting for freedom, even after the lunch-counter sit-ins in 1960 (and at the Royal Ice Cream Parlor in 1957), the demand for equality that summer came out of the blue—and was rather a rude surprise, at that. Opposite this photograph there was one of the mayor's committee. The caption for this picture read: ". . . and Durham Citizens Went To Work."

What is most interesting about this page is a subliminal impression created by an accident in its design. Or perhaps the person who laid out the page was compelled by an unconscious need to tell the truth. Directly below the picture of the demonstrators ran an article, with its headline printed in a typeface several points larger than that used for the photograph's caption. In effect, the headline appears to be the caption for the photograph. Beneath the picture of black people massed in the Howard Johnson's parking lot is the legend "The Progress."

On the other side of the page, beneath the photograph of the DIC, is another article and another headline, which also appears to refer to the photograph. Under the picture of the eleven men in suits (all but two of them white) seated around a heavy wooden table—sober, calm, deliberative men, one of them with his pipe held judiciously in the air as he listens—are the words "The Problems."

Three years later, after a period that whites would describe as one of "good race relations," an independent report comparing conditions in nine American cities characterized the situation in Durham: "The poor remained poor, with dusty gravel streets, unemployment, and some of the nation's most squalid housing." For all its achievements, concluded the report, the movement simply "ran out of goals and then ran out of gas."

CHAPTER EIGHT

> A group of poor folks thought we could get
> something done by talking it out. It just wasn't
> worth a damn. Nobody listens. It wasn't just a
> question of race. I'm Negro and some of the others
> are white. It just doesn't work.
>
> —Resident of East Durham

AUGUST 1965

The Department of Social Services was located in a single large open room on the ground floor of the Durham County Courthouse, three floors below the jail. The proximity of the two enterprises stemmed from the fact that both welfare and the jail were administered by the county. But the many young mothers who entered the imposing gray building each day to apply for aid grasped instantly what lay behind the convenience of geography: the judgment that here sinners came to justice. Indeed, everything that happened inside the DSS office was meant to hammer into these women the notion that society considered them criminals of a kind. The intake workers (underpaid white women who formed the bottom rung of the DSS staff) treated the poor, mostly black women with the same sullen disinterest and easy contempt with which the white jailers held the black men who arrived in handcuffs three floors above.

Ann, too, entered the DSS office reluctantly. She didn't want to go on "relief," but diabetes had so weakened her body that a doctor had told her she risked permanent injury and possibly death if she didn't give up housework. Taking a seat by the door, she noticed that the old linoleum floor wore a haze of scratches and grime. The hard plastic chair made Ann's legs and back ache and was as filthy as the floor. When a worker at last called her name, Ann walked over to a large desk where a white woman hunched over a stack of papers. Ann looked for a chair, but saw none. She realized that she was meant to stand during the interview. When the white woman finally glanced up, she gave Ann a look that was naked in its assessment: too fat, too poor, too black.

"What do *you* want?" she asked, loud enough for everyone in the enormous room to hear. Several pairs of eyes turned toward Ann. She explained her situation: how she couldn't work because of her health, why she lacked a hundred dollars for rent, about all the things her two girls needed.

"And where's the father?" the woman asked, smiling.

"I don't know."

The welfare worker laughed and looked over at a co-worker. The other woman smirked. The interrogation continued for twenty minutes. The woman behind the desk asked even more personal questions while Ann, standing before her, was forced to explain her life—with a special emphasis on her problems— to a roomful of strangers. At last, the woman dismissed Ann with a brusque wave. She would be notified when a decision had been reached.

Ann left the room and walked out of the building and down the limestone steps to the sidewalk. She proceeded east on Main Street a half block and turned south onto Roxboro. A block later she crossed the railroad tracks and then headed east again on Pettigrew. She turned onto Fayetteville Street after about a third of a mile, took it a short way to Lakewood, crossed over to Old Fayetteville Street, walked the block down to her own street, Fowler, and, reaching her house, opened the front door, walked in, and sat down in an old chair, clutching her purse in her lap as she waited for the rage to subside.

A few days later, Ann was cleaning her house when she was interrupted by a knock on her door. Two strangers stood on the doorstep, one a small woman with a light brown complexion and curly hair and the other a striking dark-skinned man in his early twenties. The man explained that he and the woman worked for a new antipoverty organization and wanted her to attend a meeting that night. Ann eyed them skeptically. Why should she bother herself with a meeting? she asked. As if on cue, the woman launched into a passionate speech about the need for poor folk to work together to find solutions to their problems, about how the government would never be interested in them until they banded together and forced the power structure to pay attention.

Ann couldn't argue with the claim that the government ignored poor people. The memory of the DSS office was still fresh in her mind. But she didn't have any faith that a group of poor people could change the system. When the pair asked if she was having any problems, she sighed and led them on a short tour, pointing out the tub, which was tilted at an awkward angle, one leg through the rotten bathroom floor. She flushed the toilet and a fountain of water gushed toward the ceiling. She turned the front porch light on and off by stamping on the floor. Worst of all, she told them, she was being evicted for falling a month behind on the rent and had nowhere else to go.

The tall man said he thought that Ann was being treated badly. Maybe they could help. He said they could find the money to pay the back rent, but first he thought he and Ann should visit the landlord the next day. Now would Ann attend the meeting that night? She laughed. If it got the landlord off her back, she'd go to a dozen meetings. The man scribbled down an address and told her they'd see her at eight o'clock. Then they shook hands and left. Through the cracked front window, Ann watched the pair stroll briskly up Fowler Street. When they were out of sight, she dropped the scrap of paper on the kitchen table and returned to her housework.

Howard Fuller left Ann's house shocked that shotgun shacks still existed in American cities in the 1960s. But, then, Durham had been one surprise after another ever since the twenty-four-year-old Fuller had arrived on the evening of May 3, eager to begin his job as a community organizer. Fuller could not believe there were dirt streets in Hayti. Although he had grown up in a poor section of Milwaukee, the roads there were paved. Durham was also the first place he had encountered a black community so clearly divided along class lines. The slumlords he knew up North were all white. Here, a black man pocketed Ann Atwater's money for that pitiful shack—and threatened to toss her family into the street because she had trouble making the rent. That was how white people treated blacks, not how blacks treated one another. All of this defied Durham's reputation as a model for the New South, a public relations line Fuller heard often when he first arrived.

"Of all the Southern states," residents boasted to the newcomer, "North Carolina is *moving!*" And the fair city of Durham, they assured him, was the jewel in that liberal crown, home to Duke University, tobacco and textile factories, North Carolina College, and a solidly established black middle class, with deep roots set down nearly a century before.

And yet . . . how was one to account for Hayti—for the darkened, misery-filled streets and rat-infested houses that Howard Fuller visited every day; for the homes with gaping holes in the roofs, in which the residents were forced to wear raincoats *inside* during bad weather; for the poverty and hopelessness that permeated the neighborhoods? If Durham was so different from other Southern cities, so liberal on racial issues, so prosperous for both blacks and whites, then what was the meaning of Hayti?

It would clearly take some time for Fuller to grasp this new environment. It was like crossing a large body of water at night using stepping-stones hidden below the waves. But challenges had always excited him. Although he had been an excellent student, college had been a tremendous social test. As the only black student at Carroll College in tiny Waukesha, Wisconsin, Fuller struggled to talk and act in ways that minimized the distance between himself and his classmates. He succeeded too well. His white friends eventually assured him that they considered him "not really black." That made him uneasy enough, but even worse were his trips home. On one holiday visit, he was hanging out with old friends, telling them some anecdote about school, when a strange look suddenly clouded his friends' eyes. He heard how he sounded to them: the voice of a stranger, a *white* stranger. He would later joke that he had been around white people so much that he had forgotten how to dance, but at the time the situation was excruciatingly painful. When he tried to revert back to his old self, he found he couldn't remember exactly who that person was. To reestablish his links to the black community after graduation, he accepted a scholarship from the Urban League to pursue a master's degree in social work at Case Western Reserve University in Cleveland, Ohio. There, he joined CORE and immersed himself in the fight for public school desegregation, participating in many demonstrations, including an all-night sit-in at the school board.

In return for his scholarship, Fuller had agreed to work for at least one year for the Urban League. He fulfilled this obligation by moving to Chicago, where he became an "employment specialist," placing black workers in a variety of jobs. Fuller was prepared to shake up the city, to overthrow the status quo—but the Urban League took a more methodical, "go slow" approach. He told friends that he spent his days "finding a Negro who was just the right color brown to fill a job slot." The groundswell for change that had begun in Greensboro in 1960 had spread throughout America, and Fuller ached to contribute to this struggle. His longings would have been familiar to W. E. B. Du Bois, who, when he was almost exactly Fuller's age, had written in his diary:

> I rejoice as a strong man to run a race. And I am strong—is it egotism or is it assurance? . . . I therefore take the world that the Unknown lay in my hands & work for the rise of the Negro people, taking for granted that their best development means the best development of the world. . . . I wonder what will be the outcome? Who knows?

Fuller, too, was unsure what the outcome of his efforts would be. When an old friend from Milwaukee called to ask if he would be interested in working as a community organizer for Operation Breakthrough, a new agency in a poor section of Durham, he jumped at the opportunity.

And now he had his chance. The small gathering settled down to business at a home in Ann's neighborhood. Ten people sat in a room which would have accommodated a few dozen, but Fuller showed no signs of disappointment with the low turnout. He was prepared to build the movement around a nucleus of a few dedicated individuals, carefully listening to what each person had to say, and how they said it, mindful of the bruised feelings that hid beneath bluster. He answered their concerns one by one, enumerating their rights and explaining how to wring justice out of various government agencies. The enthusiastic group met for several hours, and it was well past midnight when Ann asked the final question: "When we gonna meet again?"

Early the next morning, Fuller knocked at Ann's door and the two of them strolled the few blocks to the office of her landlord, a charter member of Durham's black elite, a wealthy and powerful man named Henry M. Michaux, Sr. He had been active in local politics for decades and had earned a place in local history in 1938 as one of the first blacks to serve as a delegate to the Democratic County Convention. Michaux was used to being treated with deference and did not know what to make of Howard Fuller. At six feet four inches, Fuller loomed over Michaux and branded the landlord's treatment of his tenant "shameful." The young man informed Michaux that he had the back rent money, but would turn it over only after certain repairs were made. Michaux had never been confronted by one of his tenants before, and certainly not in the company of an articulate and highly educated black man who talked breezily of "numerous housing code violations." The landlord thrashed about like a man tossed into frigid water. Why, he had no idea that something was wrong with Mrs. Atwater's house. No one had told him. He was a busy man with many properties. Of course, now that the matter had been brought to his attention, he would send a man out there that day to fix things up.

Ann left Michaux's office in a happy daze. She had never heard of anyone successfully challenging a landlord in Durham before. When the surly handyman showed up that afternoon to nail up a few boards, he seemed an angel from heaven wielding a hammer. True, the faucet in the bathroom still leaked. And the ancient electrical wiring was as likely as before to burn the house down. In fact, she thought, what the house really needed was the wrecking ball. But still, something important had changed. Although she could not put a name to it, she felt the change in her heart, which was suddenly buoyant, expectant.

Howard Fuller harbored no illusions about what he was up against: he quickly saw through the "jewel of the New South" palaver. "Took me about three weeks to discover that what people were telling me was that the [hotels were] integrated and you could go in the front door of the theaters," he recalled later. "Other than that, in terms of being progressive, they weren't telling me anything."

The city's national reputation was eroding. A study by a team of eminent political scientists concluded that Durham was ruled by "orthodox conservatives" who were not "concerned with the deteriorating economic position of White or Negro labor." To these men "poverty was a punishment for sins," not a condition to be remedied—and most especially not by government intervention. The study also skewered Durham's reputation as a model for race relations, revealing that three of the four most influential white businessmen in Durham— members of a ruling "inner clique"—considered blacks to be genetically inferior to whites. The fourth believed that this was true in nine out of ten cases, but granted the possibility of the exceptional black individual. Even Watts Hill, Jr., himself a member of one of Durham's leading families, described the city's leaders as "highly conservative, divided for many years, easily panicked, motivated to act only by the strongest pressure, quick to relax, and above all short on leadership."

Fuller understood that there are two routes to power in America—money and people—and dollars were in short supply in the neighborhoods he was trying to organize. Of the 9,000 people living in Hayti, only 800 earned over $3,000 a year (the poverty line for a family of four). And while Durham had one of the largest black middle classes of any city its size in

America, Fuller knew better than to count too heavily on this group for financial support. The black elite might attach itself to a movement that had already proven itself, but it would not supply leadership for such an effort. And if its members considered a plan too radical—that is, if it threatened *their* interests—they would dig in their heels and work quietly against it.

The only answer was to use what Hayti did have: people. Fuller based his work on the principle he had learned at Case Western, the belief that if conditions were to improve for poor people, they themselves would have to implement the necessary changes. Lip service had been given to this idea months before Fuller's arrival. A grant proposal for the organization declared that "the basic responsibility to break the cycle of poverty lies within the community." But none of those involved with the group at that early stage could have predicted how far Fuller would push that mandate. In this, Operation Breakthrough differed from most other antipoverty agencies that provided services to the poor. Soon after arriving in Durham, Fuller explained his passionate belief that empowerment was necessary because "there are other kinds of poverty too, in addition to economic deprivation."

> There is the poverty of not knowing, of being "left-out" in community affairs, of lack of self-respect . . . Operation Breakthrough is seeking to help the poor to break these shackles of poverty, too . . . [and helping them to] deal with their own needs in relation with the rest of the community, and [they] are gaining a new feeling of self-worth and self-respect as they speak out and set into motion considerations they had previously felt were hopelessly barred from them.
>
> All of Operation Breakthrough's programs hark back to the original consensus that the dignity and worth of the individual must be acknowledged and promoted if the individual, himself, is to be able to make maximum use of any new opportunity for self-help that might be offered him.

Under Fuller, Operation Breakthrough would be dedicated to empowerment and self-help.

Most people who came in contact with him during his years

in Durham sized up Fuller as a seasoned and self-assured strategist whose every step was part of an intricate master plan for achieving clearly defined goals. Fuller thought it best to let people believe this fiction, but the truth was that he had no master plan. In fact, Fuller had come to Durham with high ideals but no goals beyond resident empowerment. The brilliant young organizer was experimenting, and always hoping that a misstep wouldn't cause the entire enterprise to blow up in his face. He had help in this effort from several people, including publisher Louis Austin, who, though aging and in ill health, was as pugnacious as ever. When Fuller first encountered resistance from the black elite, he dropped in on Austin at the offices of the *Carolina Times*. Austin, who had spent forty years publishing a paper with the motto "The Truth Unbridled," advised Fuller not to pull his punches.

"Now, Fuller," Austin told him, "you've got to understand what these people are like. If you keep doing this they're going to get mad at you. But you've got to keep . . . doing . . . these . . . things."

Austin taught Fuller to take on the upper class in the black community with the same zeal and uncompromising spirit that he used in confronting the white power structure. Fuller, who had never known his own father, developed a deep, almost filial affection for the older man.

Floyd McKissick, although increasingly busy with national CORE politics, also helped when he could. McKissick was one of the first people in Durham to meet Howard Fuller, and as one of two people who interviewed him for the job as community organizer, McKissick was partly responsible for bringing him to town. From McKissick, Fuller learned about strategy and, at least as important, about how to speak in a way that would move and motivate people. McKissick had a knack for translating complex ideas and for incorporating the audience's responses into his speeches. At a church meeting in rural North Carolina, Fuller watched, enthralled, as McKissick played to the "Amen corner," encouraging the listeners to shout out agreement with his words. It was a powerful lesson in oratory that Fuller would always remember.

As Operation Breakthrough got underway, the poor women of Hayti quickly stepped into leadership roles. Much to her own surprise, Ann Atwater was one of these leaders. She went door to door throughout her neighborhood, telling people about how Operation Breakthrough had helped her force the powerful Henry M. Michaux to repair her house. She discovered that she liked talking to strangers. Even more startling, people seemed to like listening to her and to be genuinely inspired by her arguments. It was more than startling, she decided, it was a miracle. After all, she was just another poor black woman struggling in anonymity to raise her children in the slums of Durham. God had placed this talent for communication, for touching others, deep inside her. And there the gift lay, dormant and unsuspected for years.

She would be a missionary for justice. Soon her familiar bulky frame huffed along the unpaved lanes of Hayti. She became known as "that Breakthrough woman" who could help you get things done. She was especially interested in housing issues. When asked what issue was most important to them, four of the five neighborhood councils organized by Operation Breakthrough that summer responded "housing." In fact, housing was a fundamental and perennial concern, dating back to slavery days, a festering sore which was often decried by community leaders, white and black, but which never seemed to heal.

In the 1920s, some 80 percent of black Durham residents lived in substandard housing, a figure that remained unchanged in the Hayti area four decades later. When the federal government set up the Housing Authority in 1934 to help local governments replace substandard housing, many cities rushed to grab their share of the half-billion-dollar program. Durham did not. Despite a clear and pressing need, subsidized housing wasn't considered, primarily because it ran counter to the economic interests of slumlords who held powerful positions in and out of government. The situation was so blatantly corrupt that even the conservative *Morning Herald* was moved to cry foul: "Several members of both the city council and the board of county commissioners are known to be heavily interested in 'shanty property' and it is unlikely . . . that they would support a movement which might seriously destroy or curtail their earnings."

These powerful men managed to keep all federal housing assistance programs out of Durham for a decade and a half. The Durham Housing Authority was finally created in 1949 and a city housing code was drafted in 1956—both measures that should have helped poor residents but, in fact, accomplished little. The Housing Authority was headed by a former cotton mill executive named Carvie Oldham, who ran public housing with the same autocratic and ruthless style that had marked his tenure in the mill. The housing code was rarely enforced, and its most important mechanism, the power of the city to correct code violations and bill landlords, was not once exercised by the city council, which oversaw housing issues. Powerful real estate interests dominated the city government even more completely in the 1960s than in the 1930s. The city council included "one lawyer who owns two apartment complexes as well as other real estate, two savings and loan presidents, one banker, one broker, one builder, two members associated with building supply concerns (one the president) and one insurance salesman. In addition the mayor's wife's family has extensive real estate interests in Durham."

The influx of federal urban renewal money was supposed to be a coup for Durham's poor. As the program developed, however, it was more like a coup de grace for an already ailing district. The city made good on its promise to bulldoze blighted areas, demolishing thousands of derelict houses and hundreds of crumbling businesses in Hayti. The problem was that they were never replaced. Entire neighborhoods disappeared into the insatiable maw of urban renewal, displacing residents into an already tight housing market. With well-practiced gallows humor, poor blacks dubbed the process "urban removal." Most of the true renovation occurred downtown, the home of the business elite, black and white, and the main beneficiaries of the program were the members of the Durham elite: construction companies, landlords, and lending institutions.

A "gentleman's agreement" among Durham real estate

agencies to keep blacks out of predominantly white neighborhoods exacerbated housing problems. When the U.S. Supreme
Court outlawed community zoning by race in 1917, segregationists had to develop another means for achieving this same
exclusionary end. They devised the "restrictive covenant."
Under a clause written into the mortgage contract, home buy-
ers agreed never to sell the property to "excluded parties"
(those prohibited varied depending on the section of the country, but blacks and Jews were the groups most commonly
excluded). When the courts overturned this method of discrimination in 1948, real estate brokers employed a variety of
methods to keep blacks literally in their place. As always,
Durham presented itself as a model of tolerance and racial
goodwill in housing, but a Duke sociology student found real
estate agents there performed the same tricks used across the
country. Posing as a prospective home buyer, the student telephoned several agents, waiting a few minutes to reveal that the
home was for a Negro family. Most of the agents shifted gears
after learning the buyer's race and steered him to houses in
all-black areas. When one agent was informed that the buyer
was black and was asked if that made a difference, he said,
"Just to be honest with you, it does." Another agent recommended a black realtor. "All our houses are in white sections,"
he explained. "We don't think we have anything where you
would be happy. I'm sure you would want to live where your
children would have playmates."

The tightly knotted issues of housing and race have troubled
generations of Americans, black and white, liberal and conservative. On the right, segregationists such as Jesse Helms often
inveighed against open housing laws, with Helms citing in his
editorials the few (but always existent) blacks who agreed with
his reactionary positions. "[Negroes] will find that you cannot
sue a man and make him want to live next door to you," Helms
quoted one such black man. "You must keep your community
as clean as the white man's community. You must keep up your
home as well as he does . . ." To segregationists, blacks hadn't
yet proven themselves decent and responsible citizens; they
needed to *earn* the privilege to live among whites. Of course, in

their silent and grateful hearts, segregationists believed that day would never come, for they considered blacks to be inherently, and therefore unalterably, inferior to whites. "It is time," Helms pontificated in a 1960s TV editorial, "to face, honestly and sincerely, the purely scientific statistical evidence of natural racial distinctions in group intellect."

The familiar theme sounded by Helms's showcase Negro— that blacks simply had to maintain their property better— denied the reality that most blacks did not own their homes. Like Ann Atwater, they lived in rental housing, often held by slumlords who were more interested in collecting monthly rent checks than in making needed repairs. But there is an even more fundamental error at work here, and that is the misapprehension common to both conservative whites and some elitist blacks that what poor blacks really wanted was to live next door to whites. As if poor blacks, in their simplemindedness, believed that proximity to whiteness conferred a blessing, a kind of miraculous dispensation from the travails of poverty. Poet and playwright Amiri Baraka (previously LeRoi Jones) confessed his past misreading of black intentions in this regard:

> [T]he concerns I once dismissed as "middle class"—buying a home and moving into "white folks' neighborhoods"—are actually reflective of the essence of black people's striving and the will to defeat segregation, discrimination, and national oppression. There is no such thing as a "white folks' neighborhood" except to racists *and to those submitting to racism*. [Italics in the original.]

By and large, of course, poor and working-class blacks merely wanted what whites wanted: decent housing, available only in "white neighborhoods." As singer-songwriter Nina Simone sang in her 1963 song "Mississippi Goddamn": "You don't have to live next to me / Just give me my equality." In their unquestioning acceptance of their own superiority, whites were unable to entertain the possibility that many blacks considered living next door to whites as *the cost* of obtaining adequate housing. This blind spot was evident in a letter printed in the *New York Times* concerning the play *A Raisin in the Sun*. In Lorraine Hansberry's Pulitzer Prize–winning work, a black family—the Youngers—clashes over how to use the insurance money paid on the father's recent death. The mother ultimately uses the small fortune to move her family out of their crowded ghetto apartment and into a "little old two-story" house with a small yard—in a white area. The white letter writer suggested that this amounted to a "happy ending," to which Hansberry countered, "If he thinks that's a happy ending, I invite him to come live in one of the communities where the Youngers are going!"

Ann quickly found a focus for her housing work that fall, in two incidents that would galvanize the black community in Durham over the next few years.

In September 1965, a white landlord named Abe Greenberg bought more than a score of properties in East Durham and promptly raised rents, although he had not made any improvements to the dilapidated houses. Greenberg, who already owned a similar number of houses in the section, was expanding his holdings to exploit the housing crunch caused by urban renewal. Edgemont, where the properties were located, was a tumbledown, racially mixed neighborhood, once a mill village, known euphemistically in the mid-1960s as "transitional." Desperate for low-cost housing to replace their demolished units, blacks moved in and the lower-class whites who could afford to leave sold their property at a loss and fled to the suburbs. What Greenberg had done was nothing new, even for a predominantly white area, but the fact that he raised rents on so many properties at the same time (by a whopping 25 percent in some cases) brought the long-simmering resentment to a boil.

"I think your actions . . . are morally reprehensible," the director of the neighborhood community center wrote Greenberg. "Either the rent should be lowered or the buildings should be made worth what you are charging." Greenberg ignored the letter.

At about the same time, a local neighborhood organization set up by Operation Breakthrough also demanded that the landlord lower rents or fix the houses. The group warned Mayor Grabarek about the situation and asked that the council deny Greenberg's request for a zoning waiver that would allow him to build even more properties in Edgemont. "It is time to call a halt to the practice of allowing houses to deteriorate while building further houses which are then allowed to deteriorate," argued the organization. As usual in these cases, the city ignored the pleas of residents and granted Greenberg the zoning variance he wanted. Durham's building inspector did visit Greenberg's properties, however (as required by law), and notified the landlord that his houses were substandard.

At the same time, another tempest was brewing in the nearby all-black public housing project McDougald Terrace. The 380 families living there were targeted by Operation Breakthrough organizers for one of the first neighborhood councils, but because there was a tenants' group already in the project, Howard Fuller instructed the Operation Breakthrough employee, a young NCC student named Joan Alston, to attempt to operate through the existing organization. That older group was no protest organization. Members devoted themselves to innocuous good works—sending get-well cards, planting flowers on the project grounds. As she tried to elicit grievances from residents, Alston encountered a wall of suspicion and fear. The tenants were convinced that if they talked with the community organizer, the executive director of the DHA, stern Carvie Oldham, would evict them. Durham's tight housing market, combined with Oldham's well-known dictatorial style, gave teeth to the threat. After several weeks, residents trusted Alston enough to whisper complaints about unfair treatment, high rents, and summary evictions. A majority of tenants, young mothers, said that what they really needed was help in forming a day-care center in the project. With such a center, they said, they would be able to go to work and in time earn enough to move out of the project. Thanks to Alston, the issue was put on the agenda for the regular August tenants' meeting. With Operation Breakthrough's backing, a record 100 residents met in the main hall at McDougald Terrace that morning, eagerly anticipating a discussion about day care. They were stunned when the cooperative president quickly adjourned without taking up the matter. Oldham had gotten wind of the plan.

In the silence that followed the adjournment, Alston shouted out that residents interested in forming a day-care center should stay after the meeting. About twenty women met and formed the Mothers' Club, electing a young mother named Joyce Thorpe president of the group. Three days later, Thorpe received an eviction notice. The DHA refused to provide any reason for its action, but there was no mystery about what had happened. By assuming a visible leadership role, Thorpe had challenged Carvie Oldham's authority.

Howard Fuller recognized at once that Thorpe's eviction presented a crisis. At the organization's prompting, a tenant had made a stand. Now that she was slapped down by the authorities, all eyes were on Fuller's group. Would they finish what they had started, or would they abandon Thorpe and go on to other issues? If Operation Breakthrough was to have any credibility in the community, it had to show that it would support residents. Fuller immediately organized a picket line. Soon sixty demonstrators were marching outside the Housing Authority. In reporting the incident, the local press gave the impression that all of the protesters were residents of McDougald Terrace. In fact, fewer than ten actually lived in the project. Although many more residents wanted to support Thorpe, they feared reprisals by the vindictive Oldham. The majority of the picketers were NCC students whom Fuller had recruited to "fill out" the picket lines.

Fuller turned next to one of his mentors in Durham, lawyer and civil rights leader Floyd McKissick. McKissick agreed to represent Thorpe, determining that her case marked an important test for the rights of public housing residents. "Tenants can not be evicted without due process," argued McKissick through the labyrinth of hearings and motions as the case spiraled up through the judicial system—from a local justice of the peace to the North Carolina Supreme Court, then to the federal courts, until finally reaching the U.S. Supreme Court two years later. Although the Court's ruling was ambiguous, as a result of Thorpe's case the Department of Housing and Urban Development ordered housing administrators to show cause when evicting tenants of public housing and to set up an appeals process.

With faith in Operation Breakthrough, a hundred residents formed a new organization—the Tenants' Club—to handle grievances with the DHA. After an intense lobbying campaign, which included letters, petitions, and more picketing, Carvie Oldham agreed to meet with tenants to hear their grievances—an important first. For Joyce Thorpe (whose eviction order was stayed by the North Carolina Supreme Court pending resolution of her case), the meeting with Oldham proved the power of direct action.

> They knew if we were willing to get out there and jeopardize ourselves as to not even having a place to live when we came back . . . we didn't know what we were gonna have anywhere to live or not. And I think they felt like that if they were willing to do this, that then we were really serious about what we were doin' . . .

The meeting, however, was a bust. Carvie Oldham (whose diminutive physical stature and imperial temperament made comparisons with Napoleon inevitable) sat at the head of the room, arms folded defensively, while angry tenants rose to their feet, one after another, and complained about problems at McDougald Terrace. After two hours, Oldham simply got up and left. The DHA head had probably been ordered to attend by some high-ranking city official, most likely Mayor Grabarek. A few weeks later, the DHA board tried another tack. Responding to heavy pressure by Floyd McKissick and J. J. Henderson, the DHA's only black board member, the Housing Authority met with tenants, and this time agreed to make a number of changes. As time dragged on and none of the agreed-upon policies were implemented, however, many residents became disheartened.

Despite Howard Fuller's personal commitment to confrontational politics, Operation Breakthrough was limited in many ways as an organization. Along with federal funding came restrictions on activism. In addition, many board members did not share Fuller's vision of resident empowerment. Victor S. Bryant III certainly did not. Bryant was a prominent Durham attorney and a member of one of the city's grand old white families. His grandfather, the first Victor, had presided over Durham's turn-of-the-century White Supremacy Club. Victor III was far more enlightened, but his liberalism was paternalistic, rooted in noblesse oblige. As the board's first chairman, Bryant saw the organization as a means to inculcate the values of education in the poor—to "get the children started in the right direction"—not as the activist, even militant association of poor blacks, devoted to challenging the established order in housing, welfare, and politics, that Howard Fuller wanted.

Fuller made Bryant uneasy. And so did Ann Atwater as she became more involved in Operation Breakthrough. The white attorney knew how to deal with the older black male business elite. In Bryant's opinion, Fuller and Ann too often "approached things more on a racial basis." This view was shared by Mayor Grabarek, who used his position on the board to carp about what he saw as the organization's many flaws. "Too many of our city's best leaders [are] not on the board," he complained, adding that Operation Breakthrough "duplicated services of the other agencies." These disagreements provoked many heated debates between the board and Operation Break-through's staff.

It seemed evident to Fuller that class identification was a large problem within the organization. Some board members owned substandard property in the Edgemont area. If residents won their battle with the slumlord Greenberg, these other landlords would likely have to fix up their houses, too. "If you were going to fight a war on poverty," reflected Fuller, "how could you have the enemy on the board?"

Within these constraints, Fuller pushed on. His personal charisma and innovative strategies won many battles, but as early as the fall of 1965 Fuller had already realized the need for a new organization, one less hamstrung by federal and local bureaucracies. A plan unfolded that November after the five Hayti neighborhood councils had merged into one area-wide council. In January, the Area Council, 300 members strong, split off from Operation Breakthrough to become United Organizations for Community Improvement, or UOCI.

Ann Atwater gladly moved over to the new organization, free to pursue her goals. She participated in UOCI's first annual meeting, where a crowd of 200 area residents (all of them black and nearly all women) met in the stifling Hillside High School gymnasium on a hot and humid Saturday morning in May 1966. After electing leaders, the new UOCI members were thrilled when veteran civil rights leader C. T. Vivian, an intimate of Martin Luther King's at the SCLC, addressed them. Vivian began by saying he had been shocked by conditions in the "Magic City."

"I have ridden through the streets of Durham," he told the hushed crowd. "Never before have I seen a Southern City that looked so much like a depressed backward country." He spoke, too, of the possibilities for progress. He preached eloquently about the importance of creating a true community out of the miasma of Hayti. "There is a big difference between living in a part of town," he pointed out, "and having a community—one is just rows of houses, the other is a place of oneness together."

The way to form that community, said Vivian, was by working together to demand that the power structure change. "We are not going to stop demonstrations in this nation until we have good housing and political power. There is something about demonstrating that does something for you, for your dignity; it tells the truth." Ann was just one of many who called out "Amen" to Vivian's observations. She knew intimately that "something" Vivian spoke of—that sense of dignity and truth about society and self that Ann had experienced almost daily since joining Operation Breakthrough.

The new organization wasted little time putting Vivian's message into action. At the close of the meeting, UOCI's newly elected president, Rubye Gattis, a twenty-eight-year-old mother of four, led members out of the gym and they headed downtown, en masse, bringing traffic to a standstill. The marchers were ostensibly protesting the School Board's recent decision not to take part in a federally funded jobs program, the Neighborhood Youth Corps. The six-member board, all but one of whom were white, had turned their collective back on 200 summer jobs for low-income teenagers rather than accept "federal intrusion" into Durham's affairs. Clearly, though, UOCI leaders were putting Durham on notice: the go-slow approach was dead. The days of back-channel negotiations—with moderate, middle-aged, wealthy black men speaking for poor residents of Hayti—were over. Now they would have to deal with an angry army that was young, poor, militant, and mostly female. This was the real message of the march that sultry May afternoon: We are here, and we're not going away. Durham would have to "get real" about its problems or it would pay a price for its intransigence.

That same message was directed at another audience. Howard Fuller and UOCI leaders wanted the black elite—the biological and cultural descendants of Merrick, Moore, and Spaulding—to understand that a new day was dawning in the Magic City. It was as difficult at first for the black upper class to swallow this message as it was for the white leaders of Durham. "Fuller and his movement embarrass other Negro leaders," observed Louis Austin, who had never let up on his attacks on the black elite's complacency. "Most of today's adult Negro leadership is hopeless. The Future is in these young people."

In an interview conducted at this time with an NCC student, Austin described what he called the "dual personality" of the black ruling class. "On the surface," he said, "they stand for the same things you stand for. But this is sometimes deceit, for while they do this, they are sometimes working in subtle ways to defeat the cause." And a SNCC organizer surely had Durham's famous black elite in mind when he sounded a similar note a year earlier in a report sent to the group's national headquarters: "There is a powerful and rich black bourgeoisie in the larger urban areas of this state. . . . They work within the framework of the same power structure which has kept the mass of the black people in this state in their present economic and political straits."

It wasn't just white landlords who opposed major reversals

in housing policy. Since the turn of the century, blacks had owned at least as much rental property in Hayti as had whites. Booker T. Washington had praised this anomalous situation when he had visited Durham back in 1910. Despite the obvious benefits to some individuals from this arrangement, most blacks suffered under it, as black landlords, like their white counterparts, had an economic incentive in maintaining the status quo. A 1969 Duke University study of housing issues in Durham touched on this sensitive issue of black landlords, concluding that while these black elite "have sometimes sought such changes like the end to discrimination, these men have not supported sweeping code enforcement and other far-reaching measures. . . . Had Greenberg been forced to make large improvements, other substandard landlords (which included several blacks) would have likely come under similar pressure."

Ironically, this disenchantment with Durham's black elite among poor blacks came just as the former group realized its apotheosis. The month before UOCI stretched out its fledgling wings, the venerable North Carolina Mutual had opened the doors to its handsome new headquarters, with pomp and circumstance unrivaled in Durham's history. The building was a twelve-story showcase of modern architecture, all glass and concrete, rising like a mirage from the site of Benjamin Duke's old estate, Four Acres. The Mutual had thrown a five-day-long "Dedication Festival," a gala event that included a formal banquet held, not on the NCC campus, but in Duke University's "Great Hall." Opening-day ceremonies had been attended by scores of dignitaries, black and white, from North Carolina and throughout the country and abroad, causing Vice President Hubert Humphrey (who delivered the dedication address) to joke from the podium that he hadn't seen as many "federal officials in one place" at the same time "since the last Cabinet meeting." The new building sparkling in the North Carolina spring sunshine was a source of pride throughout the black community, but it was a pride alloyed with cynicism for Durham's poorest black citizens. An elderly black man summed up this attitude when he said of the Mutual's resplendent building: "I bet a colored man can't even get a loan up there anymore."

These problems were not new. In its long history, Durham's black aristocracy had only rarely been up to the task demanded of it by W. E. B. Du Bois in his concept of the Talented Tenth, that small fraction of the black community blessed with extraordinary resources and abilities and committed to the "uplift of the entire Race." They had, after all, rejected the Sturm und Drang of Du Bois for the accommodationism of Booker T. Washington. And if the early Martin Luther King, Jr., was a bit too radical for their tastes, they viewed the Royal Ice Cream Parlor sit-ins led by Douglas Moore with something akin to horror. But what economically affluent group was ever consistently radical, affiliating itself with the aspirations of the poor? Certainly, black leaders in Durham did more to support improvements for impoverished blacks than white leaders ever did to help poor whites. True, they needed to have their consciences pricked and their interests threatened before they would take a stand for "the Race." They acted slowly and without resolve, they backtracked, they obfuscated, they spoke with a small hesitant voice when what was needed was a howl. But at the end of the day, they usually came down on the side of the poor black community. This pattern held true in the mid-1960s. By the summer, a visitor to Durham would note: "The old line Negro leadership, seeing the initiative slip away from itself is rushing to Fuller's bandwagon." In time, all seven of Durham's most powerful black organizations would sign a statement publicly endorsing UOCI's "protests against intolerable conditions under which many of the citizens of Durham are forced to live."

Ann's life soon revolved around her work with UOCI and Operation Breakthrough. She fearlessly confronted white authorities with such relish that she earned the nickname "Roughhouse Annie." Nonviolence was a tough notion for Ann to embrace, but she tried not to strike back when police shoved her or when white hecklers spat on her at demonstrations. "I wanted to stomp them into the dirt," she recalled later, "but they told me if you wanted to have a part in it, you had to be cool." Still, she wasn't shy about using her bulk to intimidate her opponents.

In early June, community leaders focused attention once again on landlord Abe Greenberg's refusal to bring his Hayti properties up to code—and on the city's refusal to press the issue. The Edgemont Community Council decided to picket Abe Greenberg's real estate offices in downtown Durham. Ann and other UOCI members joined the ECC in carrying signs reading: GREENBERG, MY ROOF LEAKS; GREENBERG, FIX OUR HOUSES; and GREENBERG, MY HOUSE DOESN'T HAVE SCREENS. The city's media ignored the demonstrations, probably hoping that the protesters would give up and go home if they were denied the attention they obviously wanted. Instead, the demonstrators interpreted the snub as a challenge and stepped up their efforts. They renewed their demonstrations and added new picket lines: In front of Greenberg's home (signs: YOUR NEIGHBOR IS A SLUMLORD and MY CHILDREN SLEEP WITH RATS, MRS. GREENBERG), outside City Hall (IS THE MAYOR GREENBERG'S MAN?), and at black Southeastern Business College, to protest the involvement of the school's president, David Stith.

Stith, an up-and-coming member of Durham's black elite and a personal friend of Greenberg's, saw himself as the best-qualified mediator. A recent unsuccessful candidate for the city council (with Greenberg's support), Stith very likely thought that playing peacemaker in this contentious issue would look good on his résumé in future political campaigns. He had seriously misjudged the situation, however, and his own role in it. Protesters quickly decided that Stith was on Greenberg's side. Worse, they saw the college president as trading on his skin color to prove a solidarity with the black residents of Edgemont, a solidarity that did not, in fact, exist. Why, they wondered, hadn't Stith sought out the leaders of the ECC before this crisis? To many residents Stith seemed less interested in solving their problems than in taking the heat off Greenberg. Stith was suddenly embroiled in a bitter racial battle, horrified to find black protesters walking a picket line outside his office carrying signs reading: STITH, ARE YOU BLACK OR WHITE?, UNCLE TOM STITH, and GREENBERG'S NIGGER. When Ann and other protesters showed up at Stith's home that afternoon and began marching up and down his sidewalk, Stith lost his temper and had his handyman hose them down. Soaking, the demonstrators continued to march. Soon after this incident, as he was leaving his house, Stith saw Operation Breakthrough vehicles dropping off more picketers just around the corner from his house. Furious over what he considered an undeserved personal attack on his integrity, Stith set off alarms about Operation Breakthrough's misuse of federally funded cars. Fuller's enemies pounced on the possible violation.

The *Morning Herald*, sanctimonious as ever, editorialized:

> There is a proper course in protesting substandard housing, and Operation Breakthrough would have been well advised to have counseled the Edgemont Community Council to follow it. This newspaper has every confidence that desired results would have been obtained by following that course. The course is not nearly so spectacular as picketing, but Operation Breakthrough can be more effective in relieving poverty if it disregards the spectacular and follow[s] regular procedures in undertaking to correct undesirable conditions.

The paper noted, almost as an afterthought: "It must be added too, that it is incumbent upon the city to enforce its building code"—as if the writer was unaware that the city's repeated failure to enforce the code had sparked the demonstrations in the first place.

Fuller's boss, Robert Foust, backed the decision to bring in organization vehicles, reasoning that the primary purpose of Operation Breakthrough was, after all, to help neighborhood councils. "If [an action] is beneficial to them," he told a reporter, "then that's it."

But this explanation only antagonized foes of the antipoverty group. The day after the *Herald*'s mini-lecture in civics, Nick Galifianakis (a Democratic candidate for Congress) lashed out at "Durham's Operation Breakthrough mess." Calling on his Washington connections, Galifianakis brought a congressional committee staffer to town to investigate the possible abuse of federal funds. While the investigator reported finding

serious problems with the organization, particularly concerning sloppy accounting procedures, critics successfully countered that the investigation was nothing more than a "partisan
fishing expedition" initiated by a candidate for public office.
The immediate storm over this affair blew over, especially
after Operation Breakthrough banned vehicles from transporting picketers, but a far more serious controversy quickly
escalated, one that reflected the national schism that had been
growing in the coalition of interests known collectively as the
civil rights movement since 1963.

At the end of July 1966, Howard Fuller spoke before black
residents of Woodland, North Carolina, an isolated and impoverished rural hamlet in the northeastern corner of the state.
He told the crowd that he had not come as a representative of
Operation Breakthrough, insulating the organization from
what he was about to say. "I come here as a black man, come
to talk to a bunch of beautiful black people."

> Now people are always telling us; you Negroes shouldn't
> push so fast . . . and, for goodness sake, don't you Negroes men-
> tion black power. . . . So I'm telling you, it's gonna be alright as
> long as you keep saying "yes, sir" and "no, sir" and you keep on
> shufflin' and eatin' watermelon, everything's gonna be alright,
> and we ain't going nowhere . . . you know what your problems
> are . . . and I'll tell you this . . . all that stuff about services is o.k.,
> but if you don't get organized . . . if you don't fight, you ain't
> gonna get nothing, you ain't gonna get nothing. You gonna have
> to get together and you got to identify the enemy. And the
> enemy is anybody, white, black, polka dot, or tweed who tries to
> keep you down.

There was nothing in what Fuller said that day that he had
not already repeated dozens of times in Durham during the
past year—except for the phrase "Black Power." Across America, that combination of words was new and significant,
although it meant different things to different people. To some,
it was a liberating assertion of racial pride; to others, it
announced the increasing importance of political rather than
social goals in the ever-evolving battle for black progress.

Some saw the phrase as wrongheaded and divisive, freighted with racially exclusionary shadings that would diminish white support. Still others heard in the cry "Black Power" a frighteningly literal call to arms, an invitation to open rebellion and violent revolution. In fact, each interpretation was true, in the sense that adherents of the different positions—and dozens more—existed in that churning and heterogeneous group known, with deceptive simplicity, as black America.

While the internal battle over goals and methods had been building within the movement, it first broke into the open that June—a little more than a month before Howard Fuller's speech in Woodland—during a major civil rights march through Mississippi: the James Meredith March Against Fear. Meredith, who had integrated that state's university system in 1962, launched a solo 220-mile walk from Memphis, Tennessee, to the Magnolia State's capitol in Jackson on June 5. His purpose was to encourage black rural residents to register to vote. As he crossed the state line into Mississippi, a white man hidden in a clump of bushes shot Meredith from behind with a shotgun, seriously wounding him. Gathered around Meredith's hospital bed, leaders from three civil rights organizations—SCLC, SNCC, and CORE—vowed to complete the march for the fallen activist. The next day, hundreds of black and white protesters met on the road where Meredith had fallen. In the lead were Martin Luther King, Jr. (representing SCLC), Stokely Carmichael (SNCC), and the new head of CORE, Durham's Floyd McKissick.

McKissick's selection to manage CORE after James Farmer's retirement that January was a harbinger of the coming battles over Black Power—in all its ambiguities. The old civil rights organization—so powerful in 1964 that Jesse Helms had attacked it as "the thought-control center for the Negro population of America"—had been steadily losing influence, members, and money. Militants within the organization saw the election as an opportunity to install a new, more activist leadership—one which would reenergize a movement that had stalled after winning most of the battles against legalized segregation. A CORE insider later summed up the board's choice between educator George Wiley and Floyd McKissick as a choice between a "brilliant university professor married to a white woman and a down-home lawyer who sounded black." The characterization of McKissick was patently unfair. There was no question of McKissick's own brilliance: he had helped design one of the earliest sustained sit-down protests against Jim Crow and helped to guide the most famous of these efforts—the Greensboro lunch-counter protest. He had also recently argued successfully before the Supreme Court in the Thorpe case. The list of his achievements was long and distinguished. But it was equally true that a militancy among younger blacks and a concomitant mistrust of all whites worked against Wiley and for McKissick. Even King, the black leader most committed to the traditional path of multiracial coalitions and nonviolence, would soon grow frustrated with the movement's stagnation. He was becoming convinced, he wrote, that the greatest stumbling block to true freedom "is not the White Citizens' Councilor or the Ku Klux Klanner, but the white moderate, who is more devoted to 'order' than to justice . . ."

The already frayed coalition started to unravel in Mississippi on a sweltering June day as King led the marchers in singing the civil rights standard "We Shall Overcome." A large contingent of young marchers fell silent when they reached the lyrics "black and white together." When King asked why they had stopped singing, the young people informed the venerable leader (who was himself only thirty-seven years old), "This is a new day; we don't sing those words any more. In fact, the whole song should be discarded. Not 'We shall overcome,' but 'We shall overrun.' " Soon after this incident, SNCC leader Stokely Carmichael employed the chant "Black Power" to fire up marchers, who were enduring harassment and violence at the hands of white small-town residents and even more vicious attacks from the police—as the federal government ignored King's repeated requests for protection. The expression Black Power electrified the militant blacks aligned with SNCC and CORE, shocked King, and disgusted more conservative black leaders.

In a heated discussion with King, Carmichael defended the phrase. "Martin," he reasoned, "you know as well as I do that practically every other ethnic group in America had done just this. The Jews, the Irish and the Italians did it, why can't we?" McKissick also defended the phrase, terming it an inevitable response to the "dashed hopes and mangled dreams of a people and a result of the ineffectiveness of the nonviolent movement." Leaders such as the NAACP's Roy Wilkins would have none of it, however. "No matter how endlessly they try to explain it," he said icily, "the term 'black power' means anti-white power . . ."

By the time the weary marchers trudged into Jackson, the furor over Black Power had eclipsed discussion of voter registration, the march's ostensible purpose. Longtime civil rights organizer Bayard Rustin concluded that those two words had "touched off a major debate—the most bitter the community has experienced since the days of Booker T. Washington and W. E. B. Du Bois." But the debate over the meaning of Black Power seemed, at first, abstract to many (especially white) Americans—until Chicago's predominantly black West Side was rocked by three nights of bloody rioting, beginning on July 12. To critics, these riots clearly resulted from the Black Power movement. "America is being led like a lamb to the slaughter," tolled Jesse Helms, that bell of Southern conservatism. "Americans need to stop protesting, marching, looking [*sic*], burning, destroying, threatening, posturing and loafing. They need to start minding their own business again, go back to work, regain respect for decency and personal responsibility, and to pray for God's forgiveness for what they have deliberately tried to do to America."

Howard Fuller's use of the phrase Black Power—against this backdrop of contention and violence—stirred a hornet's nest in both the white and black communities. "Antipoverty Worker Urges Promotion of Black Power," shouted the headline in the state's most important newspaper, the Raleigh *News & Observer.* The buzzing occasioned by his action would not diminish for years. Even Louis Austin, Fuller's behind-the-scenes supporter and father figure, attacked the radical, nationalist wing of the Black Power movement, judging it to be "no better than the Ku Klux Klan," and predicted that "the call for black or Negro separatism from the mainstream of American life is a foundation and an objective that within itself is certain to come to no good end."

As the controversy over ideology swirled through Durham, activists struggled to keep the focus on the issue of housing—continuing to press the city for action against Abe Greenberg, the Edgemont slumlord who found endless excuses for not bringing his properties up to code. Rats still crawled through gaping holes in floorboards. Inclement weather drifted through broken windows. Busted water pipes forced residents to cart water from neighbors' taps. That August, nearly a year after buying the houses, Greenberg's lawyer asked the city to extend his client's deadline for making repairs, citing insufficient man-power to get the job done. The head of the Edgemont Community Council, Nathaniel Brown, fired off a bitter letter to Mayor Grabarek: "Mr. Greenberg appears to be right in his assumption that we are helpless in finding Administrative backing of any kind of help for our desperate situation . . ." He concluded with a warning that was particularly ominous, coming just a month after the Chicago riots. If the city did not compel Green-berg to upgrade his houses, wrote Brown, "we will have lost all faith in what Durham can do for its poor. We will be placed in a desperate position and we will act accordingly."

On the night the city council was to deliberate Greenberg's case, Ann Atwater and 100 other Hayti residents met at St. Joseph's Church to plan strategy. They decided to take a restrained approach, letting their presence at the meeting—a block of 100 black citizens—speak for them. They would applaud when Nathaniel Brown explained the residents' posi-tion and remain silent after the mayor spoke. If the extension was granted, they would silently file out of the chamber. Their plan of action formulated, the crowd left for City Hall.

One can imagine the reaction of the mayor and city council members as some 100 poor black people walked into the chamber of city government. In Durham's long history, few blacks of this social stratum had attended these meetings. Perhaps unnerved by the silent mass of black faces confronting him, the mayor delayed discussion on housing. Debate on Greenberg's request for an extension was scheduled for the early part of the meeting, but Grabarek departed from the published agenda and skipped to other matters. Running out of issues, the mayor finally turned to housing. As planned, the black residents applauded Brown's reassertion that Greenberg should not be granted another delay in repairing his properties. This statement was reinforced by C. E. Boulware, a respected and dignified NCC professor, who, with deft wit, thanked the august body for providing the residents of Edgemont with "two hours away from their leaking-roofed houses on this rainy night."

With little discussion, the council did the expected and granted Greenberg his sixty-day extension. The action surprised no one. Still, members of the ECC were unprepared emotionally for the letdown that followed the council's ruling. As the *Morning Herald* had recently lectured, they had followed the "proper course in protesting substandard housing." It had gotten them nowhere. The city's action was a crushing blow and many people simply drifted away from the ECC.

Ann Atwater reacted differently. Each time the men of Durham flexed their muscle, she redoubled her efforts to break up their game. Like several women in UOCI and Operation Breakthrough, Ann seemed to draw her energy from the white power structure's intransigence. The more they dug in their heels, the more she was determined to yank control from them. "You can't let them treat us like this!" she cajoled her peers. More often than not, people came along. And if they sometimes attended a meeting of UOCI just to move the large, persistent woman out of their doorway, that was all right with Ann.

While there were other vigorous and committed women in UOCI, Ann stood out as a natural leader. Her militancy frightened some, but it attracted many more to the cause. Ann personified Black Power. In early 1967, Howard Fuller recognized her potential as an indigenous organizer and offered her a seventeen-week training course as a community action technician (CAT). It was a large commitment and Fuller told her he'd understand if she declined. After considering the offer, Ann concluded that the Lord had called her to this work, and if it was His will, how could she refuse?

Each day Ann reported to the basement of the Scarborough Funeral Home in Hayti. The classes began at eight-thirty in the morning and ran until midafternoon. The trainees, poor men and women like Ann from across North Carolina, sat on folding chairs and studied how to involve people in community projects. They learned about the rights of welfare recipients, about housing codes, about how to prod the city council and various governmental agencies. But mostly they learned to stand up for themselves when they were in the right and never to back down.

For a high school dropout like Ann, all this was heady stuff. She had never been a good student, but now she thrived in the CAT classes. She discovered she had an excellent memory for important information and a knack for separating the essential from the superfluous. She was the star of her class, and when the training was over she could (as she herself put it) "kill anybody that wasn't already dead." Even before graduation, UOCI hired her to supervise its neighborhood workers, a position which carried with it the chair of the group's housing committee and a seat on the board of directors. Suddenly, Ann was a player. She pulled together picket lines, marches, mass rallies, and demonstrations.

Part of Ann's success was due to her commanding physical presence; she knew how to exploit her bulk. As Patrick Wallace, UOCI's assistant director, observed, "There is something very effective about someone as big as Ann informing the mayor that the black community won't tolerate further ghettoization." She did not use her size as a mere bluff, however. When a School Board official refused to listen to her and tried to throw her out of his office, Ann grabbed the telephone from his desk and hurled it at his head. She missed; but the man sensed a standoff and the two sat down and discussed the issue Ann had come to talk over.

Her tenacity and size were backed up by resourcefulness

and creativity. She saw how welfare caseworkers kept clients in the dark about their rights, justifying arbitrary actions by citing mysterious regulations. Ann's solution was to channel accurate information to welfare recipients. She developed several techniques to secure this intelligence. Once, she organized a picket outside of the DSS offices, and while workers were distracted by the commotion, Ann went inside, located a copy of the department's thick regulations manual, and smuggled it out. She found a copy machine, reproduced the manual, and returned the original. Then she walked out of the building with the handbook tucked under her coat and called an end to the picket. From then on, when caseworkers argued that, for example, regulations didn't allow clients to own vehicles, the client would point out that according to regulation XXX, recipients could own a vehicle—if the net worth was under $500—without suffering any loss in benefits. Welfare workers were stupefied.

Before her face was widely recognized at City Hall, Ann spent hours walking the halls of that building, ferreting out the confidential meetings of various boards and commissions that controlled Hayti. Being socially invisible had its advantages. She slipped into the back of these gatherings—just a tired, heavy, middle-aged black woman searching for a place to rest her feet as she dealt with some bureaucratic runaround. Ann secretly took notes and fed the information to Fuller and others, who used it to challenge the city about these closed-door hearings. For several anxious months, city officials drove themselves crazy trying to figure out who was leaking information to UOCI. Ann quickly developed into a tough negotiator in meetings with various city agencies. Marveling at Ann's vast knowledge of federal housing laws, a HUD consultant admitted that "she knows more than most bureaucrats in Washington." Without exaggeration, UOCI's Patrick Wallace called her the "leading spokesman for the poor in terms of problems with public and private housing."

Ann was soon a power to be reckoned with at City Hall, at the DSS offices a few blocks away, at the public housing projects, and wherever poor black people protested unfair treatment. She was loved by many Hayti residents and feared, though often respected, by her numerous foes in Durham's officialdom. But some white residents truly hated her. When she rose to speak at city council meetings, councilman Charles Steel, a hard-line segregationist, turned his swivel chair to present his back to her, rotating around again only after she had finished speaking. Out on the streets of Durham, she encountered even more naked hostility. One man in particular troubled her. He often showed up at demonstrations, a short, muscular white man with a face so contorted by hatred that Ann wondered if he was unbalanced. He was usually in the company of a small group of other angry-looking men. "Crackers," she sized them up silently. She pretended to ignore the man but made a mental note to be more careful than normal when he was around. She knew he was dangerous—there was no mistaking that. She did not know, but would not have been surprised to learn, that the angry white man was the leader of the local Ku Klux Klan: C. P. Ellis.

CHAPTER NINE

> We are supposed to be proud of [Durham], but
> no one tells us what to be proud of. Leaders take
> no stand on community problems. They act as
> though by being silent about them, problems will
> just disappear. Race problems, economic
> development, city planning—they treat them all the
> same—do nothing, say nothing.
>
> —White resident of Durham

C. P. Ellis' ascent to power in the Ku Klux Klan paralleled Ann Atwater's own steady climb through the ranks of community activists. The two had a surprising amount in common. As a poor white laborer, C.P., too, was locked out from the traditional Southern institutions of power. Labor unions, an avenue for upward mobility for Northern workers, had been rendered ineffectual or were demolished altogether by the Dixie plutocracy. The one-party Democratic rule in the South had created a system that was corrupt and undemocratic in the extreme, but since the demise of the Populists, the votes of poor whites could be taken for granted—just as the Republican Party had earlier taken black voters for granted.

When challenges to white elite rule arose, all the new Bourbons had to do was inject race into the campaign. A century of propagandizing ensured that the race card trumped all others. Even Durham's enlightened Mayor Grabarek would play this devil's game. Grabarek had come into office preaching racial tolerance, making a historic journey into the heart of the black community the night after assuming office. But by the spring of 1967, he was doing poorly in the polls. Almost as a reflex, Grabarek turned to racial politics, buying newspaper ads proclaiming, "I will not get the bloc vote!" (meaning the black vote), and telling white voters that although he had tried to be fair, "fairness is not enough" for blacks. Grabarek won by an 11-point margin. Liberal North Carolina governor Terry Sanford had earlier used the same tactic in his 1960 campaign, telling reporters he would not "seek or want or accept approval by the NAACP."

C.P. felt as at home in the Klavern hall as Ann felt surrounded by residents of Hayti at her UOCI meetings. The Klansmen shared a similar past of poverty and failure, were haunted by the same familiar demons, and hated a common enemy. They loved George Wallace and Jesse Helms and despised Martin Luther King and Floyd McKissick. Besides their well-known rallies where they burned crosses and preached race hatred, the Klan hosted regular dances, shooting matches, barbecues, bingo nights, and fishing trips. When a woman fell ill, Klanswomen looked after her children and brought covered dishes for the family. For C.P. and other poor marginalized whites, the Klan served as an extended family, providing a release from the squalor, tedium, and isolation of everyday life and promising the hope—misguided as it was—that in white supremacy a better day was coming.

C.P. joined every Klan committee he could, and quickly earned a reputation as a tireless worker. Like Ann Atwater, he was surprised and delighted to discover that others respected him. At the weekly meetings, C.P. found his voice. As he gained confidence, he spoke out more forcefully. Before long, he was elected to the position of chaplain—or Kludd—of the Klavern. C.P. loved life in the Klan. He loved the pageantry and mystery of the ceremonies, the camaraderie of the men, but he was not ambitious, and he would have been content to continue in his mid-level role forever. Change came suddenly and unexpectedly. The Exalted Cyclops, Jack Murray, telephoned one evening and asked C.P. to stop over at his house. When C.P. arrived, Murray took him into his bedroom and closed the door. The older man explained that he was in bad health—working in the tobacco factory had ruined his lungs and heart. He had to resign his position with the Klan. He had discussed the matter with the state leader, Grand Dragon Bob Jones, and the pair had decided that C.P. was the best man to succeed Murray as Exalted Cyclops of the Durham Klavern.

There were no objections to C.P.'s elevation at the next meeting and so he donned the scarlet robe and repeated the sacred oath of leadership. It was a sublime moment for Paul Ellis' boy, the uneducated son of an uneducated linthead standing before several hundred of his peers, recognized as a leader in the battle to restore the beloved South. The inside of the Klavern hall, with its looming neon cross and Confederate flags, was a world away from the Hayti funeral home where Ann Atwater received her CAT diploma, but for C.P. and Ann, these locations would always remain special places, the mise-en-scènes where each assumed the liberating burden of responsibility and self-sacrifice.

Under Grand Dragon Bob Jones, the Klan grew quickly in North Carolina in the mid-1960s and even critics of the group allowed that the awning salesman from Granite Rock was "personable," "easy to talk to," and a "go-getter." Jones constantly crisscrossed the state, attracting thousands of mostly poor whites with his message of white supremacy. By 1965, federal investigators called North Carolina the "most active Klan state" in the country. A report issued by the Anti-Defamation League concurred with this assessment, naming the North Carolina branch of the United Klans of America "the best run state organization." Investigators counted some 112 Klaverns spread throughout the Tarheel State, with an estimated 8,000 to 9,000 members. Posters announcing Klan rallies, bearing the slogan "Be a Man, Join the Klan," became a common sight in store windows and on telephone poles in small towns and major cities across the state. Hundreds of rallies were staged in North Carolina during the 1960s, drawing as few as 100 to as many as 3,000 curious and generally appreciative participants. The attention flummoxed state officials, who were still struggling to cast North Carolina as "different" from the Deep South. Lieutenant Governor Robert Scott minimized the news of Klan activity in the state, quipping, "When I first saw the press report [about increasing Klan membership], I said to myself that it just confirms the impression I've gotten that the people in North Carolina are a bunch of joiners."

While both Grand Dragon Jones and Imperial Wizard Robert Shelton (who lived just over the border in South Carolina) frequently visited rallies across North Carolina, the day-to-day administration of each Klavern was left largely up to its EC. When C.P. took over that position for Unit Nine, he made few changes. At the weekly meetings, members spent hours cursing out Martin Luther King and other national black leaders, calling them Communist dupes and worse. As UOCI exerted more power in Durham, Howard Fuller received similar treatment. Frequently, someone would suggest that these traitors be "eliminated," but calls for assassination never went beyond the talking stage in Durham. More hours were spent discussing news items gleaned from Jesse Helms's editorials and from various Klan publications. In the statewide newsletter "NEWS from KLANSVILLE," Klansmen learned of nefarious plots against whites such as fluoridation and gun control. One such cause célèbre that shook "Klansville" for a time was the "Negro blood" scare. The plot was outlined under the headline RED CROSS BLOOD BANKS PEDDLE CONTAMINATED NEGRO BLOOD. According to the article, during hospital transfusions thousands of whites were routinely receiving the blood of blacks with sickle-cell anemia. "When sickle cell contaminated blood is given to ailing white patients," warned the newsletter, "severe damage can result." It continued:

> When alien race-mixing propaganda finds its way into the classroom and Sunday School, there to poison the minds and moral[s] of this nation's youth, it is clear [sic] a matter for serious concern. But when the same propaganda reaches into the hospital clinic and operating room to jeopardize the lives of the sick and dying, it is nothing short of criminal.

Another source of information for discussion at the Klavern hall was the national UKA magazine *Fiery Cross*. In appearance, *Fiery Cross* was a step up from the crude mimeographed "Klansville" newsletter. The magazine was typeset and included many photographs. But the articles were just as crude, featuring alerts about various threats to the white race. Traditionally, the greatest perceived threat was sexual—the threat of inter- marriage and race mixing. It is no surprise, then, that *Fiery Cross* was obsessed with the question, and it devoted a section in every issue to photographs of black men and white women together. "Along the Black Front" sometimes found actual interracial couples to feature. Photographs of Sammy Davis, Jr., and his white wife walking hand in hand along a beach or kissing in public or dancing at a nightclub were a staple. But more commonly the mere physical proximity of men and women from different races was enough to earn a place in the magazine. A particularly ludicrous example of this potential miscegenation was a 1968 photograph of Pat Nixon dancing with a black man at a White House function. Earlier, the Klav- ern had been upset by the shocking news that Secretary of State Dean Rusk's daughter had married a black man. What particularly galled the Klan was that the union could have been prevented. "[Dean Rusk] could have stopped the relation- ship by sending her to an out-of-town private school, to Europe, or could have whaled the daylight out of her and run the nigger off with a shotgun," complained a Klan document from this time.

Something about all this talk bothered C.P. It certainly wasn't the racist content; he was as repelled by miscegenation as other Klansmen, and was ready to lay down his life to oppose Communism. But gradually during his first year as EC, he began to tire of the never-ending discussions about these mat- ters. What's the point of sitting in the hall all the time com- plaining about Communists, Jews, and niggers? he wondered. Where is this *getting* us? Howard Fuller certainly didn't waste all his time in meetings running down whites. He and his peo- ple were *out there*, marching, demonstrating, picketing, putting pressure on the government. Maybe, thought C.P., it was time for the Klan to quit worrying so much about secrecy and more about effectively communicating its views. When he men- tioned his concerns to another Klan officer, all he got was a blank stare. So C.P. decided to start off slowly and obliquely down this new, more open road. He, however, sent out feelers to individuals who he thought might be sympathetic to the Klan viewpoint, people in positions to help the cause: policemen, firemen, low-ranking city officials. A surprising number of them responded favorably to the Klansman's overtures. Within a short time, C.P. had built up a small network of friends within the city government who would keep him posted on developments of interest to the Klan. When UOCI applied for a permit to hold a rally, C.P. would know about it well in advance of the event. His informers updated him about relevant items on the agendas of various city and county boards. The cooperation convinced C.P. that he was leading the Klan in the right direction. He felt so confident that he even wrote a letter, on Klan letterhead, introducing himself to the North Carolina State Bureau of Investigation and inviting them to attend a Klavern meeting. "I have nothing to hide," C.P. declared to the state agency responsible for investigating the Klan. "We are proud of the U.K.A. and are ready to die if we must to see that our children and your children are not raised under a Communist, socialist society." He signed the handwritten letter "C. P. Ellis, President, Unit #9, United Klans of America." The SBI ignored his invitation.

While he held back on telling the members of his Klavern about his plan to go public, C.P. did convince several other men to join him in regularly harassing black protesters. They showed up at picket lines and shouted insults at the demonstrators, calling them niggers and monkeys and telling them to go back to Africa. The demonstrators ignored the men, but C.P. could tell that his group rattled them. One protester annoyed C.P. more than the others: Ann Atwater. Obese and very dark-skinned, she was at nearly every rally and demonstration C.P. attended, ordering people around and mouthing off to the white authorities. The large black woman violated all the unwritten rules that, to C.P.'s way of thinking, constituted the beloved Southern way of life. She was a woman, a *black* woman, and she was clearly in charge of many demonstrations. She moved her great bulk around with the swaggering confidence of a white man. She would look anyone—man or woman, black or white—in the eye and tell them to go to hell if she felt like it. C.P. would have loved to take Ann Atwater down a notch or two.

In the spring of 1967, it looked as if Durham was in for another "long, hot summer." Summertime riots had become an annual event in America's inner cities, starting with the Los Angeles Watts conflagration in 1965, and the climate in Durham that spring was particularly volatile. In April, a group of young blacks were charged with tossing firebombs into Duke Forest, just outside of town. Opinion was divided among whites over whether the youths were on a training mission or were actually trying to cause damage. Most whites were certain, however, that the incident was related to Stokely Carmichael's visit to Duke a month earlier. The white community was particularly rattled when they learned that the car driven by the young firebombers belonged to the local antipoverty agency— and was assigned to Howard Fuller. Fuller explained the auto had been used without his knowledge, but his enemies added this latest incident to their quiver despite the fact that Fuller was never charged with any crime.

Tension rose still further over the next few months as a routine decision about the placement of new public housing escalated into a battle over ghettoization. Developers designed a 200-unit project to provide low-cost housing for families living in the path of the new crosstown expressway. Construction of replacement housing had been one of UOCI's demands, and as head of the housing committee, Ann Atwater had fought hard for it. A private developer wanted to build the new units on a twenty-two-acre site on Bacon Street in the middle-class section of Hayti. New schools had already been erected in the area to handle the influx of students, and the city council anticipated granting a zoning variance needed to commence work on the project at its usual Monday-night meeting on July 17. Grabarek and council members were shocked when 150 angry UOCI members, supported by a large number of black homeowners from the area in question, showed up that night.

"[There seems] to be a great conspiracy in Durham to expand and enlarge the great Negro ghetto," one distraught resident of the neighborhood told the council. "In the name of human decency, I beg of you not to allow the apartments to be erected at the location on Bacon Street."

The black community wanted the public housing units built in a different location, and virtually anywhere outside of the already overwhelmingly black section of Durham would have pleased them. Blacks saw Bacon Street as just another instance of being herded into ghettos—overcrowded, isolated from the rest of the city, and lacking in public services. "We are tired of being ghetto bound," Ben Ruffin, the executive director of UOCI, told the mostly uncomprehending council. "Urban renewal has provided us with a one-way ticket to the ghetto and the southeastern part of the city. We do not want any more projects in this area."

Howard Fuller told the council, "The whole situation is highly political, because I think that you don't want Negroes living with white folks and you know that those white folks that voted for you all don't want it."

> If you'd enforce [the housing code] you wouldn't have to build projects in the first place. But you refuse to enforce that code because . . . many of you are realtors. . . . I didn't come to beg, and I didn't come, you know, with my hat in my hand, because we've come up here too many times with hat in hand. We come up here this time on the basis of we're just tired. . . . We're tired of you white folks turnin' down everything that will benefit Negroes.

All of this was greeted with shouts of support by the black people in the chamber and by icy and uncomprehending stares from most of the whites. Fuller's conclusion was even more divisive.

> [Y]ou all better wake up, you all better wake up, you all better wake up to what's happening, and you better listen, because these are the voices of the people, and they're people that you have forgotten, they're people that you have pushed across those railroad tracks, they're people that you have moved out of urban renewal areas so that you could get that nice expressway. . . . You better start listening to them. . . . 'Cause they're tired, and

194

they're frustrated, and people who get tired and frustrated do things they wouldn't ordinarily do.

Coming from an advocate of Black Power, a man who had been linked, however tenuously, to a recent firebombing incident, Fuller's statement had a powerful effect on the council—and on the city as a whole when reports of the council meeting appeared in the morning paper. It wasn't just Fuller's statement that sent waves of dread through the white community. Ann Atwater had warned that Durham's inaction risked riots. Another woman added that if the desires of the black community were once again disregarded, "right here in Durham will be another Vietnam."

Where blacks merely maintained they were issuing warnings, whites heard implicit promises of violence. And the possibility of mass insurrection was heightened in everyone's mind by the riots already spreading across the country. Even as Ann was addressing the council, a few hundred miles up the eastern seaboard, Newark, New Jersey, was burning. National Guard troops raced through the area in armored vehicles dodging sniper fire and shooting at shadows. The headlines in the Durham paper the morning after the council meeting left little doubt about white fears: ANOTHER "NEWARK" THREATENED HERE.

Mayor Grabarek ended the meeting by postponing any decision on the Bacon Street project and appointing a committee to look into black demands. Where whites claimed to be acting prudently and thoughtfully, blacks perceived delaying tactics. Black Durhamites remembered all too well the Greenberg affair—only the latest example in a century of foot-dragging. "They are just biding their time," said one black man bitterly. "Committees, studies and reports will not solve the problem. We want action and we want it now."

A majority of blacks felt that their demands were fair and reasonable. Moreover, they considered that they had already demonstrated patience and forbearance in the face of decades of neglect and outright hostility on the part of the white town leaders. Their portrayal in the press the next morning as unthinking hotheads bent on destroying Durham only confirmed black residents' belief that they could not get a fair hearing in the city. A staff memorandum to the head of the North Carolina Fund written at this time opined that all the speakers had really stated at the controversial meeting was: "(1) Durham, please face up to the many problems that have accumulated over many years; (2) do something about the minor problems like street signs, sidewalks, bus service and spraying for roaches; and (3) commit yourselves to take positive action in solving the major and more complex problems." That was not, however, what the white community heard.

At 7:30 on Wednesday evening, July 19, Fuller, Ruffin, Rubye Gattis (president of UOCI), and a few others met at St. Joseph's Church to prepare for a mass meeting that would commence at 8:00. Fuller, who would not speak at the meeting, counseled participating neighborhood leaders to avoid inflammatory rhetoric. The situation was much too volatile already, he told them, and the crowd would be hard to control if emotions were stirred up.

At 8:00, around 200 residents of Hayti, including about fifty children and a sprinkling of white adult supporters, gathered in the church. The first order of business was to escort "persons not well known to the group"—mostly whites and reporters from the white media—out of the building. That done, the meeting opened with prayers and hymn singing. Rubye Gattis did an admirable job of reviewing the events of the previous two days. She was followed by two speakers, both community residents, who raised the pitch of the meeting with their complaints about the city's treatment of poor blacks. One woman was speaking vigorously against the city's housing policies when the church's PA system went out. Gattis turned to Ann Atwater the one person in the room who didn't need a microphone to be heard. Ann added her own outrage to the previous speaker's passionate remarks. She had missed the pre-meeting, where leaders had stressed the need for calm. Even if Ann had been there, she would not have complied; it simply wasn't her way. In a few minutes, Ann had the crowd whipped up, with cries of "Amen!" and "Tell it!" echoing off the church rafters.

"It appears the only way to get action is to hit the streets and go downtown!" she shouted. The meeting applauded in thunderous agreement. Afraid that things were spinning out of control, Gattis quickly interceded. The microphone had been fixed and she asked Ann to sit down as she presented the next speaker. The woman who followed Ann recited a dry list of grievances. After hearing four complaints, Ann couldn't stand to listen anymore. She wasn't about to sit there and watch as the energy she had drawn out evaporated. She jumped to her feet.

"You have heard enough," she shouted. "You said you were ready to hit the street. Let's go downtown and finish this meeting."

The crowd charged out of the church.

Ruffin and Fuller jogged along the line of agitated protesters ensuring that the march didn't turn into a melee. They completed their trek to City Hall without incident, and after a short speech by Ben Ruffin, turned around and headed back to Hayti. As the marchers came to the corner of Main and Roxboro, they passed a pile of bricks at a construction site. Some teenagers in the ranks gave in to temptation. Ann was right behind them and saw them run over to the pile, scoop up a few bricks, and lob them through nearby store and car windows. No one was injured, but the resulting six broken windows were prominently featured in news stories about the march the next day. The destruction confirmed white suspicions about the violent intentions of Durham's blacks.

At a special meeting of the city council the next morning, Mayor Grabarek announced the formation of a commission to "provid[e] a forum for all parties interested in public housing." The mayor was clearly hoping that the tactic that had worked so well to end demonstrations and marches in 1963 would succeed once again. But leaders of UOCI were less than enthusiastic about the new commission, since they were well aware that such a forum already existed in the city council meetings themselves. A collective groan went up from the large crowd of blacks in the audience when Grabarek announced that no decision had been reached on the Bacon Street issue. Disappointed and angry, Rubye Gattis still managed to present the carefully composed public face of UOCI—reasonable yet resolute—as she responded to the council's latest action (and inaction).

> We do not believe that Watts and Newark are the answers. . . . But unheard protests lead to frustration and the accidents that have created difficulties in other cities. We sincerely hope that last night's broken windows will be the last broken windows in Durham . . . We are more concerned with broken lines of communication with the total community. . . . We pledge ourselves to work with any members of the Durham community who genuinely want to listen to the voices of the poor whom we represent.

Howard Fuller and other black community leaders had no plans to mount further demonstrations at that point, but Mayor Grabarek changed that. The mayor asked the governor to mobilize National Guard units to patrol the streets of Durham, a move that insulted the black community. Something had to be done, as a North Carolina Fund staffer later put it, to "show that we are unafraid and that the city must do more than show how fast the police forces of the state and the National Guard can be mobilized. . . . I honestly believe," concluded the man, "if the mayor had not mobilized the National Guard, there would have been no march."

A march was organized for that night. Before the demonstrators left St. Joseph's Church, Fuller and Ruffin stressed the need for discipline. Any kind of violence, like the brick-throwing incident of the previous march, would be used as a justification to crack down on demonstrators by the city and county police, state troopers, and National Guard troops that lined the streets of downtown Durham. Marchers were cautioned not to pick up anything they might innocently drop while downtown; the authorities might think they were arming themselves with stones. The threat of violence didn't just come from law enforcement officers, marchers were told; waiting for them downtown were members of the Klan.

This was probably just a hunch, but it was an accurate one. C.P. had learned about the rally that afternoon in a phone call from one of his informants, a city arson inspector. The man had asked C.P. to provide additional security downtown and the Klansman was only too happy to oblige. His daughter, Vicky, was working in a drugstore just off Five Points, where the rally would be held, and C.P. was afraid that she would be caught in riots. He rounded up ten other men and stationed them along the intended return route of the march. The damage to store windows had occurred on the march *back* to the church on Monday, and C.P. figured that was when something would happen this night, too. He made sure his men were prepared. Most of them carried handguns. Beneath a long coat C.P. carried a shotgun, and in his pockets were more shells.

Two hundred marchers headed downtown, through streets lined by glowering law enforcement officers. At Five Points, Ben Ruffin was addressing the demonstrators when a bottle flew out of a crowd of whites across the street, striking a black man in the face, opening a large gash above his right eye. A group of young blacks took one look at their injured comrade, blood streaming down his face, and ran off in the direction the bottle had come from. Howard Fuller suddenly appeared before them, a wooden cane in his hands. He suggested that it would be a good idea for the young men to return to the rally. They agreed.

As the demonstration ended and the marchers turned to head back to St. Joseph's, C.P. alerted his men to get ready. He fingered his shotgun, removing the safety. C.P. felt certain that the time had come to take back his city, indeed to reclaim the South. He would prefer to shoot Howard Fuller or, better yet, Ann Atwater, but, he told himself, one way or the other, *somebody* was going to get shot that night. He had no fear about what the police or National Guard would do when the Klansmen fired the first shots. Wasn't he there at the request of a city official, after all? He was merely helping to restore Durham to order.

But as C.P. waited, fate took the matter out of his hands. The marchers changed their plans, returning to Hayti by a different route than the one C.P. had staked out. He watched them head off in another direction and considered finding a new position with his men. But that would be difficult to do. Besides, he considered, there would be other chances. As the last of the marchers disappeared, C.P. told his men to go on home. He acted disappointed in front of them, but secretly he was flush with excitement. C.P. had begun his campaign to take the Klan out of the Klavern hall and into the public arena.

CHAPTER TEN

[Y]ou don't hear much about poor whites in this
state. Year after year they plant corn, paint
houses, fix cars or work at seasonal jobs and live
off welfare in the off-seasons. Their children quit
school at sixteen and go into the army, the jails,
the state hospitals; when troubled times come, they
join the Klan and do the rabble-rousing for the
middle class. But they never speak up for
themselves. With no traditions of organized
political activity behind them and nobody to look
to for help since the New Deal, they live in apathy
and despair. Gentle and violent Southerners, they
are the silent ones, the forgotten.

—ELIZABETH TORNQUIST

C.P. prayed his nervousness didn't show. Dressed in a faded
green suit, he felt awkward standing before the microphone
and bathed in bright lights. He was glad now that he had convinced two other Klansmen to accompany him to the city
council meeting on his maiden voyage into mainstream
Durham politics. He hoped the three of them presented a suit-
ably menacing picture. The handgun each man wore in his
belt helped, but C.P. was used to speaking at the Klavern hall
and at rallies. This night he was not standing before friends
and he hoped he'd come off well.

It was a cool fall evening, after the hot summer of 1967. C.P.
still hadn't convinced his Klansmen of the wisdom of his strategy to go public, but he had grown tired of waiting and had
decided that, with or without the Klan, he could in good con-
science expose himself to the spotlight. The perfect opportu-

nity arose when the chairman of the North Carolina Good Neighbor Council, David Coltrane, told a gathering at the state capitol that the Klan was "directly or indirectly involved in all the brushfires last summer in Durham . . ."

C.P. was determined to set the record straight. "We deny the statement by Coltrane that we were responsible for the racial tension in the city of Durham," C.P. said, reciting his carefully composed statement. "We challenge Mr. Coltrane and Mayor Grabarek to bring forth evidence to prove that we were responsible for any such tensions."

Short and sweet. C.P. felt better after he sat down. The many blacks who now regularly attended city council meetings glared at him but he relished the smiles and nods directed at him by many whites in the audience. He even thought that he had detected sympathetic expressions on the faces of a couple of councilmen, too. He almost regretted having used an alias. At the last minute, he had hedged, introducing himself as C. V. Anderson, vice president of the local Klan. Next time he would use his real name and position, he decided.

He began attending meetings regularly, and not just of the city council. The Klansman showed up at sessions of the county Board of Supervisors, the School Board, the Housing Authority, and many other official bodies where he would argue against policies beneficial to blacks and for practices and procedures that upheld "conservative Southern values." When school officials conceded to black demands that the rebel anthem "Dixie" be banned from school functions, for example, C.P. was there to fulminate, although unsuccessfully, against the decision. He protested even the small amount of money the city dribbled out to provide services in black sections of town. Before long, white residents of Durham were calling C.P. after each of his appearances. "We're damn glad *somebody's* saying what you're saying," they told him.

And it wasn't just Durham's poor white neighborhoods that supported him. Residents of upscale Hope Valley also wrote C.P. with their thanks—sometimes enclosing a check to support "your important work." His fans included some high-ranking city and county officials who called to thank C.P. for saying publicly what they felt but could not say. Councilman Charles Steel was a particular ally, informing C.P. when he expected opposition from blacks toward the conservative agenda. Carvie Oldham, head of the Durham Housing Authority, was also a frequent caller, notifying the Klan leader whenever a particularly contentious meeting was scheduled so that the Klansman could attend and back up Oldham's position. Sometimes C.P. visited these men in their offices, but the meetings were always "unofficial." They explained that they had to be careful about appearing to be too close to the Klan; blacks and liberals could make things very uncomfortable for them. C.P. assured them that he understood. It was enough that these representatives of official Durham confided in him. He considered them his friends, or, at the very least, colleagues who, under different circumstances, *could* be friends, and he believed that they felt the same way about him.

As head of the local Klan, C.P. worked with many of the leading racists in the region. Of course, he was on intimate terms with the Klan's state leader, Bob Jones, and Jones' wife, Sylvia, head of the women's auxiliary. He also knew and respected Imperial Wizard Robert Shelton, the UKA's chief executive officer. J. B. Stoner, a lawyer and head of the National States' Rights Party, visited C.P. on recruiting trips through Durham. Stoner was a virulent anti-Semite, whose Confederate flag vest delighted C.P. With experience organizing Klan units in several Southern states, Stoner was as violent as Shelton, and would later be convicted in the 1958 dynamiting of a Birmingham, Alabama, church. He convinced C.P. to sign on as a state organizer for the National States' Rights Party, but the busy EC had no time to recruit members for the neo-Nazi group. He also met several times with another States' Rights leader and ardent white supremacist, Dr. Edward Fields. C.P. was impressed that the far right included a doctor (and only much later learned that Fields was a veterinarian).

C.P. also worked with leaders of other racist organizations in Durham. There was a branch of a competing Klan group, the Knights of the Ku Klux Klan, led by a former member of the UKA Klavern, a saturnine housepainter named Lloyd

Jacobs. C.P. wasn't sure what to make of Jacobs. He both admired and was repelled by the other man's rabid commitment to the cause of white supremacy. C.P. considered himself a radical, but Jacobs was clearly cut from a different cloth— one that was beginning to unravel. Jacobs was forever predicting the imminent collapse of the United States government. A state investigator who attended one of Jacobs' open-air rallies in 1967 reported that the Klan leader told his followers that before the next presidential elections "all the lights in America would go out at the same time, that all the power plants would be blown up simultaneously, that chlorine would be dumped into all cities [*sic*] drinking water, roofing tacks distributed upon all super highways . . ." Jacobs condemned the war in Vietnam as a conspiracy to kill off white boys so that white girls "would get so hard up that they would marry and intercourse negroes." Jacobs attended city council meetings, but only sporadically, which was a good thing, in C.P.'s view, since Jacobs' diatribes left listeners with the impression that the man was unhinged.

On the other end of the racist spectrum were Joseph High, a small businessman who headed the Durham County Citizens' Council (formerly the White Citizens' Council), and an old-style Southern gentleman by the name of Garland Keith, who ran the Citizens' Committee for Law and Order. High and Keith were smooth and respectable where C.P. was rough and, despite the numerous calls of support, still somewhat disreputable. Keith, in particular, possessed an aura of dignity. He dressed impeccably and had the manners of a grandee. C.P. never heard him utter the epithet "nigger," not even when the two were alone. All forms of obvious vulgarity were anathema to Keith. When an overheated young Klansman once used the word "damn" in Keith's living room, the older man took him outside and lectured him: "You and I share a lot of common values. But I'd appreciate it a great deal if you wouldn't use bad language in the house if my wife's at home." Beneath his Old South gentility, however, Keith was as opposed to desegregation as any Klansman and worked the system expertly to frustrate changes in Durham's social order.

Less fastidious than his comrade, Joe High was pure New South. During the initial battles on school desegregation, he used his prodigious energy to organize a chapter of the White Citizens' Council. High was also a survivalist and fancied himself to be a karate expert. He spent free weekends instructing C.P.'s men in combat techniques and firearms training, strutting around in the woods outside of town, barking orders and wearing an 8 mm Mauser strapped on his hip. But High's ability to go mano a mano with blacks and Communists in the impending race war was called into question after he shattered his hand while attempting to break a piece of plywood, karate-style.

Despite differences in style, the three men worked well together and even shared an overlapping membership, with some of the milder members of C.P.'s organization forming the radical wing of High's and Keith's groups. It was a symbiotic relationship: C.P. provided Keith and High with a day-to-day connection to the more militant segment of Durham's racist society, and Keith and High added a degree of credibility to the overtly racist movement that C.P., as a Klansman, could never have obtained on his own. The pair also gave C.P. entrée to City Hall and Durham's business community. The city manager was a chum of Keith and High, and C.P. accompanied the two on several visits to his office. C.P. even arranged a meeting with Mayor Grabarek, although it was held at the CPA's business office in the Central Carolina Bank Building and the atmosphere was not terribly warm. But by and large, C.P. found that "the doors of city hall were just about open to us. Nobody shut the door in our face." The Klan viewpoint could always find a hearing in the highest reaches of Durham's civic life.

One important achievement of C.P.'s term of office was the construction of a new Klavern hall just outside of town. Although only a nondescript single-story structure, the building was concrete proof, literally, of the Klan's new prosperity and acceptance. Most of the money for the building was raised by the working-class Klan membership, but even more importantly, a significant amount of the funds arrived as secret donations from middle- and upper-class supporters. A venerable bank underwrote the construction of the new meeting hall. Following a long Klan tradition of secrecy, the building was officially the headquarters of an organization called the Town and Country Sportsman's Club. Klan units throughout North Carolina sported similarly vague titles—Ponderosa Pistol Club, Hunters Club, Saddle Club, Lee County Improvement Association, Fine Fellows Club. Locals all knew what these clubs were: units of the Ku Klux Klan. Out front flew two flags: the Stars and Stripes of the United States and the Stars and Bars, the battle flag of the Confederacy.

C.P. had believed leading the Klan into the public sphere was the right move, but he was unprepared for the huge success of that effort. The meetings with city and county officials, the back-channel support from polite Durham society, the swelling membership roles, the new Klavern hall—any one of these taken individually was a significant feather in C.P.'s hood. Together, they were an astonishing tour de force for racism in the Magic City. C.P. felt more than vindicated; he felt valued. If the night of his initiation into the Klan was a homecoming, his acceptance into Durham's civic life was the discovery of a previously unknown extended family. True, they moved in a different social world than C.P. They talked and dressed differently. They drove new cars, vacationed at summer houses more commodious than C.P.'s tiny frame house, and kept fine stables of horses instead of a chain-link kennel with a couple of dogs inside. But for all the differences, there was no mistaking the family resemblance. They were white people all, with faces turned to the cynosure of race. C.P.'s only miscalculation was in believing that because Durham's white elite despised blacks, they did not also despise him.

Howard Fuller knew that if whites considered Operation Breakthrough as an exclusively "black" organization, it would limit the group's effectiveness. To counter this perception, Fuller and others tried to recruit low-income whites from C.P.'s own neighborhood into Operation Breakthrough and UOCI. "If the new UOCI could begin to bring in white residents, the organization's strength and scare power would quadruple," observed a visiting community organizer in 1966. "It would scare the pants off the Mayor and leading business-men." But impoverished whites were battling a century of pro-paganda telling them that blacks were the sole cause of their problems. Despite organizers' best attempts, mudsill whites could not overcome the whispers of the past—or the shouts of the present. "America is being transformed into a fiery jungle of violent lawlessness," thundered Jesse Helms (the racial code word "jungle" appeared frequently in his television editorials). "There are chuckles in the Kremlin these days. . . . What is needed most is enough law enforcement, whatever the cost, to put down any further rebellion." To make common cause with reviled blacks, the dupes of Communists and despoilers of Southern women, would be to betray America and the South.

Fear of Communism had all but destroyed Americans' ability to deal with the complexities of class issues, or even to recognize that class differences exist in this country. In this, as in so many areas, W. E. B. Du Bois was far ahead of his country-men and -women. In his book *The Souls of Black Folk*, published in 1903, he declared, "The problem of the twentieth century is the problem of the color-line," but he reassessed this oft-quoted formulation in the introduction to a 1953 edition of his classic book. On the eve of *Brown* v. *Board*, Du Bois wrote:

> I still think today as yesterday that the color line is a great problem of this century. But today I see more clearly than yesterday that back of the problem of race and color, lies a greater problem which both obscures and implements it: and that is the fact that so many civilized persons are willing to live in comfort even if the price of this is poverty, ignorance and disease of the majority of their fellowmen.

Few individuals—black or white—shared that insight. One who did was playwright Lorraine Hansberry, the author of the Pulitzer Prize–winning play *A Raisin in the Sun.* After a passionate and eloquent defense of the civil rights movement at a 1962 conference in Carnegie Hall (called to protest the

McCarthyite tactics of the House Un-American Activities Committee), she called for immediate change in the South's social system, and shocked the audience by adding:

> And I say this not merely in behalf of the black and oppressed but, for a change—and more and more thoughtful Negroes must begin to make this point—also for the white and disinherited of the South, those poor whites who, by the millions, have been made the tragic and befuddled instruments of their own oppression at the hand of the most sinister political apparatus in our country.

However, appeals for interracial cooperation among the lower classes never gained much of a following during those Cold War years. In Durham, as throughout the nation, poor blacks and poor whites regarded each other with hostility from their respective ghettos.

With C.P. and the Klan exerting pressure from the far right, it became harder than ever for Durham's black community to win concessions from the white power structure, or even hold on to the gains already achieved. The marches of the summer (which whites saw as "black riots," even though most of the violence had come from whites) were seized on by conservatives as a pretext for getting rid of Howard Fuller, "that militant from Chicago." Leading the charge were two of North Carolina's representatives to the U.S. House, Nick Galifianakis and James Gardner. "There is a definite agitating element" in antipoverty agencies in Durham, Galifianakis insinuated, and asked the FBI's assistance in uncovering the "troublemakers." Congressman Gardner went even further, demanding a full investigation of the North Carolina Fund and its parent organization, the Office of Economic Opportunity (OEO), and the withholding of all funds from Operation Breakthrough. The FBI was unable to tie Fuller to any crimes and NCF director George Esser, Jr., backed his man, adding a warning to all those who would attempt to kill the messenger of urban grievances. "[S]erious problems can arise in Durham," cautioned Esser, "or any other American city, if problems . . . are not faced directly . . ." Others leapt to Fuller's aid, including Louis Austin.

The attempt of the Durham White Power Structure to have the salary of Howard Fuller cut off, with the hope of ridding this city of his presence or the leadership of the underprivileged of his race, is one of those nasty techniques sometimes resorted to by white people in administering reprisals to any Negro who stands up and demands his rights or the rights of his people. The case of Howard Fuller can be reproduced again and again in every southern state or wherever Negroes have suffered the injustices of racial discrimination and attempted to demand their rights.

Fuller also received support from unlikely quarters. Watts Hill, Jr., chairman of Home Security Life Insurance, and a member of one of Durham's leading families, defended the head of Operation Breakthrough in a letter to OEO director Sargent Shriver. Fuller "is the single person most responsible for there not being riots in Durham," wrote Hill. "Had he been withdrawn from the picture, there would have been a leaderless mob." The black elite closed ranks around Fuller. In his typically phlegmatic manner, Asa Spaulding, head of the North Carolina Mutual, defended the beleaguered militant, stating, "I doubt seriously that removing Mr. Fuller from the Durham community would be a better cure of its ills than his remaining here as a reminder of its ills until they are cured."

Thanks to these endorsements, Fuller's job was saved, but the attacks enraged many in the black community, foremost among them Ann Atwater, who was by this time completely devoted to the charismatic leader. The injustice of the situation confirmed Ann's view of Durham as a conservative-to-reactionary town masquerading as a progressive one. She reacted as she always did to adversity: by redoubling her efforts to force change on the reluctant city. She spoke at a dozen city council meetings, demanding a halt to the Bacon Street project. While black leaders had tried to defuse the situation after the tense marches of the summer, by that fall tempers were flaring again. After the council once again refused to consider moving the housing project out of the predominantly black section, Ann led a group of over 100 angry blacks into the council chamber, where a statement was read clearly designed to play on white fears: "We believe that to continually push Negroes into well-defined areas will create animosities which could become as explosive as Watts . . . Newark, or Detroit. . . . If you do not wish to aid us in the perpetuation of progress, then we shall not aid you in the preservation of peace."

A week after that meeting, Ann and a small group of other Durham blacks traveled to Washington, D.C., to air their grievances before officials at the Department of Housing and Urban Development. The bureaucrats assured them that Bacon Street was just one of three such projects planned for their city—the other two of which would be built in predominantly white neighborhoods. On the return trip, the Durham delegation debated whether they could trust the federal authorities on the "package deal" and decided that experience dictated skepticism. (In retrospect, it was a wise decision. The two other projects were never built after white residents objected to them.)

Ann headed another protest at an October meeting of the city Planning and Zoning Commission. She warned members of the commission that if they approved the variance to allow construction of the Bacon Street project, they were inviting trouble. Blacks would do everything in their power to prevent the increased ghettoization of Hayti. In a surprise move, the commission voted unanimously not to recommend the zoning change. Ann was delighted, but decided not to take the heat off the city council, which could still reject or accept the commission's decision. A Sunday prayer meeting/protest on the City Hall steps attracted a crowd of 450. Four days later, the contractor who had been selected to build the controversial project suddenly pulled out, citing "fiercer than usual" opposition. The council finally saw the handwriting on the wall and killed the project.

It was Ann's biggest victory yet, but she had little time to savor it. The other battles over housing raged; there were no signs of victory there. Most of the complaints centered on Carvie Oldham, mandarin of the Durham Housing Authority. Oldham objected to many of the specific changes Ann demanded in her role as chair of the UOCI housing committee, but his real problem was with the current *attitude* of public housing tenants, which was, to his mind, insufficiently servile. As the ranking white man in charge of the lives of black tenants, the reactionary Oldham felt it was his duty to uphold the immutable Southern social hierarchy. Blacks must defer to white rule. To treat black tenants as equals ran contrary to the Southern way of life. Also following tradition, Oldham blamed the change in attitude on outside agitators. It was evident to Oldham that antipoverty workers had sparked trouble among the otherwise contented tenants. "We had tenant councils of a sort prior to Operation Breakthrough," he explained, "but they weren't as antagonistic as the councils formed by Operation Breakthrough." Oldham did admit that activists had forced some needed changes, but the former cotton mill manager immediately added huffily that "this could have been done solely by negotiation, without the picketing."

Charges against Oldham's imperious rule ranged widely, from unfair administrative procedures to threats and intimidation. Residents recognized that Oldham's repressive policies were the work of a Bourbon mind, one which sought at every turn to deny black tenants their dignity. They saw, only too clearly, that Oldham was bent on re-creating in the public housing projects the world of the plantation. Unmarried women who were thought to be pregnant were subjected to physical exams. One housing official roughly poked a young woman's abdomen to determine if she was pregnant. Satisfied that she was, the official sneered at her, "It felt good going in, but it's going to be hell coming out."

A common tenant complaint concerned invasive attempts by officials to prove that single women were living with men— a violation of both housing and welfare rules. In one such case, the manager of a project grew suspicious when she saw a truck parked outside a unit rented by a young single mother. The manager later said she "accidentally" used her master key to enter the woman's apartment and discovered a man sitting on a sofa in the living room. She called the welfare department to have the family's public assistance cut off, and then reported the violation to the Housing Authority, starting the eviction process. Luckily, the woman contacted Ann, who investigated the incident and determined that the man's truck had broken down in the lot and that he had used the woman's telephone to call a garage. He was waiting for the repairmen to show up when the manager "happened into" the apartment.

In intimidating residents, Oldham's employees often relied on the Durham police. This was the case during a rent strike at McDougald Terrace, when, late one night, a Housing Authority official showed up at the apartment of one family participating in the strike, accompanied by a uniformed policeman. The pair informed the family that they had come for the rent. When the tenant told them what they already knew—that the money had been deposited in an escrow account—the officials left, but returned a half hour later and demanded that the man come downtown with them. The fate of black men in white prisons was, of course, well known to the family, and the tenant's daughter, who was already ill, grew terrified, pleading with the policeman not to take her father. When the girl fainted, the two men left, but they returned early the next morning and repeated their demand. The child, now frantic, collapsed into a coma. She died within hours.

An official city commission looking into abuses by the Housing Authority later catalogued many of these problems. "The entire Lease," wrote the panel, "is worded so that the tenant promises everything and is responsible for everything while the Housing [Authority], as landlord, promises nothing and is responsible for nothing." The report concluded: "the despair of the tenants . . . is justified."

Demands for Oldham's ouster were routinely ignored by the city, however. As usual, the city council refused to rule on specific complaints about the Housing Authority, referring them to "the proper committee"—Durham's necropolis of grievances.

On December 12, a meeting between the Housing Authority board and tenants turned into a four-hour shouting match as many black residents vented long-simmering frustrations. Some turned to the old traditional verbal mockery to reveal hidden truth. In the poor neighborhoods, Mayor Wense Grabarek was known as "Mr. Smooth-it-over," leader of the

"You must understand our position" men. The city housing inspector was dubbed "See no evil" man. And the city council was renamed the board of "It takes time." While important as emotional safety valves, such expressions did nothing to change outward circumstances and the pressure for change escalated. Louis Austin, his aging finger still on the pulse of black Durham, warned in a *Carolina Times* editorial that the residents of Hayti would not be patient forever: "Durham citizens are sitting on a veritable powder keg."

That warning was certainly apt in Ann Atwater's case. As the person responsible for seeking solutions to housing problems, she had reached her limit of tolerance. She had traveled to Washington, D.C., to obtain justice, and had come away with a promise she knew was worthless. She had seen her mentor Howard Fuller vilified. She had worked to keep marches peaceful, even though she would have preferred to "bust up" Durham. Nothing seemed to work. Each victory (and there were few of *those*) was accompanied by another setback. And now the same white leaders of Durham who attacked Fuller embraced the head of the Klan. She had no proof that Oldham and C.P. were working together, but she strongly suspected it. She had sat through several city council meetings and had seen members of the council smile approvingly as the Klansman spoke about preserving "the Southern way of life." Ann knew all about the "Southern way of life," and to her, boiled down to its essence, it meant "that black folk will not have a voice."

And yet, she was determined to be heard. If impassioned speeches before the council and endless peaceful marches downtown wouldn't draw the attention of city officials, perhaps it was time to send a stronger message, one that white people could not ignore, a message that would force Mr. Smooth-it-over to act.

Three nights after the contentious housing meeting, just as the issue of the *Carolina Times* containing Austin's characterization of Durham as a "powder keg" was hitting the streets, Ann drove her old battered car to where city workers had torn up a section of roadway in Hayti. Such areas pockmarked the landscape, as urban renewal chewed its way through black Durham. This particular crater was lined with oil lamps the size and shape of bowling balls. Through the night, each orange tongue of flame flickered from a wick at the top. Ann stopped her car beside the hole and lingered a minute. When no other cars drove by, she rolled up to one of the flaming metal balls and opened her door. With some effort, she reached down and scooped up the ball. It was a cold night and the warm metal felt good on her hands. She blew out the flame and carefully placed the oil lamp on the floor of her car. Then she drove off in the direction of McDougald Terrace, where a small knot of men waited, smoking cigarettes and talking in hushed voices.

The Durham papers deemed the firebombing of Housing Authority offices front-page news. Hay stored in a section of the building had caught fire and caused much damage before firemen had arrived and put out the blaze. Ann Atwater read the short article and noted with a certain satisfaction its tone of alarm. Now maybe the city would get the message. Over in the poor white neighborhoods of East Durham, just a mile from where Ann sat, the article about the fire did indeed stir considerable interest. There, C. P. Ellis fumed over news of the firebombing. Why didn't the police crack down on these Communists? he wondered aloud. At the next Klan meeting, there was more talk about shooting Howard Fuller. Within the police department itself, white officers started a pool to see who could come closest to predicting the date on which the black leader would be killed.

The only positive reaction to heightened tensions over housing, and one almost certainly not linked to the fire itself, was the change in the Housing Authority's practice of waiting a year to reevaluate rent when the head of a household left. The period was shortened to a month. The small concession—just one of perhaps a hundred much more important demands—placated no one. Progress in employment practices was just as slow in coming. Reacting to pressure to hire more blacks, the Durham Merchants Association, unveiled in February 1968 an ambitious program to train fifteen young blacks for business positions. The "Durham Retail Institute" was supposed to run twice a week for eight to ten weeks, but it was dropped after only a single session, when UOCI representatives objected to what they considered a demeaning and racist emphasis on issues such as grooming and good hygiene.

As with housing, blacks kept a laundry list of grievances over unfair white business practices. Topping the list was the fundamental issue of jobs. "There is obvious discrimination when you look in stores and see nothing but white faces," pointed out a black leader. "Those white sales clerks have no more ability than Negroes who have jobs paying much less." Blacks accused white store owners of screening them out of higher-paying positions (giving jobs to "the more qualified," who "happened to be white," but never releasing the results of tests), promoting white employees over more experienced black workers, and tokenism. "They think one Negro with 200 whites proves 'I am an Equal Opportunity Employer,'" protested one black antipoverty worker. "They token us to death." The fight for jobs was an old one, and little had changed in Durham since Louis Austin protested discriminatory hiring practices in 1953. Writing in the *Carolina Times* with his trademark trenchant humor, Austin had pointed out: "The question of seeking employment is not one of upholding southern customs or not upholding them, it is a question of eating. We would like to inform our white fellow citizens that on our side of the fence, food is an important matter." Fifteen years later, food remained an important issue to the poor citizens of Hayti.

Frustration over the lack of progress in housing and employment issues kept tensions high in Durham, with only a spark needed to touch off an explosion. It came in mid-February, blown over the border from a conflagration on the campus of South Carolina State College in Orangeburg. Students at that black school had been protesting since February 5 a segregated bowling alley in town, with demonstrations growing in size and intensity over the next few days. On February 8, state and local police, erroneously believing that one of their officers had been shot by demonstrators, let loose a fusillade into a crowd of students gathered in front of a dormitory. Firing rifles, shotguns loaded with double-aught pellets (the largest manufactured), and a variety of handguns, police poured round after round into the crowd. Thirty-three students were wounded in the hail of gunfire, some of them with as many as eight separate wounds. Three of them died, including Samuel Hammond, an eighteen-year-old freshman who had been shot once in the back, and Delano Herman Middleton, a seventeen-year-old high school student shot three times in the arm, once in the hip, once in the thigh, once in the side, and once in the heart. Lying on the ground next to Middleton was Henry Smith, eighteen years old and also dying, the result of five gunshot wounds. Several witnesses later testified that a patrolman walked up to Smith, mortally wounded but still conscious, and struck him with the butt of a gun. As the dying pair were being dragged across a field to a rescue vehicle, one patrolman told them, "If you'd been home where you belonged, you wouldn't be in this fix." The wounded streamed into (an all black) Orangeburg hospital. A horrified hospital employee asked a policeman what had happened. "A couple of these niggers got stung with birdshot," he replied matter-of-factly. Later that night, another patrolman wistfully told a colleague over his police radio, "You should have been here, ol' buddy; got a couple of 'em tonight."

The Orangeburg massacre did not generate the same national outrage and agonizing self-examination as would the killings of four white students at Kent State University two years later. But American blacks, for whom death at the hands of the police was far from unprecedented, viewed the slaughter of its young college students as a moment of special ignominy. The outrage in Durham was typical of black sentiments across the nation: malign neglect was bad enough, but the killings of their neighbors to the south indicated it was once again open season on Southern blacks. A week after the killings, blacks in many cities held demonstrations to grieve for their dead, to show communal solidarity, and to vent outrage. On February 15, Ann Atwater and Howard Fuller escorted a crowd of several hundred blacks, mostly students from NCC and Duke, for a memorial service at Five Points Park. Two small fires were ignited in the park, both of which were immediately put out. When demonstrators set fire to a coffin as part of their protest, the firemen at the scene doused the flames and then turned their hoses on the crowd. Pandemonium erupted, with people running in all directions to escape the cold blasts of water. When the hoses were shut off, baton-wielding police chased the demonstrators. The scene was reminiscent of Birmingham, only on a smaller scale. An official investigation of the disorders later ruled that city police and firemen "used unnecessarily harsh and repressive measures to deal with the young Negroes. . . . [This] caused the violence and disorder . . ." Despite efforts by Howard Fuller and Ann Atwater to calm the situation, a score of angry black teenagers sped down Main Street, tossing garbage cans and bricks through a dozen store windows. During the melee, Fuller was arrested for assaulting a police officer. Fuller's crime had been to intercede when he witnessed a policeman about to strike a black man in the head with his baton even though the man's arms were already pinned behind his back by another officer. The police maintained that Fuller tried to prevent them from arresting the other man, a charge which Fuller denied. As Fuller himself was being arrested, the policeman taunted him with the baton, repeatedly prodding him in the stomach and then sticking it between his legs and twisting. Fuller pulled the stick away from the man. The policeman later claimed that Fuller also struck him in the mouth, a charge Fuller called "a goddamn lie." The six-foot-four activist added, "If I ever assault a cop, he's going to leave there with some physical markings."

Ann saw Fuller being hauled off and she followed on foot to the jail, just a few blocks away. Still soaking wet from the fire hoses, she planted her large body in the doorway of the building. "You ain't gonna put me out!" Ann hollered when several officers gathered around her. "Howard didn't do nothing. I ain't going nowhere til you release him!" With several other demonstrators milling around, the police were loath to use the kind of force necessary to move the 390-pound respected community spokeswoman. From her position in the doorway, Ann blocked traffic in and out of the jail, all the while using her oversized voice to curse anyone who came near her. Fuller was quickly processed and released.

The Anvil, a local alternative paper, dispatched reporters into the streets to gauge public reaction the morning following the disturbance. Not surprisingly, they found that Durham's views of the preceding stormy night were largely divided according to race. A black man waiting for a bus spat out, "They should have burned the whole place down." An older, less militant black man regretted the window breaking but added, "I don't see [whites] apologizing to us about anything." Another elderly black man pointed out that his people had tried working within the system for years, with little result. "Well, what you going to do?" he asked the reporter wearily. "You try and do what you can. Sometimes you go too far, sometimes you don't go far enough; you just never know till you try. We're just doing what we have to."

White opinion was far less sympathetic. Many moderates exposed their ignorance of life across the railroad tracks by griping, "We've given them houses, schools, jobs, everything they wanted. Now what?" Others were even more hostile. "We ought to shoot them but not with hoses," said one man. The reaction of white businessmen whose windows had been smashed was understandably bitter. "What happened in Orangeburg is their business," said the manager of Kress. "[The violence] doesn't do anybody any good, except the glass companies." But among Durham whites in general, most of whom still lived in the belief that Durham had "good race relations," the reporter found "puzzlement and frustration." For them, the only way to explain the recent troubles was to roll out the old Southern chestnut about trouble-causing outsiders. Durham whites "were almost unanimous in their indictment of outside agitators," reported the *Anvil* writer. "The feeling is that without them there would be no trouble; that the Negro people of Durham are by and large peaceful and satisfied." That anyone could continue to believe this notion is testament not only to the persistence of myth but, more importantly, to the failure of white leaders and institutions, including the press, to tell whites the truth about their city. Later that summer, when a far greater explosion would rock Durham, another reporter for the alternative *Anvil*, Elizabeth Tornquist, would put her finger squarely on this problem of white ignorance. "The black people have learned what goes on because they have had to," she would write. "The white people have been able to survive knowing nothing. Now, however, when they desperately need to understand what is happening, they have no handle to get hold of the situation."

For a week and a half following the February violence, Mayor Grabarek refused to comment on the troubles. Finally, he issued a terse statement saying, "We shall enforce the law equitably and equally for all people in the community." The statement, which was clearly designed to mollify conservatives, received an icy reception in Hayti. A week later, the mayor did nothing to enhance his reputation with Durham's blacks when he testified at Howard Fuller's trial. For once not wearing his red carnation, the mayor was asked to describe Fuller and replied, "He has a proclivity for vexation." Blacks and whites alike scratched their heads at Grabarek's abstruse testimony, but it was clear the mayor was no friend of Fuller. (Fuller was acquitted on the assault charge and convicted of resisting arrest—a ruling that was overturned on appeal.)

In the wake of February's chaos, whites were less interested in the causes of the violence than in whether or not it could happen again. When asked that question, UOCI's Ben Ruffin shrugged and tossed the question back: "Durham will have to decide that by the way they respond to [black] grievances . . ."

In an interview with the *North Carolina Anvil*, Howard Fuller was more explicit about how Durham could avoid creating the need for more demonstrations: the city, he said, needed to "quit talking and do." About job discrimination "in downtown stores where black people are pouring in their money." About a school system that continually improved programs and facilities for wealthy white students while the inner-city poor schools (which were 45 percent black) went begging. About the perennial housing problems: "enforce the codes . . . put some streets in . . . make [Hayti] a place where people . . . can live." What frustrated Fuller the most was the fact that blacks weren't demanding that all these problems be fixed at once. They merely wanted the city to take some small but substantive steps toward resolving these long-standing issues. "Then," he explained, "you've got something to show. Something to say to people. It's not pacification. It's movement."

> I'm never going to tell a person don't take a job because it's pacification. I tell him to take the job and understand it's a first step to bringing about significant change. Always look ahead. But in a place like Durham they won't do a damn thing. The mayor sits up there showing people he's big daddy and in control. And the whites want to prove they run the city. Well, everybody knows it so they don't have to prove it every day. But it's that kind of attitude that brings on an explosive situation. . . . I keep saying that it is possible to bring change without violence but that it is getting less and less possible because they won't do anything.

Three days after the interview, rather than integrate its annual Miss Durham pageant, as demanded by UOCI, the Durham Junior Chamber of Commerce voted to cancel the event altogether. A month later, on March 18, a commission appointed by the mayor eight months earlier to look into the full spectrum of black grievances issued its long-awaited report to the city council. It recommended no substantive changes in housing, employment, or schools. It did, however, refer several times to the city's unshakable commitment to "effective communication."

Durham's white community considered the document a blueprint for racial comity, prudent yet magnanimous. But most of Durham's black citizens never even learned of its existence.

CHAPTER ELEVEN

> On the tainted air broods fear.
> —W. E. B. Du Bois

News that Martin Luther King, Jr., would visit Durham on Thursday, April 4, 1968, boosted the spirits of a beleaguered black population in the Bull City. King would be stumping throughout the Tarheel State for his longtime friend, black gubernatorial candidate Dr. Reginald Hawkins. Although the civil rights leader was beloved in most black communities, Durham felt a special connection to King because of his crucial 1960 visit in support of the lunch-counter movement. Some 1,500 people had been enthralled by King's soaring rhetoric in White Rock Baptist Church that February night, and, human nature being what it is, by 1968 the number of Hayti residents with their own vivid memories of attending that historic rally had swelled to several thousand. Durham had clasped King to its heart nearly five years before he had been awarded the Nobel Peace Prize, and so residents couldn't be blamed for assuming a proprietary interest in the reverend's illustrious career. They felt, and not without at least some justification, that they had helped propel King on his meteoric rise. King, the product of Atlanta's black *grand monde*, also had many friends and acquaintances among Durham's black upper classes, including John Wheeler, president of the Mechanics and Farmers Bank, Duke professor Samuel Cook (the school's only black professor), and John Stewart, head of Mutual Savings and Loan. Wheeler, Cook, and King had been classmates at Morehouse College, while the older Stewart was an intimate of King's father and had known the future civil rights leader when "Little Mike" (the name Martin came later) was a precocious toddler.

Durham whites were, as a group, far less sanguine about King and his impending North Carolina tour. Two days before the visit, a letter printed in the *Morning Herald* condemned King as a Communist "ring leader." Charges that King was Red were not new, but they had increased in number and vitriol in the past year, particularly since King had announced his opposition to the Vietnam War. Jesse Helms used his TV editorials to abrade King's reputation, denouncing him as "a sham, an agitator, a fellow traveller with known communists." According to Helms, the inner-city violence of the past several summers could be laid at the feet of the supposedly meek minister: "King can wave his Nobel Peace Prize to his heart's content," declared Helms, "[but his movement] is about as non-violent as the Marines landing on Iwo Jima, and it is a 'movement' only in the sense that mob action is moving and spreading throughout the land." Others might be fooled, but Helms assured listeners in January 1968 that his own finely pitched ear discerned in King's voice "the crackle of anarchy and the threat of violence."

If Hayti had been excited over King's visit, residents were doubly disappointed when they learned that the trip had been canceled. On Wednesday, April 3, King telephoned Hawkins from Memphis, Tennessee, with the news that events there required his continued presence in that city. King, who was in Memphis to support striking sanitation workers, told Hawkins that he just couldn't leave at that time. A march led by King the previous week had turned violent, with some protesters smashing store windows, and now, the civil rights leader told his friend, "non-violence is on trial" in Memphis. King felt he had to lead another march to prove that nonviolence could work. A crestfallen Hawkins assured King that he understood.

The following evening, on the day he was supposed to have been in Durham, King was standing on the balcony outside his motel room in Memphis, cigarette in hand, joking with supporters, when a single shot fired from a high-powered rifle struck him in the face. King collapsed, quickly lost consciousness, and at 7:05 P.M.—barely an hour after the shooting—was pronounced dead.

News of the assassination stunned black Durham. It was as if the bullet that had struck down King had also pierced Hayti's much-bruised heart. When approached for comment by the press, the normally unflappable Asa Spaulding could only choke out that the news "was so shocking and distressing that it has not only left me speechless, but also not able to think clearly." As the wave of sorrow, shock, and grief spread across the black district, people King's age or older could be seen standing on sidewalks, in corner markets, or riding the bus home from work with tears streaming down their faces. The young, even those who felt that the African-American apostle of non-violence was an anachronism, reacted with anger. North Carolina College students drifted into the large campus auditorium throughout the evening, at first just to console one another and then to plan a reaction to the assassination. Howard Fuller lived just across the street from the campus, and a contingent of students came to his door, to invite the respected activist to their meeting. Inside the auditorium Fuller found a seething crowd, impatient to unleash its fury in a march on downtown Durham. The students expected the militant Fuller to join them, but were surprised when he spoke against their idea. Fuller knew that a demonstration under such emotional circumstances would end in violence. He recalls: "(A), I didn't think it was the way to respond to King's death given who he was, and, (B) I thought people were going to get killed." Fuller endured calls of "Uncle Tom" but held fast to his view, eventually convincing the students to wait until the next morning to hold the march.

Fuller arrived home to find a frantic Adam Clayton Powell, Jr., almost incoherent in his concern over becoming the assassin's next target. Powell had spoken at Duke University earlier in the week and had stayed on as houseguest two doors down from Fuller. He rambled about King's death being just the first in a plot to wipe out black leadership, and to placate Powell, Fuller was forced to spend that tragic night, gun in hand, outside the house in which Powell slept.

C. P. Ellis was working at his gas station when the news of King's death came over the radio. He let out a cheer, like a football fan after a decisive touchdown. His phone began ringing almost immediately. He told excited Klansmen on the other end of the line to come down to his gas station to celebrate the shooting. C.P. set out Coca-Cola crates for the men to sit on and they drank beer and laughed until late into the night. King—whom the Klansmen called "Martin Lucifer Coon"—represented the entire spectrum of attacks on Southern values, and so in his death C.P. and his men saw the defeat of liberalism and the restoration of "the American way of life."

"Well," he told the men, "that's it. We've stopped it." And they all nodded in agreement. C.P. didn't know who had shot King, but he was certain that the assassin was part of the white supremacy movement.

C.P. lifted his beer bottle into the air and called out, "To the gunman!"

The other men raised their bottles and repeated the toast.

Early the next morning, Ann Atwater and Howard Fuller joined students for a memorial service for Dr. King at the NCC chapel. Speakers stressed the need to refrain from violence during the march, both out of respect to the memory of King and to avoid providing police with an excuse to massacre demonstrators. No one had forgotten the Orangeburg shootings.

There had been larger marches in the past decade, but none of them matched in tone, the gravitas of this slow cortege through the streets of Durham. When the crowd at last arrived at City Hall, a brief prayer service was held before speakers from nearly every segment of Durham's black community eulogized their fallen leader. Someone in the crowd lowered to half-staff the United States flag flying in front of City Hall. Finally, just as rain began to fall, the crowd launched into a chant demanding that Mayor Grabarek come out and receive a list of demands. The mayor complied. Standing before the crowd of mourners was the conciliatory Grabarek of old, the white leader of rare compassion. First, he thanked his recent adversary Howard Fuller for preventing violence on the previous night. Then he told the crowd that he had already contacted the White House for permission to fly the United States flag at half-staff for a period of mourning. And he promised to work toward fulfilling the other demands—a city council proclamation honoring King's memory and the cancellation of public school on the day of King's funeral. "I seek your understanding in this difficult time for our nation," Grabarek concluded. The demonstration ended with another short prayer service and then the crowd drifted off slowly, the mourners reluctant to separate on the sorrowful day.

Jesse Helms's television editorial that evening was salt in the wounds of black North Carolinians. Of course "men of good will" all "regretted" the murder, said Helms, but he implied that King himself was responsible for his own death since he "may have participated in the creation of an atmosphere of terrible tension at Memphis." Helms reminded his listeners that he had in the past charged "that violence stalked [King's] heels, that indeed he provoked it" by his protest methods. "And our greatest fear about those methods has now been confirmed," said Helms with evident satisfaction, "by the murder of Dr. King." There would be no mea culpas from Helms concerning his own role during the past eight years, inflaming far-right hysteria about King's "Communist links."

Tarheel blacks did not need Jesse Helms's stinging insults uttered over the body of their fallen leader to push their anger over the edge. Riots had already broken out in other cities, including several in North Carolina, on the night of King's death, and not even Howard Fuller's admonitions could contain Hayti's rage forever. On Saturday night, April 6, it erupted, as firebombs exploded throughout the city. An apartment complex owned by slumlord Abe Greenberg was one of the first structures to go up in flames. The Southern Railroad station was hit. A café burned, and so did a furniture store, an A&P grocery store, several abandoned houses, a dry cleaners. In all, eleven buildings and several cars were set on fire. Many other stores had their windows broken. Durham was a city under siege. Units of the National Guard were sent to fire stations during the night. Police decked out in riot gear closed all restaurants and patrolled downtown streets. All vehicles attempting to enter the city had to pass through checkpoints. Thinking that the long-awaited race war had begun, C.P. sat until just before dawn on the front porch of his small house, gun in his lap, watching the orange glow of fires flaring up first in one direction and then in another, waiting for the black shock troops of Communism to come marching up Pleasant Drive. Ann Atwater spent the better part of the night creating decoy gatherings, drawing police attention away from sites she knew had been targeted for the torch.

On Tuesday, a funeral service was held in the modest red-brick Ebenezer Baptist Church where his father had presided for three decades, and in which young "M. L." King, Jr., had preached his very first sermon at the age of eighteen. Now he was dead before his fortieth birthday, a tape recording of one of his last sermons serving as his own funeral oration. "Every now and then I think about my own funeral," King's familiar voice echoed eerily through the packed church. Keep it simple, he advised. Just say "that I tried to love and serve humanity." After the service, King's bronze casket was placed on a simple mule-drawn farm wagon for a crosstown procession that ended in a cemetery created in 1886 by former slaves who had refused the indignity of burying their dead at the back of the local graveyard.

In Durham that noon, a group of fifty whites observed the day by raising the American flag outside City Hall from its position at half-staff, while the rest of the group sang a rousing chorus of "Dixie."

The violence continued over the next week, despite a 7 P.M. to 6 A.M. curfew imposed by the mayor and the deployment of National Guard troops throughout the city. When it was all over, several buildings had been wholly or partially burned—including another house belonging to Abe Greenberg—and the windows of dozens of businesses lay in shards on the sidewalks. Sporadic gunfire was heard on several nights, although no injuries were reported.

Throughout this week, students at Duke University staged their own unusual protest. It began on Friday, April 5, the day after King's assassination, close to 500 students and faculty marched to university president Douglas Knight's mansion to present him with a set of four demands. The first two were not unexpected, given the circumstances: they called for Knight to

226

add his signature to an advertisement that would appear in the *Morning Herald* in support of a day of mourning, and for the president to resign from the segregated Hope Valley Country Club. It was the last two demands that elevated the protests to a different plane. The young men and women outside the president's door insisted that the school's underpaid, and mostly black, maintenance staff be guaranteed a $1.60 minimum wage, and that Knight appoint a committee of workers, faculty, and students to decide on collective bargaining and union representation for maintenance workers. The smooth slide from social to economic demands would surely have pleased King, who was engaged in a similar struggle in Memphis at the time of his death, but the unusual demands confounded the university president. He invited 200 demonstrators into his house, where—after two hours of negotiations—he announced that he had no immediate response to their demands. Refusing to accept no answer for an answer, the students settled into the nonplussed Knight's house to await a substantive reply. Knight's condition, though, was more serious than simple perplexity. Citing exhaustion and, later, the effects of a recent and ongoing bout with hepatitis, Knight departed the campus, leaving the students no negotiating partner. (In addition to any medical problems, he may have been relieved of his authority by the university trustees; a year later, that body forced Knight to resign.) The demonstration then shifted from the president's house to the main quadrangle, where the crowd of protesters swelled to over 1,500 and began a "Silent Vigil" (which was anything but silent).

The cooperation between students and staff and the focus on working-class issues were unusual, if not unique, among the campus protests of this era. Duke University itself was not simply a white bastion, but a middle- and upper-class white bastion, accurately described as "a pleasant, sheltered place . . . where 'nice kids' came for four years of beer, basketball game[s], and studying." The poor white textile workers of the 1960s would have understood very well the sentiments of a tobacco machine operator who, in the 1930s, called Duke "just a place where rich men's sons go and live in luxury four years and come back to drive us in cotton mills, mines, in fields and these tobacco plants and work our day-lights out so they can have [a] big, fine building like at Duke." And yet these privileged protesters did not allow their actions in support of maintenance workers to be blurred by the other contentious issues of the day. During a mini-concert by Joan Baez on the Quad, her husband, antiwar activist David Harris, spoke at length about draft resistance. Finally, one protester stood up and informed Harris that "the Duke Vigil is not a draft resistance vigil. Our main object here is for the employees at Duke." When Harris persisted in denouncing the Vietnam War, he was hissed into silence by the crowd.

As news of the singular protest spread, messages of support for the vigilers came from around the country. Duke alumnus William Styron sent a note expressing his "fullest sympathy and support." Robert Kennedy, then running for President, telegraphed: "By your actions in support of employees who seek recognition for their bargaining rights, you set a standard that all should emulate." King's old friend from Morehouse, Duke professor Samuel Cook, magnanimously credited the vigil with keeping violence to a minimum in Durham, claiming that "the Vigil did more to prevent the riots than the curfew because . . . [it] provided hope and encouragement to the Negro community at a crucial hour." While reporting the professor's comments, a journalist for the Duke student newspaper pointed out that such a moderating influence was questionable at best, since most black residents simply didn't know about events over on the university campus for several days— Durham's two main newspapers refused to cover the developments until they could no longer ignore them. The larger black community in Durham was less than enthusiastic about the vigil when they did learn about it. Middle-class white students expiating their guilt over the death of Martin Luther King— that was how many viewed the demonstrations. But as the focus remained on the plight of the low-paid black workers, many blacks began to take notice. Eventually, even Howard Fuller gave qualified support, calling the action "significant."

"Just like the Memphis Garbage Workers Strike," Fuller

said, "it shows where we have to go." The vigil was "a possible method for both black and white to work together to attack these problems." This racial coalition in pursuit of class goals would not last, however. Black nationalism, with its move to purge all whites, was ascendant. Richard Nixon, who as a law student at Duke, had alienated many of his (white) classmates with his diatribes against Jim Crow, was, in April 1968, well on his way to winning the presidency by playing the race card, further polarizing an already dangerously divided America with his antiintegrationist "Southern strategy."

Despite Fuller's lukewarm endorsement of the vigil, he was suspicious of whites' commitment. A few weeks before the vigil, he had spoken to this issue directly. A reporter had asked if he was "in favor of a black/white coalition." "No," Fuller had said. "Right now I'm in favor of black people getting a coalition among themselves."

The Duke vigil ended a few days later when Wright Tisdale, chair of the Duke trustees, announced that a minimum wage of $1.60 for nonacademic staff would be phased in over the next several months. Knight's membership in the Hope Valley Country Club—a symbolic issue and probably a moot one in the president's absence—was his own affair, and the discussion about union recognition would commence when Knight "felt better." With a touching naiveté common in this era, many students believed that they had "wrought a revolution." Tears filled many eyes that last day of the protest in the Quad as Wright Tisdale, a perfect symbol of the enemy—aging, white, a vice president at Ford, even his name a WASP caricature—linked arms with students and sang a chorus of "We Shall Overcome." Not everyone was convinced. One cynic later wrote: "Under his breath, perhaps, [Tisdale] sang it like it really was: 'I shall overcome, you have been overcome.' "

Howard Fuller shared that skeptical view. "[The students] felt they had achieved a victory by sitting on the grass," he said as the vigil ended. "When the Union members vote and say we accept fully the conditions offered, then I'll say it was a victory."

But the victory at Duke was real enough—only less encompassing or durable than many believed. If they had not wrought a revolution, the students had at least forced the pace of social evolution. The vigil had raised the consciousness of many white students and of the university as a whole, causing both to question their role in what they had previously regarded as the best of all possible systems. As in some radical retelling of *A Midsummer Night's Dream*, society's normally invisible workings had been made briefly visible. And yet, what a black friend wearily explained to one of the vigil's organizers conveyed a far greater truth: "You whites can do your thing and go home. We blacks can never quit."

The hot spring that began in Orangeburg stretched into another hot summer, with angry protests flaring up both in the black community and before various city bodies. Fed up with the Housing Authority's intransigence, leading 150 protesters, Ann took over a meeting between the city council and representatives of the DHA. The tenants occupied the seats used by the city councillors to hold a "mock hearing" concerning grievances. There were more turbulent council meetings, and several incidents of arson involving DHA property. Ann boasted to friends that she "could make a Molotov cocktail better than the man who invented it."

Ann and C.P. sparred directly at city council meetings. The encounters were usually tense, with potential violence roiling just below the surface, but sometimes these confrontations were also tinged with comedy—as in the contest for seats in the council chambers. Both Ann and C.P. always brought with them a phalanx of supporters, creating an overflow crowd. In order to deny the Klansmen seats one evening, Ann's group arrived at the meeting early and occupied all the empty chairs. C.P. and his men stood seething in the back of the room during the meeting. The next time, C.P. brought his men even earlier, taking all the available seats by the time Ann showed up with her contingent. Unwilling to concede defeat even in this symbolic battle, Ann devised a strategy that turned the bigots' own racism against them. When a chair next to a single Klansman was left vacant, one of her black supporters immediately sat down. The plan worked perfectly. The horrified Klansman who found himself sitting next to a black person jumped to his feet, freeing up another chair—which Ann's people immediately filled. This process continued down the row—a kind of domino effect—the room filling with the scraping of chairs and the spluttering of unhappy Klansmen, until all of C.P.'s men were once again standing red-faced at the back of the room, while Ann's army of black activists sat comfortably at the front.

But one council confrontation between Ann and C.P. nearly ended in bloodshed. The September skirmish took place during a council discussion over forming a human relations Commission, primarily to hear alleged incidents of race discrimination. The issue, like all issues involving race, was extremely contentious. Blacks had been alternately asking for and demanding such a body for more than a year. Even some whites were bothered by the council's foot-dragging. When appointed to a council committee to look into the proposal during the summer, one councilman refused, angrily protesting, "The council knows the need for a human relations commission, and it has failed to act . . ." The committee was appointed, however, and chaired by C.P.'s secret friend, the segregationist Charles Steel.

The debate over the HRC was even more acrimonious because it took place in the middle of a black boycott of white businesses, called by a new protest organization, the Black Solidarity Committee for Community Improvement, generally known as Black Solidarity or by the initials BSC. The group was led by A. J. H. "Howard" Clement III, a radical young executive with the North Carolina Mutual. In July, Clement had presented the Durham Chamber of Commerce with a list of eighty-eight demands, covering nearly every area that concerned the city's black population—including the formation of a Human Relations Commission. Until the demands were met, the BSC would sponsor a boycott of selected white businesses.

Feeling the economic pinch, white store owners cried foul. The vice president of the Durham Merchants Association complained, with some justification, that the business community was being blamed for all of Durham's ills. But in the pages of the *Carolina Times*, Louis Austin chided the businessmen, reminding them that "the greatest and longest boycott ever conceived, perpetrated or conducted has not been by the BSC or other civil rights organizations in this country, but by the white so-called Christian church where the doors are open on Sunday mornings, as well as other days of the week, 'for whites only.' " The power structure of Durham had better pay attention to the boycotters' demands, recommended Austin, or they would be "setting the stage for a successor that will make the B.S.C.C.I. look like a prayer meeting band."

This was the backdrop to the night on which the city council was to vote on forming a Human Relations Commission. The chamber was packed. People stood in the hallway, craning their necks to watch the proceedings going on inside. The audience seated in the chamber was a conglomeration of Durham's various racial factions; there were contingents from UOCI, the BSC, the Klan, and the White Citizens' Council. During the discussion period, one white man went to the microphone and made the dubious claim that cities with such commissions "suffered more violence than Durham." He was met with hoots of derision from blacks in the audience. Then C.P. took his turn. The Klan leader was never diplomatic when speaking about blacks, but on this night, perhaps fired up by the recent events, C.P. was particularly mean-spirited. He was, he would later admit, "mean as the devil that night." He told the crowd, "We're just simply tired of niggers taking over Durham," and went on to rail against the Communist plot to destroy his town using "ignorant niggers." Councilman John Stewart, still grieving over the death of his friend Martin Luther King, Jr., declared, "I don't have to listen to this," and stalked out of the room. A black minister got to his feet and told C.P., "You better learn how to say 'Negro.' " C.P. fired right back, "I'll learn to say 'Negro' when you learn to say 'four' instead of 'fo.' " C.P.'s performance was so extreme that Louis Austin, who had witnessed many displays of hostility directed toward blacks in nearly forty years running the *Carolina Times*, devoted an editorial to it. "God forbid," wrote Austin, "that any black man of this nation or anywhere on this earth will ever be capable of . . . such an exhibition of race hatred and ignorance as that displayed . . . at the Durham City Council meeting last Tuesday night."

Ann, too, was used to racist talk, especially coming from C.P., but, like Austin, she was shocked by the Klansman's hateful vulgarity that night. Sitting a few rows back from the microphone, she listened to C.P. curse her and her people. Then something inside of her snapped, and she reached into her purse and pulled out a knife. As C.P. continued his harangue, unaware of what was going on behind him, Ann rose to her feet and headed toward him. She kept her eyes on her target: a spot on his neck where she intended to shove the knife home. Fortunately for both C.P. and Ann, she had to climb over two of her friends, and they grabbed her before she could complete her lunge. As quietly as possible, they disarmed Ann and calmed her down. They explained that she was playing into C.P.'s hands. "You act up, and they'll throw you into jail," one whispered. "You don't want that." The meeting ended without bloodshed—and with the council creating a Human Relations Commission. It was a small victory. The establishment of another official body for communication and not action was, despite C.P.'s opposition, unthreatening enough to receive even Charles Steel's vote.

As the Christmas season approached, Durham was as bitterly divided as ever. Howard Clement of the BSC rejected an attempt by merchants to settle the dispute before their most lucrative period. Instead, Clement organized "Black Christmas." Blacks for several counties around were urged not to shop in Durham that Christmas. Instead, black churches set up "shopping centers" in their basements, and chartered buses to transport shoppers to Raleigh and Greensboro. The churches distributed bags of toys to 300 Durham families. The BSC staged a Christmas parade at the same time the white Merchants Association held its annual event. Over 20,000 enthusiastic people showed up for the Black Christmas parade in Hayti, cheering as groups representing dozens of black organizations marched by. Children scrambled for the candy tossed by a black Santa Claus.

To most whites, the reasons for the boycott that was devastating downtown merchants were mysterious at best and mean-spirited at worst. *Anvil* reporter Elizabeth Tornquist asked white shoppers at a suburban mall what they thought of the boycott. One young man had not heard about the boycott and so Tornquist began to explain what was happening. "[A]s soon as I reached the word 'Negro,' he said, 'Oh, I wouldn't want anything to do with that sort of thing.' " The reporter asked two elderly ladies about the boycott. "[They] clucked their tongues and said sweetly, 'We don't approve of such things at all. No, we don't approve.' And I could hear them saying it again and again to each other as they strolled away." Another shopper, a girl of high school age, thought the solution was simple: "If they would only work, wouldn't they have what they want?"

Howard Fuller had heard these same evasions and questions—from whites and from some conservative blacks. "I am amused," he told a BSC meeting, "when [they] ask 'Why the boycott? All you are doing is destroying our nice race relations.' What nice race relations? We have never gotten anything in this town without fighting."

At a mass meeting in late December, Ann lashed out against those who termed the boycott an example of "black lawlessness." "[S]ince 1896," she cried, "they've had an open housing law; they've disregarded this law in Durham. Since 1865, they've had a civil rights law, [which has also been ignored]. . . . I don't see how any Christian could not support the boycott."

Remarkably effective, the boycott reduced sales between 15 and 20 percent for a total loss to the targeted businesses of around a million dollars. Maintaining the campaign after Christmas proved more difficult, however, and in February it was called off. While the boycott wasn't a complete victory, the number of concessions achieved was striking. Blacks were appointed to fill two vacancies on the Housing Authority board. Downtown stores made good on their promises to hire and to promote more blacks. Strides were made in private housing, with a black real estate agent given access for the first time to multilisting services. New fire-fighting gear replaced outdated equipment at the main Hayti fire station.

The protests did not ebb, however. Ann was as busy as ever, particularly since fewer concessions were won in her domain of housing than in any other area. Even her continuing health problems didn't slow her down much. That spring she left her hospital bed to lead a march. Her rotund figure dressed in hospital gown and slippers at the head of the demonstrators inspired many less committed Hayti residents to battle on. Ann had received national attention late in 1968 when *McCall's* magazine profiled her in a feature titled "What Can One Woman Do?" She felt she could not slow down because there were now too many people depending on her. "Two years ago I could walk the streets and pass people and they never bothered to speak with me," she told the magazine writer. "Now, both black and white have taken notice of me. They speak, they stop and ask questions. When I go to a meeting, they know who I am. If I say anything, this is more or less the way it goes."

While that last assertion is partly bravado, there was much truth in it, for Ann felt acutely the responsibility her new influence brought. Her struggle against Carvie Oldham's fiefdom persisted, but progress was always measured in inches. A private study evaluating Durham's civic government in 1969 blasted the DHA, informing embarrassed officials, "There is little evidence that the Authority is willing to accept any responsibility for solving the social problems of its tenants or to permit tenant councils to have a voice in the policy-making process. . . . To date, the Authority has seemed desirous only of preserving its current status." The city fathers were used to more circumspect criticisms—when criticism could not be entirely avoided. Such a blatantly negative report was unprecedented. The city promptly buried it.

C.P. was also kept busy—in his case, with Klan activity. Besides his public appearances to present the Klan viewpoint, and his secret meetings with various municipal and county officials, C.P., like any good party leader, was laying the groundwork for the Klan's future, organizing a Klan Youth Corps. The idea for the project originated with Imperial Wizard Robert Shelton, but with very little guidance or assistance from the national organization, C.P. fashioned a Youth Corps, which reflected his values and priorities. C.P. understood the strategic value of cultivating new blood for the organization, but even more, he identified with the hunger many working-class white children felt for an organization such as the Klan. These teenagers were growing up in a time of extreme change, tossed about as the social order danced beneath their feet. And the changes did not appear to benefit them. The true level of poverty among North Carolina whites during the 1960s was extreme: nearly half of the manufacturing jobs in the state were in textiles, one of the lowest-paid segments of the industry. Because of this, factory wages in the Tarheel State vied with Mississippi's for last place in the nation. The poor white children of the South were caught between worlds. Blacks were their historical enemy, and, outside of the factories and except on election day, whites of means simply had no use for them. The elite of Durham sneered openly at them whereas middle-class whites tried to put as much distance as possible between themselves and their poorer cousins. The one group possessing the intellectual framework to understand the problems and aspirations of poor whites—white liberals—by and large detested "rednecks." It was ironic, but liberals believed in the South's racial Manichaeanism almost as completely as Jesse Helms—they just aligned themselves with the folks on the darker side of the color line. As one journalist put it: "[Liberals'] guilty response to the racial oppression of one group of poor people has produced a vindictive toleration for the economic exploitation of another." The 1969 film *Easy Rider*, with its stereotyped portrayal of cracker violence, typified the fear and loathing most liberals, particularly Yankees, felt for poor white Southerners. The best of the true progressives—always a small group, in the North or the South—did attempt to reach out to this rejected crowd, but they were usually rebuffed. Poor whites had been weaned on the Southern catechism of hatred for blacks and unions and an abiding suspicion of intellectuals. Overtures by anyone friendly to these groups—or, God forbid, members of one of them—received short shrift in the poor white sections of Durham.

Joseph Butler, a pseudonym, was typical of the young men attracted to the Klan Youth Corps. Although he was born in

1954, Butler grew up in a world remarkably unchanged since the late 1800s. Until he was a teenager, his family lived in the country several miles from Durham, tending a small farm of tobacco and corn using a team of mules. It was a difficult life, full of hard work and little money, but one that had the compensation of stability. Boundaries and relationships were hierarchical, drawn with a straightedge: men dominated women, parents dominated the home, and whites dominated blacks. As in many rural white families, Butler grew up in close proximity to black people. He was raised by a black nanny and his constant playmates as a boy were the children of a neighboring black family. He would never forget the time he was working out in the fields with a hired hand, an elderly black man named Ivy, when the man set down his hoe and sang "Dixie." Some thirty years later, tears would fill Butler's eyes as he recounted that day, recalling that the black man sang the rebel anthem "with more reverence than any white man I've ever heard sing it. And it sounded damn good." Because of these daily cordial interactions, Butler believed he "understood" blacks. Then he moved to Durham and his world was turned upside down. "All these black militants screaming 'Black Power!' scared the hell out of me," he remembers. "What the hell is this? I wondered. I didn't want to see that change. . . . I think more than anything else I was afraid of change itself rather than of any kind of conditions that change might ultimately bring about."

The Klan, with its promise to hold back change, naturally appealed to a young boy such as Butler. Like C.P., Butler had been weaned on the old Southern epic tales about Robert E. Lee, Stonewall Jackson, Jeb Stuart, and Nathan Bedford Forrest, and so he, too, believed in the South's possible redemption. When Butler saw a handbill advertising the Klan Youth Corps, he immediately joined up. The gangly white kid with rural roots was affable and intelligent, and it wasn't long before he was voted vice president of the Corps. What Butler liked most about the Klan was simply the opportunity to engage in activities with other conservative whites his age— high school students who wouldn't make fun of him for his clothes or old-fashioned values. Another part of the draw was C.P. himself. The Klan leader genuinely liked young people and had a knack for communicating with them that was rare for men his age. Butler also liked the new public path that C.P. was blazing for the Klan. As an officer of the highly visible Corps, Butler was invited to talk about the organization around town. In time, he became a good public speaker, even feeling at ease making presentations before the city council.

At its peak, there were around 150 active members of the Youth Corps in Durham, with a core group of perhaps thirty highly committed individuals. They gathered each Tuesday night at the Klavern hall, well-groomed youths in neat rows, dressed in their uniform of black shoes, blue khaki pants, and a white shirt with a UKA emblem embroidered over the left breast. Once a month there was an invited speaker. These guests included Joseph High (from the Citizens' Council), city councilman Charles Steel, at least one county commissioner, a uniformed policeman, and the county sheriff, Marvin Davis. According to Butler, most of the guests talked in general terms about civic responsibilities or about the dangers of illegal drugs. They did not dwell on racial issues per se. "No one ever came out and said, 'Hey, you guys are doing a great job, just keep your sheets ironed,' " he recalls. But there was plenty of "race talk" when guests weren't around. C.P. taught them about "the Jew-communist plot to destroy the white race." Copies were passed around of the virulently racist *Fiery Cross* and the even more explicitly anti-Semitic *Thunderbolt*, the organ of the neo-Nazi National States' Rights Party.

The Corps participated in several cross burnings with the adult Klan members, always in the context of a rally. And there were out-of-town trips. C.P. drove a vanload of Corps members down to Tuscaloosa, Alabama, to celebrate Imperial Wizard Robert Shelton's release from a federal penitentiary. (Shelton had served almost a year for contempt of Congress after refusing to make public the UKA's membership list.) They traveled to Granite Quarry, North Carolina, to visit the Tarheel Grand Dragon Bob Jones. Then there were a few rallies around the state to socialize with other Klan units. Plans for a Klan junior auxiliary for girls ran aground after one of these trips, when the older Klan women heard about an impromptu swimming break that involved teenage girls. Somewhere in the retelling, the swimming suits the participants actually wore were removed from the story and the innocent diversion became a nude debauch. That was the end of the girls' division of the Klan Youth Corps. Although Corps members rarely participated in Klan demonstrations, Butler and some others once joined a delegation of local Klansmen on a trip to Richmond, Virginia, to protest school busing. With representatives of other violent far-right groups, the Klansmen—young and old—ringed the house of James McMillan, the federal judge who was the author of the busing plan, tearing down a section of his fence and burning him in effigy before the police stepped in.

As with the adult Durham Klan unit, however, most of the Youth Corps's work was focused on perceived local problems, and, given the tender age of Corps members, that meant problems in the schools. Butler led 400 white Durham High students in a walkout to protest Black Culture Week. ("Probably 100 had convictions about it," admits Butler. "The rest probably wanted an excuse to get out of school.") He also fought, unsuccessfully, to continue the practice of playing "Dixie" at football games and to keep the Stars and Bars flying outside the school entrance. The activities of the Corps, like those of its parent Klavern under C.P., were primarily nonviolent, although talk about "killing coons and kikes" abounded in both groups. Members of the Youth Corps were involved, however, in C.P.'s most blatant act of violence, a brutal and stupid affair that was given an undeserved element of romance with the label "the shoot-out."

No pacifists, C.P. kept his Klavern out of acts of violence for purely strategic, political reasons, but the constant talk of racial hatred created a perfect climate for violence, and small acts of aggression did erupt from time to time. Once, while waiting for a traffic light to change on his way home from work, C.P. spotted a long-haired white man, a quintessential hippie in C.P.'s eyes, in the car next to him. The young man returned C.P.'s stare and flashed him the peace sign. Before the light could change, the Klansman jumped out of his car, ran around to the driver's side of the other vehicle, and punched the startled driver in the face. As blood trickled from the man's nose, C.P. returned calmly to his car and drove off. There were similar assaults over the years during which he headed the Klan. Given the animosity in Durham during those years, and C.P.'s own fury against a world he couldn't control—and his tendency to always carry a gun—it was amazing that he hadn't shot anyone.

In the early evening of September 4, 1970, C.P. received a phone call. He was sitting in his little house behind the gas station, about halfway toward his usual goal of inebriation. On the other end of the line a Youth Corps member was nearly incoherent with fear and rage. It took C.P. a minute to understand that another Klan youth had been robbed of his bus money by a group of blacks outside a Sears store. C.P. told the boys to wait outside Sears; he would be right over.

A few minutes later, C.P.'s old Buick screeched to a stop in front of the store. In the car with the Klan leader were two members of the Youth Corps. Not able to find the youth, C.P. drove slowly toward downtown, hoping to find the boy or his assailants. He spotted a lone black man and pulled over. Leading the young Klan members, C.P. walked up to the man and pulled out the .38 caliber revolver he kept in his back pocket. He put the gun to the frightened man's head. "Hey, nigger," he said, "you seen a little white kid running around here?" Shaking with fear, the man stammered that he hadn't. C.P. liked how afraid the man was. He softly crooned into the man's ear, "I've always wanted to kill a nigger. I think I'm going to make you the first one." He cocked the gun's hammer, producing the desired devastating effect. C.P. laughed and released the man, delighting in the sight of him running for his life down the street.

The Klansmen returned to the car and continued their hunt. Soon they saw a group of three young black men and C.P. once again pulled over. A member of the Youth Corps got out of the car and demanded, "You niggers seen a little white boy running down here?" They had chosen the wrong group to try to intimidate. "What do you mean, 'nigger'?" one of them snapped. C.P. barked out some obscenity. Instantly there was a flash of light and the pop of a small-caliber handgun. The Youth Corps member grabbed his lower leg, cried, "I've been hit," and jumped back into the car. C.P. whipped out his gun and began firing at the men as they ran down the street. One man, Linwood Earl King, was hit in the left leg and fell into the street. C.P. pushed the gas pedal to the floor and rushed the wounded Corps member to Duke Hospital. It was C.P.'s friend, Sheriff Marvin Davis, who showed up at C.P.'s house five days later, bearing a warrant for his arrest. C.P. was indicted for assault with intent to kill.

The Klan rallied behind the Durham Exalted Cyclops. Grand Dragon Bob Jones immediately took the gun C.P. had used in the shooting and fired several rounds from it, using bullets dipped into wet sand. The process changed the barrel markings so that the police wouldn't be able to link the gun to the assault. C.P. hired a locally respected lawyer, E. Carter Harris, Jr. On his first visit to his lawyer's office, C.P. was accompanied by Joe High and Garland Keith. During the interview, Harris became convinced that the two were using C.P.'s case to promote their own racial agenda.

"They were going to bring [Klan leader Robert Shelton] here from South Carolina and they were going to make a black-white issue of it," recalls Harris. "It seemed to me they didn't care whether he got convicted or not. I told them, 'Listen here, I'm not going to be a part of this. If you want me to try and get him off, I will. But I'm not going to be part of any stage show. You're talking about bringing this firebrand up here and letting him talk about race all through the trial.' I said, 'if he's found guilty, the judge has to give him time.' These guys were just using him. They just puffed him up and made him think he was something. I felt sorry for him. That was one reason I wanted to try and get him off."

For his part, C.P. was worried about Harris' casual demeanor, but when the trial started in October, C.P. was happily surprised to find that his attorney was "a ball of fire." He wouldn't have needed an F. Lee Bailey to get him off, at any rate. It was clear from the beginning of the trial that the judicial system was on the Klansman's side. The judge was an elderly conservative whom C.P. recognized immediately as a kindred soul. There was no hard evidence that C.P. fired the shot that hit Linwood King, and the jury of six men and seven women was surely impressed when Sheriff Marvin Davis, the man who had arrested C.P., took the stand as a character witness in his defense. After hearing two days of testimony, the jury found C.P. not guilty. Historian Allen Trelease has observed that for nineteenth-century Klansmen "the main safeguard lay not in their secrecy but in their ability to thwart legal processes if they were identified." In most cases, this was still true a century later.

After celebrating his courtroom victory, C.P. went back to serving the Klan, leading the weekly meetings, organizing the Youth Corps, and meeting clandestinely with city officials. Supporting his family was as difficult as ever, but he was glad that at least he was not in jail. To augment the small income from the service station, C.P. got a job as an unskilled maintenance worker at Duke University. The work put him into daily contact with blacks, who still made up the bulk of the maintenance staff, but like so many white Southern racists, on an individual basis C.P. was able to get along with blacks tolerably well.

He was running an errand in downtown Durham one day not long after the trial when he spotted a city councilman walking briskly toward him on the sidewalk. He had visited the man's house once (secretly, of course) and had talked strategy with him on the phone just the previous night. Well, this is lucky, thought C.P. He had forgotten to tell the man something when they had talked. As the two drew closer, C.P. smiled and started to reach out to shake hands. Just yards away now, C.P. saw the flicker of recognition in the other man's eyes as their eyes met. But instead of the smile C.P. expected, a small ripple coursed across the councilman's face. With surprising speed, the man changed his direction, turning sharply and veering into the street. C.P. watched dumbfounded as the councilman waded through traffic like a man crossing a fast-flowing river, finally emerging on the other side and then hurrying down the sidewalk. C.P. stood on his side of the street watching the other man's back until he disappeared into the noontime crowds of businessmen, shoppers, and secretaries along Main Street. Even after he could no longer see the man, C.P. remained standing on the sidewalk, replaying in his mind what had just happened. And each time he saw again the look on the man's face—first the glimmer of recognition, then, caught off guard, the other thing, the ripple—he felt a queasiness in his gut. He knew that look; had seen it often enough in his childhood when he had accompanied his father downtown. It was the look on the faces of the businessmen as they passed the pair in their worn and ill-fitting clothes, the look that began in the eyes but quickly encompassed the entire face. The mouth, twisting up at one corner, the nose and forehead wrinkled in distaste. And sometimes the look spread to include their whole bodies as they leaned away to minimize the possibility of physical contact between the two and their own selves. The only thing missing from the councilman's performance, it now struck C.P., was the word. But perhaps he would say it when he was safely back in his office. Maybe he would scurry inside, remove his jacket, and sit down at his desk. After rolling up his sleeves, he would leaf through the pink slips of urgent phone messages that had accumulated in his absence and then he would say the word under his breath and with as little thought as if he were humming a line from some half-forgotten advertising jingle. He would say, "Linthead."

Baffled and smarting from the snub, C.P. wandered down the street.

CHAPTER TWELVE

Verily, black and white workers did not fight each
other because they hated each other, but they hated
each other because they fought each other.

—A. PHILIP RANDOLPH

C.P. couldn't decide at first if the large black man sitting across
from him was crazy or just a fool. Or a third possibility: maybe
he was trying to put something over on the Klansman. C.P.
knew the FBI had infiltrated his unit—agents once had the
temerity to try to recruit *him*. Maybe Joe Becton, the new
director of the Durham Human Relations Commission, moon-
lighted as a government informer. But no, there was no mistaking Becton's sincerity—or his sanity or intelligence—even
if his desire to meet formally with the gun-toting leader of the
Durham Klan struck C.P. as foolhardy.

"Look, Mr. Ellis," said Becton, "I want to work for equality
and fairness for the *whole* community."

"Well, white folks aren't treated fairly in Durham," countered C.P., expecting an argument.

Instead, the director of the Human Relations Commission
sat back in his chair and nodded. "You're right," he said with
an unsettling directness. "There's some of you who's not."

C.P. was surprised but he was not about to relinquish his
suspicions so quickly. It was refreshing to meet openly with a
city official, however, even a black one, after years of only
behind-the-scenes dealings. In fact, it was Becton who had
insisted that all interaction between the Klan leader and himself occur in the open. He even requested that C.P. arrange for
him to speak down at the Klavern hall, to prove his sincerity.
C.P. said he'd arrange it. But as their meeting ended, he won-

245

dered to himself if the new head of the Human Relations Commission wasn't crazy after all.

Becton preferred the word "reckless." But he would remind the many who doubted his methods that it was *appropriate* to be reckless when living in reckless times. Better than most people, he knew that Durham was about to enter a particularly difficult period, after enjoying a brief peaceful interval. As head of the commission charged with improving race relations, he'd need all the help he could get. To his way of thinking, the Klansman was the CEO of the poor white community, and Becton needed him on board—to whatever extent that was possible—in the upcoming fights.

The immediate issue was school desegregation, once again and forever. Durham seemed doomed to perpetually wrestle with the issue. There were, of course, many other cities (in both the North and the South) engaged in the same Sisyphean struggle, but few of them matched Durham in the sheer amount of energy expended on this one issue over time. The problem began with the original *Brown* v. *Board* decisions, which outlawed separate-but-equal schools but did not provide any sanctions for noncompliance. Opposing forces in every school district in the country were left to work out their own solutions. With one foot jamming the brake pedal to the floor and the other just as resolutely stomping on the gas, Durham's civic engine roared deafeningly—but it did not budge from the starting line. After court battles stretching back to 1954, a federal district judge in 1970 issued a desegregation plan for the city. White parents resisted the plan by sending their children to already overcrowded private "segregation academies," starting up new private schools as quickly as possible, and by moving to the suburbs and enrolling their children in the predominantly white county school system. It was actually the acceleration of a process begun years earlier. City schools had started the 1960s with 15,000 students. A decade later, that number had dropped to 14,000, and by 1980 there would be only 9,000 students. Most pundits noticed only the change in the racial makeup of the schools, but the process concentrated poverty, not just race. It was mostly wealthy or middle-class whites who could afford to move or send their children to private schools. Left in the crumbling city schools were blacks from all economic strata—the majority were poor—and impoverished whites, including C.P.'s children.

A 1970 White House meeting on school desegregation, between a group from North Carolina and members of President Nixon's Cabinet Committee on Education, set in motion a series of events that would have a profound effect on Durham and, in particular, on the lives of C. P. Ellis and Ann Atwater. Having won the presidency by opposing "the stick" of forced busing to achieve integration, Nixon now offered "the carrot" of federal dollars for enticing voluntary efforts toward racial balance. Durham School Board chairman Theodore Speigner, the first African-American to hold that office, attended the meeting. He put the best face possible on such voluntary efforts. "President Nixon is confident in what we are doing," Speigner told a reporter when he returned from Washington. "He wants to approach this thing from the point of view of the local communities."

The primary outcome of the meeting was the announcement of $75 million in federal funds to be used by school districts to help desegregation efforts, with 10 percent of the money to go to public and private nonprofit groups willing to help schools in this effort. After months of negotiations and a long application process, the Department of Health, Education and Welfare announced it was awarding nearly $80,000 to the North Carolina AFL-CIO to carry out two programs to smooth the road to desegregation. At the press conference announcing the grant, reporters had to ask Wilbur Hobby, head of the state union, to repeat what he said the money would be used for. "Charrettes," said Hobby. It was, he explained, a French word for extended forums "to open lines of communication in order that all people might understand each other's role as it relates to desegregation problems." Reporters scratched their heads but dutifully took down his words.

If people thought that the word "charrette" was odd, the man brought in to lead the program was even more unusual. Bill Riddick could exist only in real life; he was too fantastical for fiction. When *Time* magazine devoted a full page to the charrette process in 1970, the author of the piece barely mentioned Riddick. "[He] said he couldn't write about me," explains Riddick. "I'm too weird. It would have undermined the process."

Thirty-three years old, Riddick was one of those intense men who, despite being well under six feet tall, are invariably described as huge. It was his presence that was oversized, as were his self-regard and his inventory of talents, including a Svengali-like ability to manipulate people. As a child growing up on a North Carolina peanut farm, Riddick was amazed to discover how easy it was to get people to do things—even things that were against their interests—if you played on the right emotions. "You can make a room of 200 people jump out the window," he hyperbolized (a Riddick trademark), "without yelling fire." The boy's family noticed this talent, and, fearing that he would put it to ill use, groomed him for a career in the church, one of the few positive routes open then to a black man of his abilities. But Riddick could never see himself in that role—it was too pedestrian, too predictable, too empty of the *juice* of life. And the idea of remaining in a poor agrarian setting, in any capacity, was anathema to a child with such prodigious talents and cocky self-assurance. He would later say he "escaped, not walked away, *escaped*" from the life others had in mind for him. Without having any sure plans for the future, he decided to attend A&T University in Greensboro. It was a fortuitous time and place for an ambitious, dynamic black teenager. In 1960, when Riddick was a junior, the lunch-counter movement erupted on campus. The excitement of being at the epicenter of that kind of intense experience captured Riddick and never released him. After graduation, Riddick brought his evolving radical theories on social change into an unlikely venue: he became an Agricultural Extension Agent. The Cuban revolutionary Che Guevara could have been referring to this most unreconstructed of all federal agencies, the USDA of the 1960s (particularly as it was run in the South), when he spoke of his admiration for those fighting in "the belly of the beast." After four years working on issues related to low-income rural housing, Riddick returned to the academy, earning a master's degree in social work at the University of North Carolina at Chapel Hill before working in a variety of community programs similar to Durham's UOCI. Like Howard Fuller, Riddick was a brilliant maverick, using whatever institutional structure he happened to be in at the time to achieve the purposes *he* considered important, a tendency that produced maximum results, and a similar portion of contention.

In 1968, Riddick was working as Director of Development at Shaw University in Raleigh when a colleague asked if he'd like to attend a charrette.

"A *what?*" asked Riddick blankly.

The other man explained the concept. It was an experimental technique (those words in themselves would have caught Riddick's ear) to bring a diverse group of people together to work out differences. Designed to produce an intense reaction (two more of Riddick's "hot button" words), the charrette involved a number of hours-long face-to-face meetings, held over successive nights. Of course, Riddick was intrigued. He agreed to come along as an observer. On the third night of the charrette, a group of militant black students took over the meeting and kicked out all the whites. Then they turned to Riddick and told him he was now in charge.

"It was dropped into my lap," he recalls. "I went from being an observer to managing it in five minutes."

After conferring with his colleagues, Riddick agreed to lead the sessions, on the condition that the whites be brought back into the dialogue. The black students gave in, and Riddick had found his calling, honing the rudimentary charrette into an impressive instrument for social change. It was the most challenging undertaking Riddick had taken on, requiring every bit of talent he had for piloting groups. The trick was to draw out people's deepest longings and fears, their frustrations and their dreams—while preventing these raw and antipodean emotions, once exposed, from combusting into violence. At a charrette in York, Pennsylvania, convened after a black woman and a white policeman had been killed during racial disturbances, black residents shouted out their discontent over police use of attack dogs. "If Whitey wants the dogs," cried one man, "let him vote for their use in his community!" The confrontation nearly ended in a riot, but that, of course, was the point: to release, in a controlled environment, the subterranean forces that would ordinarily result in a brawl, and then *redirect* that energy toward a healthier resolution.

For Riddick, directing a charrette was a cross between leading a marathon revival meeting and walking a tightrope for ten days straight. He found that he couldn't eat during the first week of a charrette—"My body can't process the food." Late at night, he'd crank up the radio in his hotel room, lie down on his bed and nurse a glass of Jack Daniel's, and sleep fitfully until dawn. He was like some shaman fasting during a particularly arduous and prolonged mystical rite. In fact, that was exactly how he thought of himself. He laughed at the irony: having run from a career in the ministry, he was now completely devoted to what was, at heart, a technique for spiritual redemption and renewal. He had organized and led just two charrettes when the call came from Durham.

Riddick knew the Bull City well from his days at neighboring Chapel Hill, and so he was familiar with the phenomenally successful black elite community, the light-skinned aristocrats of the North Carolina Mutual and two black-owned banks. Even in the state capital, Raleigh, Durham's black community was famous. But Riddick also knew that the black community in Durham was schizophrenic, with the majority of the population struggling just to survive in the projects at McDougald Terrace and Few Gardens or in the dozens of substandard houses that littered the black neighborhoods, despite the best efforts of groups like UOCI. If Riddick admired the achievements of the black elite in Durham—their prospering financial institutions, their well-disciplined political organizations, their spacious homes with large manicured lawns on which dusky-skinned children frolicked in safety until their time to head off to college—he also blamed them for the miserable ghetto that endured just out of sight. He decided to ignore Durham's black elite.

Instead, Riddick turned to Joe Becton for help in putting

together the charrette. As part of his obligation to include all segments of Durham, Becton suggested that C.P. be brought into the process. Not only did C.P. represent many of Durham's poor white residents but his son Timmy attended Hillside High School, the school with the greatest racial problems in the city. At Riddick's request, Wilbur Hobby, the AFL-CIO leader, telephoned C.P. to let him know about the first organizational meeting to be held at the local YWCA. "We'd like to get some people together from all walks of life," said Hobby.

"All walks of life?" repeated C.P. suspiciously. "Who are you talking about?"

"Blacks, whites, liberals, conservatives, Klansmen, NAACP people."

C.P. just sneered at the idea, saying, "Wilbur, I don't particularly like you and I don't even want to discuss it with you." Then he hung up.

The next time C.P. ran into his friend Garland Keith, the Citizens' Council leader, he told him about the crazy idea of him, a Klansman, attending the school program.

"Aren't you planning on participating?" asked Keith.

"Garland, I don't intend to associate with a bunch of niggers," said C.P., appalled that Keith would even consider the idea. It was bad enough sitting in the same room with them at city council meetings. But the older man counseled C.P. not to be too hasty. "If you don't get involved, you're not going to have a voice," he said. "*They* are going to wind up taking over that whole meeting and there won't be an opposing voice."

C.P. thought about it. Maybe Keith was right. If he attended the meetings, he wouldn't have to go on their terms. While everyone else was working to smooth the path toward integration, he could be the monkey wrench thrown into the works to slow the process down. He still didn't want to go, but he decided that he was obligated to. C.P. let Wilbur Hobby know he would be attending the first meeting.

Of course, Ann Atwater was notified. She had taken on even more importance in Durham's black community when Howard Fuller left to take a job organizing union workers in Greensboro, eventually serving as chairman of UOCI. Besides, like C.P., she had a personal stake in the issue. Her daughter Marilyn was also a student at Hillside High School. Becton had met Ann at a protest rally soon after coming to Durham, and the two had been impressed with each other. Wilbur Hobby called her about the meetings, mentioning nonchalantly that several Klansmen would be there. Ann figured that included her old nemesis, C.P. She wasn't going to allow him to take over the forum. She got on the phone, and soon had promises from eighteen black residents to show up.

At a little before 8 P.M. on a Thursday night in mid-May 1971, C.P. opened the door at the YWCA auditorium, where the first organizational meeting was about to begin. He looked inside and promptly lost his nerve. He shut the door. "I'm not going in there," he told Garland Keith. Inside the room sat many of the people he hated most in Durham—including Howard Clement, leader of the militant Black Solidarity Committee; Asa Spaulding, retired from the North Carolina Mutual; and Ann Atwater. Clement was dressed in a dashiki—an African shirt that was to the Klan leader what a red flag is to a bull. It took all of Keith's powers of persuasion to get C.P. into the room. Ann watched C.P. make his entrance, following him with slitted eyes as he found a chair and sat down. Her gaze remained on the Klansman until Bill Riddick walked up to the microphone and called the meeting to order. Riddick was a compact ball of nervous energy wrapped in a suit. He knew that the direction and success of the charrette could well be determined by what happened that night. Becton had pointed out Ann and her people to him, and he had told him, "There's your Klansman," when C.P. had come through the door, surly as a bear awakened from his hibernation a month early.

Now, as the room quieted down, Riddick explained a little about the process of the charrette, stressing the need for "open communication," and then quickly removed himself from the spotlight by posing a simple but loaded question: "Are there," he asked, "any problems in Durham schools, city or county?"

A few tension-filled seconds of silence were followed by a couple of cautious and polite suggestions that things could be better. Finally, Howard Clement jumped up.

"I just cannot sit here and let this go unanswered," he said in his booming voice. "I had hoped somebody else would give some answers." He launched into a historical disquisition on racism in North Carolina schools, tracing the roots of the issue back to the 1914 state report on Jim Crow education, which concluded that "the average Negro school house is really a disgrace to an independent civilized society . . . [revealing] injustice, inhumanity, and neglect on the part of white people."

It was white racism, concluded Clement, that was destroying the schools. He sat down.

It was C.P.'s turn to explode. The real problem in the schools, he said, was not white racism, it was *black* racism. "If we didn't have niggers in the schools," he shouted, the veins in his thick neck standing out, "we wouldn't *have* any problems. The problem here today is *niggers!*"

Riddick watched the ripples from this outburst radiate throughout the room. Ann shot up. "The problem," she yelled back, "is that we have stupid crackers like C. P. Ellis in Durham!" Riddick took it all in, not saying anything.

C.P. was back on his feet railing about black students with "African hairstyles and clothes" while glaring at Clement, who sported both. "And how come they let niggers hold an assembly, but they won't let white students hold one?" continued C.P. "I've tried to get them to let me go into the schools and speak to white kids, but they won't let me, 'cause I'm a Klansman."

In the silence that followed C.P.'s remarks, Clement stood up and thundered, "Right on, brother Ellis." It was as if someone tossed a lit firecracker into the room. "What the *hell* are you saying?" a black man shouted at Clement.

"He's the most honest man in the room," declared Clement. "He hates me and he told me. The rest [of] you white liberals have hemmed and hawed about it. You don't *really* like me either; he just has the damn guts to say it."

Riddick called a temporary halt to the meeting as the audience dissolved into several small groups. An official at NCC collared Clement at the back of the auditorium and told him he had lost his mind. After a few minutes, to get the mini-charrette back together and harness the forces unleashed by C.P., Clement, and Ann, Riddick asked "all the hypocrites in the crowd" to stand and explain, in a single sentence, *why* they felt they were hypocrites. With half the room standing, the newly elected mayor of Durham, James Hawkins, began the "self-criticism" session by admitting, somewhat obtusely, that he was a hypocrite "because I have felt a certain way before and changed my mind." Others were more forthcoming about their flaws, including one white high school student who admitted, "I've felt that I'm a liberal and the great white hope that's out to spread reform, but deep down inside I feel a black man's still a nigger." The crowd applauded his honesty. After several more "confessions" and a few more confrontations, it was time to end the initial session. Although he was very pleased with how the evening had gone, Riddick closed on a pragmatic and cautionary note. "Let's get to work," he told the group of black and white faces, "before we reach the point when Mr. Ellis says 'I'm tired of being nice because you don't know what you're talking about' and when Mr. Clement says 'I'm tired of being nice because you don't know what you're talking about.' "

As people were filtering out the door, Howard Clement approached C.P. "I want to shake your hand, Mr. Ellis," the black radical said, putting out his hand. Everyone within twenty-five yards stopped talking and looked over. But C.P. just glared at Clement's outstretched black hand as if it was a piece of garbage someone was trying to force on him. He had attended the meeting, but he wasn't about to make friends with niggers. Then he turned and stalked out of the room—even more rattled than when he had entered. Riddick, who had observed the entire interaction between C.P. and Clement, watched the Klan leader leave. Then he scanned what was left of the audience until his gaze located Ann Atwater. She was in the middle of an animated discussion with a group of perhaps two dozen people. Several members of the group were loudly disagreeing with her about something. After another minute, the voices had quieted and the group was nodding in agreement. Riddick laughed to himself. Despite Howard Clement's highly visible role at the meeting that night, there was no doubt in his mind that Ann was more influential in the poor black community. It was just as in so many civil rights organizations, he mused: the flamboyant male leaders make the speeches while the workaday women, most of them as plain as bread, make it happen. And despite Clement's radical rhetoric and carefully arranged Soul Brother appearance, Riddick had already heard who the real militant in Durham was, and he watched her working her people for a few more seconds.

Later, lying on the couch at his home in Raleigh with music blaring from the stereo, he replayed the events of that evening across the screen of his closed eyes. Two images kept returning. C. P. Ellis: hurting and hurtful, possessed of all the tedious, creaking, accumulated hatreds of the South, and yet guileless and—Riddick believed—essentially honorable. Klansman or not, and against his own will, Riddick liked C.P. The other image was of Ann Atwater: contentious, prideful, towering and immutable as a mountain. A thought occurred to Riddick. It was ridiculous, but that, of course, was its appeal. Probably *too* crazy, though, even for him. And yet, if he could pull it off . . . No, he told himself, slow down. Take it easy and see how things develop. Riddick forced himself to focus on the music for a while, until his racing mind slowed.

Over in the poor white neighborhoods of East Durham, C.P. also lay awake, thinking about the evening. In front of all those people, Howard Clement had wanted to shake his hand. And had called him "brother." It was hard to figure how those actions would help Clement in the black community. It sure didn't seem to do him any good at the meeting; blacks were furious with him. And yet, there must be an angle. C.P. couldn't believe that Clement would want to shake his hand without a good reason, a strategic one. This reminded C.P. of how, several weeks before, the city councilman had fled across the street rather than shake hands with him in public. C.P. gave a short, bitter laugh. The white civic leader was ashamed to be seen with him while the black revolutionary wanted to embrace him. And then there was Riddick. What was *his* game? He knew C.P. was a Klansman and still spoke respectfully to him. Why? It was all too crazy. He gave up trying to figure it out, turned over, and at last fell asleep.

*   *   *

The actual planning of the charrette began in earnest with the formation of a steering committee. Anyone could belong to the committee, and C.P. decided that, uneasy as he was about the whole thing, he had committed himself to the process and might as well see it through. He joined the steering committee—along with Ann Atwater, Howard Clement, Joe Becton, and a score of others—just to ensure that the white conservative point of view was represented. Organizing the charrette with such a quarrelsome crew was itself a task. Surprisingly, the conflicts weren't between C.P. and Ann; they avoided problems simply by refusing to talk to each other. But Ann and Howard Clement fought from the start. Ann made no effort to hide the fact that she considered him one of the "Big Niggers" from the Mutual, at one point calling him a "handkerchief head." When he got over the shock of Ann's hostility, he became indignant at being treated so dismissively. He would have likely been as insulted no matter who had criticized him. But the fact that the barbs were hurled by a woman, and a poor one, certainly did not make them easier to bear. Clement was, after all, a proud man, a dyed-in-the-wool member of the black aristocracy, born and bred in comfortable circumstances in Charleston, South Carolina, the son of a lawyer who had nearly won a seat in Congress. He was himself a lawyer, a graduate of Howard University and Howard Law School, and a top executive with the North Carolina Mutual, a company which his family had proudly served since 1906. But Clement also considered the attacks unjustified. He had taken part in the sit-in movement, twice had been arrested for his activities, risking his career as a lawyer (he had had to appear before the Committee on Character and Fitness of the South Carolina Bar to defend his involvement), and had defied his parents' demands that he give up the "foolishness." Even at the Mutual he had had to fight against pressures to be less militant. His employer had commanded him to withdraw from the charrette, claiming that it was too radical an undertaking and would reflect badly on the company. But Clement resisted all these efforts to silence him, and he was stung by Ann's charges. Rather than simply lash back at her, he realized that he needed to work to gain her trust, and, after some initial skirmishes, that was what he did.

But even these problems were all part of the total process. Riddick hoped that the conflict would produce an annealed group capable of directing the charrette once it got started. At one of these meetings, during a discussion about choos-ing a name for the charrette, Clement suggested "Save Our Schools," or SOS. The name appealed to the other members. It had the right tone of urgency. C.P. finally cleared his throat. "There's something I think I should tell you, and then I'll shut up," he told the group. "Klansmen in eastern North Carolina have a project of their own and they call it 'Save Our Schools.' " C.P. didn't add that the Klan SOS program was designed to frustrate desegregation, not implement it, but he didn't have to.

"Right on," said Clement with a laugh.

Another member of the committee suggested that they could still use the initials SOS, but have it stand for "*Support* Our Schools." Clement refused to back down.

"No, that's all right," he said. "I don't want to support our schools. I want to *save* them." The group, including C.P., voted to adopt the name.

While the charrette was being formed, C.P. kept his Klan unit up to date with reports at the weekly Klavern meetings. Some members were openly troubled by C.P.'s participation. Their leader's appearances before the city council had been difficult enough for many of them to swallow. But meetings *with* blacks? Sitting down at the same table with them? Talk-ing with them? No. It wasn't right. C.P. repeatedly explained the need to represent their viewpoint at the charrette, but it made no difference. "Look," he finally told the men in the meeting hall, "you've trusted me before. All I'm asking is that you trust me now. I *know* what I'm doing." But C.P. did not know what he was doing—that is, while he knew what path he was starting down, he had no idea where it would lead.

His first clue that the charrette was going to be something entirely different from the meetings he had been attending for years occurred during the third gathering of the steering committee. After the group divided up into several subcommittees, each one responsible for a different component of the charrette, they came to the task of selecting chairmen to guide the charrette. Bill Riddick would, of course, attend all sessions of the charrette, offering expertise and advice when asked, but it was a basic principle of the process that local people should be in control—preferably *two* local people, representing divergent points of view. Riddick had discussed his idea about the positions with Joe Becton—probably the only person in Durham who wouldn't think him crazy. In fact, the idea sounded quite logical to him.

With obligations elsewhere, Ann Atwater could not attend the meeting that night. Not only was she the acting chair of UOCI but she still worked with Operation Breakthrough and directed social and charitable programs at her church. And then there were her daughters, both of whom needed a lot of attention. It was late at night before she returned home, and the phone was ringing as she walked in the door. A man identified himself as a reporter with a local newspaper. She listened to him for a minute before concluding that it was a prank call. "Who is this?" she barked, too tired for nonsense. But the man *sounded* serious. It was his message that didn't make sense. She and C. P. Ellis, leader of the Durham chapter of the Ku Klux Klan, had been nominated to co-chair the school charrette program at a meeting of the steering committee that night. Ellis had accepted the job. What was her response? She had a simple answer: "No. I'm not going to work with that cracker." She hung up and went to bed.

But she couldn't sleep. All night long a newspaper headline danced before her eyes: BLACKS AFRAID OF WHITES! Finally, toward dawn, she called the newspaper and told them she had changed her mind. They should print in the paper that she would work with *anybody* to make the needed changes in the Durham schools.

C.P.'s first reaction at the meeting had been the same as Ann's: *Is this a joke?* Many of the people gathered around the table opposed putting a Klansman in charge of a school desegregation program, but, as Becton argued, reckless times called for reckless action. And certainly it was hard to think of a more reckless gambit than throwing C.P. and Ann together. After the nominations were debated, a vote was taken and the pair were elected. Still, C.P. protested. "Ain't no way I can work with that gal!" he insisted. But the members of the committee wore him down, and he finally agreed to take the job—if she would.

It was a stunned Klansman who told the group, "I'll be the first to admit that I'm a little uncomfortable." But, he continued, "whether you like me or not, you got me."

CHAPTER THIRTEEN

> My problems started when I began to comment on
> what I saw. I insisted on being accurate. But the
> world I was born into didn't want that. Indeed, its
> very survival depended on not knowing, not
> seeing—and, certainly, not saying anything at all
> about what it was really like.
>
> —MARY MEBANE,
> from a Durham memoir

The phone calls began almost immediately.

"What the fuck you doing, working with niggers?"

"Have you lost your mind?"

"You're a race traitor!"

At first, C.P. tried to explain what he was doing. But after realizing the futility of that task, he simply hung up on the calls that began early in the morning and continued long into the night. The accusations stung him. But nothing the anonymous callers said could match the effect of the voices clamoring inside his own head: *Betrayer! Liar! White nigger!* He didn't tell his unit (he hardly admitted it to himself), but he was convinced that school segregation was a lost cause. The courts had ruled. The wheels of social change were turning—slowly, but they were turning—and nothing he or the Klan could do would turn them back. All he could do was try to make the best of a bad situation and help make desegregation less painful for white children. Rich whites had no interest in making things work. Why should they? They sent their kids to private schools or moved to the suburbs. For working people like C.P., trapped in East Durham, that wasn't an option. He was doing what he thought best, what he had to do. But reminding himself of this did nothing to still the voices attacking him, not the ones on the phone and not the ones in his head.

Bill Riddick invited Ann and C.P. to dinner at a downtown café for their first meeting together as co-chairs. It was a predictable disaster. C.P. paced the floor until the food arrived, at last running out of excuses to sit down in a public place with two black people. When he finally did slide reluctantly into a chair, C.P. and Ann didn't say a word to each other. Instead, they communicated through Bill Riddick. The charrette organizer tried throughout the meal to get them to interact. Whenever Ann or C.P. said something even remotely personal, revealing how they felt about some racial issue, Riddick would prod: "Tell it to *him*" or "Tell it to *her.*" But it was an upstream battle. The two refused even to look at each other. Compounding the problem was the fact that throughout the tense meal, all around them people were gawking at the trio and whispering. C.P. was certain people were talking about his betrayal of the white race. Ann was just as sure they condemned her for getting involved with a Klansman.

Riddick didn't minimize the problems facing the pair. On the contrary, he stressed all the obstacles, pointing out how Durham residents—both black and white—were going to resent C.P. and Ann's working together. He went into detail, discussing exactly what these angry citizens might do to attempt to derail the collaboration. They could threaten them personally. They could show up at the charrette and attempt to disrupt it. They could, and almost certainly would, try to turn friends and family against them. As if Ann and C.P. hadn't already considered these possibilities—and a hundred other scenarios, too. But once he had them focusing on these dangers, he leaned back in his chair and gave them a perfect Cheshire cat smile. The situation, he said, was perfect. Just what he wanted. Couldn't be better. It was precisely *because* they were heading into the center of a racial storm, he said, that the possibility for *positive* change was tremendous.

"If you two can get together on this," Riddick told them in his best basso profundo, "it would change this community *forever.*" He leaned across the table conspiratorially, as if the three were criminals planning a heist, and dropped his voice to a whisper: "You have bought into something that is bigger than either of you are." Then he straightened up in his chair and stared at them, daring them to deny it.

There was nothing Ann and C.P. could say in response. They sat in an uneasy silence, the tinkle of silverware and the indecipherable hubbub from the surrounding tables the only sounds.

After a suitable pause, Riddick expertly shifted gears and began talking about the charrette in practical and even somewhat technical terms. The process, he said, had three goals. First, to ensure that black and white children could go to the same schools while maintaining a quality learning environment. Second, to create a dialogue among different parts of the community. The third goal, he explained, was more abstract. It was to move back, if only by a few inches, the wall that circumscribed the possible. This "goal," he allowed, was nearly undefinable, its results were unmeasurable, and its lasting effects on Durham would never be known. Naturally, it was the one that captivated Riddick.

"But if the two of *you* can work together," he said, and then flung out his arms in a theatrical gesture, indicating . . . anything and everything.

But by this point C.P. barely noticed Riddick. His ears burned with the whispers around them, and he was acutely aware of the physical presence of the large black woman just inches away. That she was capable of sitting in a chair in a restaurant and eating food was a revelation to him. Ann had ceased being human to C.P. years before; she existed only as a symbol of everything he hated about her race. He could easily imagine her carrying a picket sign and bellowing slogans while a swirling mass of angry blacks followed in her wake. And he could picture her as he had seen her so often, standing before the city council, righteous and indignant, like a black Moses before Pharaoh, commanding, "Let my people go!" But Ann doing something so ordinary as eating a meal in a restaurant—this was beyond C.P.'s powers of imagination. And yet there she sat, in a chair right next to him, devouring a plate of greasy pork chops and fried okra. He could hear the grinding of her teeth, feel the warmth emanating from her body. He sniffed, and swore he caught the scent of her hair. It certainly wasn't sexual attraction that churned inside of him, but it wasn't exactly disgust either. Unable to bear the confusion of feelings any longer, C.P. offered some excuse and hurried from the restaurant.

A few nights later he received his first death threat.

"You keep working with those niggers and you gonna get yourself shot," a man's voice said. He hung up before C.P. could respond. C.P. stood immobile, the dial tone buzzing from the receiver in his hand. Then he hung up, picked up the receiver again, and dialed Ann Atwater.

"This is C.P."

"Uh-huh," came the icy response.

"Look, I don't like you, and you don't like me." She did not dispute this statement. "But we got to do something 'cause our kids are suffering in school. If this thing is gonna be a success, you and I are gonna have to make it one. Can we lay aside some of these feelings?"

Ann chewed on her lower lip a few seconds before answering, "I'm willing if you are."

"Okay, then. I'll see you at the meeting tomorrow night."

"All right."

Ann hung up the phone and went back to fixing dinner. Now what was that Klansman up to? She considered and then quickly dismissed any idea of C.P.'s sincerity. She learned long ago that white folks could not be trusted. Still, she had been praying that the charrette would be a success. Just getting through the process without one of them killing the other would qualify it as that. But she had prayed for more. Maybe C.P.'s phone call had been a response to her prayers. Okay, then. She would give him an opportunity to prove himself. But as she continued stirring the stewpot she reminded the empty kitchen: "A leopard don't change his spots."

After the phone conversation, C.P. and Ann began talking directly to each other instead of using Riddick as a go-between. No one would have mistaken the two for friends. They spoke only when they had to and with little feeling—

except during their frequent arguments. C.P. would swear at her and she would swear right back, refusing to give an inch to his bigotry, and the fight would escalate until Riddick was forced to interpose himself between them before they started hitting each other. If it came to that, Riddick was more concerned about what Ann would do to C.P. than the other way around. At these times, Riddick wondered to himself if it had been a good idea to throw the two together after all. But when they calmed down, it was surprising what they could do. Gradually, they managed to take care of the business of organizing the charrette. Both of them were hardworking leaders—they had proved that within their opposing organizations—and they threw themselves into this task. C.P. went before the School Board to invite members to the charrette. A few of the old-timers on the board smiled as C.P. made his brief presentation. They were used to hearing from him under different circumstances. Instead of the Klansman boiling over some perceived racial slight, his hostility barely contained (and often not at all), there stood C. P. Ellis, politely explaining the purpose of the charrette. "It'll be an opportunity for citizens to express their support for their schools and also their dissatisfaction with them," he said. "We encourage you folks to leave your calendar open and come all ten days. We really want all of you people to come." It was a smiling and slightly astounded Theodore Speigner who thanked C.P. kindly for his appearance that night. None of them knew how much this appearance cost C.P. He left immediately after speaking and drove straight home, doubts howling in his ear the whole way.

Later, there was another phone call.

"I'm gonna shoot you down like the dog you are, Ellis," said the enraged voice.

"Well, buddy," C.P. told the man, "you're just gonna have to get in line."

Selecting a site for the charrette was the first real test of the new co-chairs' ability to work together. After much study, the steering committee selected the R. N. Harris Elementary School, a modern, one-story brick building. "It has everything we need," said one advisor, ticking off the benefits of the school: both a large auditorium (for full-group meetings) and many nearby smaller rooms, air-conditioning (a necessity in the sweltering Durham summer), an open schedule for July (most schools were already booked for a variety of uses during the summer), and child-care facilities. But white conservatives were not happy with the choice. Joseph Butler, the Klan Youth Corps member, attended the steering committee meeting and objected to holding the charrette at Harris. The student body of the school was nearly 100 percent black, reflecting the racial makeup of the neighborhoods to the west. The fact that the school was in a border area, with white neighborhoods just east of it, did not placate conservative critics. When blacks insisted it was a "neutral site," Butler responded peevishly, "There's got to be a site somewhere in this county more neutral than that."

The decision was debated for some time, with committee members growing increasingly frustrated. One solution after another was proposed and shot down. The charrette should be held downtown. It should be held in a white area. In a black area. Out in the country. In a church. At the Civic Center. Worn down by the arguing, one black man considered giving in to conservative white demands. "We've done it so much before," he conceded wearily, "but maybe we could walk one more mile to make this thing go through." Another black man countered that he was tired of giving in. "We're really wasting our time by all this," he concluded. "We've got a site and it might do these whites some good to come over into the black community once in a while."

The debate continued. Ann and C.P., of course, took opposing views.

Ann suggested that they settle on Harris and "work hard individually to get the people here," while C.P. charged that choosing Harris would tell conservative whites that they weren't wanted at the charrette.

"If we can't agree on a place to hold the thing," one exasperated man finally complained, giving voice to what many around the table were thinking, "we're never going to get much done once we have it."

Unable to make a decision, the matter was referred back to the committee for further study. In private, C.P. was considering conceding on the issue, just to move the program forward. But one thing still bothered him. He called Ann with his concern. "Look, Ann," he said, "if we have the charrette at Harris, who'll protect the whites coming over there?"

Ann wasn't sure exactly what he meant. "Protect them from what?" she asked.

"Why, from *blacks*, of course."

Ann was silent for a few moments. Growing up in rural North Carolina, she had always thought of the Klan as a powerful, terrifying force. It had never occurred to her before that beneath their robes Klansmen might sometimes be quaking.

"Don't you worry about that, C.P.," she said, stifling a laugh. "*I'll* protect you."

When C.P. announced that he was giving in on the issue, the other conservatives went along. If the Exalted Cyclops of the local Klan did not deem the issue important enough to continue fighting over, why should they? Besides, there was still an enormous amount to do to prepare for the charrette. The committee settled on a starting date of July 19. C.P. and Ann worked harder than ever. Surveys to determine what issues bothered parents and students were drawn up and mailed out, and the responses were processed in order to formulate an agenda. Flyers were written, printed, and distributed. They needed to line up support from leading community members. And then there were all the logistical problems of organizing a series of meetings lasting from 10 A.M. to 2 A.M. each day for ten consecutive days. It was exhausting work. But the hardest part was convincing marginalized people—black and white— to take part in the process. Ann returned to the old, slow method she had used in drumming up support for Operation Breakthrough years before, canvassing the poor black neighborhoods, trudging up and down the unpaved streets in the sweltering summer and knocking on doors.

"You hear about the charrette?" she asked those who answered her knock. Whether they had or they hadn't she proceeded to tell them all about it, using every argument she could think of to get them to come. She was used to apathy, the result of years of poverty and racism and government neglect. But this time she was fighting a new enemy. Several people told her in confidence that members of the Nation of Islam had put out the word that blacks should not attend the charrette, that it was just one more attempt to distract people with talk. Even with the participation of Ann Atwater, it was easy to make that charge stick. The history of race relations in Durham was, after all, a long line of such shams extending back for a century. Commissions, committees, councils, boards of inquiry, official investigations, delegations, panels—countless ventures to "improve race relations" that began with fanfare and ended in silence. Or worse: in promises no one believed, least of all those making them. Hadn't the city *always* tried to substitute talk for action? Now black residents were supposed to be impressed by SOS? No way, many decided. They weren't about to waste their time with another white man's game. But many others decided to attend. Some would come out of personal loyalty to Ann. Others, because they were *always* willing to give an attempt at meaningful communication "one more shot." So much had been taken from them already that all they had left was their hope, and they would not relinquish that. A few would show up out of morbid curiosity. Like people who attend auto races secretly hoping for an accident, they would come to the charrette anticipating a spectacular collision between Ann and C.P.

No one needed to go around C.P.'s neighborhood in East Durham talking down the charrette. If blacks would be there, many poor white residents didn't want to have any part of it. But others decided to attend, for many of the same reasons that brought out black residents.

As the opening night of the charrette approached, the number and virulence of the telephoned threats to C.P. increased. It wasn't just his fellow Klansmen who opposed the charrette. Mainstream groups such as the Durham Lions Club also bridled at the idea of blacks and whites working together to smooth the path to integration. The organization's bulletin ran an article about the charrette that concluded with the opinion that the city's schools would be better served if men with guns were stationed at the schoolhouse doors to take care of black troublemakers. The callers accused C.P. of taking payoffs to work for integration and routinely threatened to murder him and his family if he didn't resign his position with the charrette. He decided he needed to go public about the calls and to respond to the charges of selling out.

"In recent days tremendous pressure has been brought to bear upon me to withdraw my active support from the federally financed 'Save Our Schools' program," he told reporters. After revealing the many death threats, he explained that as the leader of the Klan he had for years tried to help white parents and students with school-related problems. But he had had little success. The charrette, he explained, was the last, best chance to help white children. "To resign from SOS now would mean we would have no voice . . . To have no voice means to have no part in the decisions and solutions made during and after the charrette, and this would turn control of the charrette over to the liberals and blacks." He added that while he would "personally be pleased to see a mass exodus [of white students] from public schools to private schools," for poor people like him that just wasn't an option. "[T]his is all we have left," he said in an emotional conclusion that was partly a plea for understanding and partly a cry of defiance. "If I can do anything to help our children as schools open this fall, I intend to do it."

Ann was also receiving criticism of her involvement. But she was just as adamant as C.P. about continuing with the charrette. In an interview with the *Carolina Times*, she, too, felt forced to explain her participation in the program.

> I've always tried to work at full capacity on any job I've undertaken. I try to work around any unpleasant hindrances and give full attention to the talk I am involved in. Mr. Ellis has the same problems with the schools and his children as I do with mine and we now have a chance to do something for them. There certainly is no deep seated love between Mr. Ellis and myself but this school project brings out problems we all have. We are going to have to lay aside our differences and work together. This will be the first time two completely different sets

269

of philosophies have united to work for this goal of better schools. If we fail, at least no one can say we didn't try.

The day before the charrette opened, the *Carolina Times* ran an interview unprecedented for a black newspaper: a frank discussion with the head of the local Ku Klux Klan. Throughout much of the interview, C.P. repeated the usual Klan propaganda. Asked about the purpose of the organization he headed, he answered that the group worked "to defeat a communist conspiracy using the blacks of our country to accomplish its plans."

"Do you really believe there is a communist conspiracy?" asked the incredulous reporter.

"Yes, I do," answered C.P., unruffled.

He advocated separate but equal facilities and charged that government programs to overcome discrimination amounted to special privileges for blacks. "It's like discrimination in reverse," he said. C.P. also echoed stereotypes about black behavior, saying that after visiting Durham's housing projects he was disgusted to watch blacks spend the time from Friday night until Monday morning drunk.

But he also said some things that must have surprised readers. C.P. allowed that perhaps the tenants in public housing felt "a lack of a future" and added, "If I thought I would never have any more than I do today I might do the same thing." (Of course, he very often *did* do the same thing, and for the very reason he named.) And, despite his parroting the conspiracy theories and racist clichés he learned from Robert Shelton and Jesse Helms, C.P. also revealed the first glimmering of a more sophisticated understanding of how Durham—and the South—actually worked.

"Our city is run by 'cliques,'" he told the reporter. "We elect our representatives but we don't have much of a choice . . ." The recognition of "cliques" was as far as C.P.'s thinking took him. Still, the interview was an eye-opener for black readers. The head of the local Klan was obviously a more complex character than many had imagined.

In the days leading up to the charrette, Durham's two white newspapers also featured several in-depth stories about the event, many of them focusing on the odd couple chairing it. The

Sunday of the formal opening session, the *Morning Herald* ran nearly a page of articles covering the charrette, including profiles of the co-chairs flanked by large pictures of them. The photographs were arranged for maximum effect. On one side of the page was a head-and-shoulders shot of C.P. dressed in his Duke maintenance uniform, the name "C. Ellis" stitched over the right breast pocket, his hair close-cropped, his features revealing nothing but an edgy wariness, the weathered and sulky face of the poor white South. Ann faced C.P. from across the page like a boxer, her massive arms folded across her ample bosom, eyes glinting out from a round face that was dark and powerful, her mouth set in a tight-lipped smile that would have taken very little effort to become a frown. The contrast couldn't have been more striking if C.P. had been wearing his Klan robes and Ann been caught as she was about to heave a Molotov cocktail.

Early Monday morning, July 19, the first working day of the charrette (there had been a formal kickoff the evening before), C.P. and Ann both pulled into the parking lot of the R. N. Harris School at exactly the same time. As they climbed out of their vehicles, C.P. called Ann over. The morning was still cool, but humidity was already creeping into the air, promising an uncomfortable day. "I want you to see something," C.P. told her, and walked her around to the back of his old Buick. He opened the trunk. Inside was a torn blanket, which he carefully unfolded to reveal a .32 caliber revolver. "I come prepared," he told her, his voice steely. It was amazing how he could change, she thought. Sometimes he was polite, almost sweet. And other times, for no apparent reason, he was angry and abrasive, his voice menacing. It was almost as if two distinct people struggled for control of the same body.

So he really was afraid to come into "enemy territory," Ann realized. She looked into his face and said, "C.P., that's your God." She pointed to the gun. Then she held up a large white-covered Bible that she carried with her. "This is mine. We'll see which one is stronger."

Embarrassed, C.P. made a show of refolding the blanket around the gun. Then he slammed down the trunk lid and walked into the school building, silent and alone.

271

The charrette got off to a slow start. Only one parent showed up for the first afternoon session. Steering committee members decided to spend the day once again knocking on doors in black and white neighborhoods to bring people in for the evening session. The effort paid off Monday night when a racially mixed group of 200 people gathered in the school auditorium for the first "arena session." The possible racial explosion that Riddick, and everyone else, had known was possible did not happen that night. In fact, everyone appeared to be on their best behavior. If anything, they were *overly* concerned about creating "an incident." When Howard Clement stood up and began his usual lecture on the History of Racial Oppression, even many blacks in the group rolled their eyes and muttered to one another, "There he goes again." Repetition had wrung from Clement's speech any controversy it might have once contained. The evening's most uncomfortable moment came when C.P. raised the old Southern concern about "the black beast"—blaming racial tension in the schools on black males trying "to force bodily contact with white females against their will." But the issue was too charged and others refused to challenge him on his claims. C.P. himself seemed a bit conciliatory later, admitting that another cause of tension was "acts of agitation by—yes—by whites against blacks."

There was even one moment of levity that first evening. A white liberal rose to make an impassioned plea for brotherhood, proclaiming that blacks and whites are, in the end, "all the same." Howard Clement angrily responded that he was sick and tired of hearing whites "repeating this thing that we're all alike!"

Sitting at the front of the room, C.P. turned around in his chair and yelled, "Right on, Howard!" It brought down the house. Clement smiled at him and C.P. grinned sheepishly in return.

At last, discussion gave way to yawns and people stumbled bleary-eyed out of the school. C.P. arrived home a couple of hours before dawn to find his wife, Mary, still awake, sitting up in bed. He noticed her red-rimmed eyes and the pile of crumpled tissues on the floor, but he said nothing. A distance had formed between the two over the years and the fact of her unhappiness was not, in itself, news to him. She had never approved of his work with the Klan, not because of any moral problems with the organization, but simply because it took time that she felt C.P. should have spent with his family. As far as she was concerned, the charrette was no different from any other of C.P.'s Klan projects—except that it claimed even more of his time. While he had been out campaigning for the "Southern way of life" all those years, she had been left to raise the children. "Abandoned" was the word she would have used. For eleven years—until he was placed in a care center—the couple's blind, deaf, and retarded son, Punkin', required her constant attention. She also looked after C.P.'s elderly mother, who lived with them in their tiny house. And after Punkin' was placed in an institution, Mary had put in long hours working at the Duke University switchboard, a tedious job that paid low wages. The years had passed with a stultifying sameness. A lifetime of hard work and poor habits, including chain-smoking, had worn her down and caused a serious heart condition that made breathing difficult. By 1971, she was bewildered by her marriage to a man whom, even after all these years, she could not say she really knew, and embittered by a life she did not remember ever having chosen.

C.P. sat on the edge of his bed unlacing his shoes. Unable to ignore her gloomy presence any longer, he finally asked, "What's the matter with you? We been getting more calls? You can't let them get to you."

"It ain't that," she said. "It's Timmy."

C.P. felt a chill pierce his heart, but he continued undressing. "What about him?"

"His teacher made fun of him in class today. Called his daddy a Klansman, in front of everybody. And some kids teased him. Said you love niggers."

"That's nothing new. Forget it."

He climbed into bed, exhausted but unable to sleep. In time, he heard his wife's labored, rhythmic breathing and knew she was asleep. But he was unable to put what had happened to his son out of his mind. He stared up into the darkness above him. He was angry, but at whom? He couldn't say at first. But as he thought about it he realized who was to blame. He was, of course. What did he think he was accomplishing with this charrette anyway? Could it possibly be worth the pain it was causing? He was there *because* of his children. But was he hurting them more by participating? He didn't know. For the first time since joining the Klan, he was beset by unanswerable questions. Before the Klan, he had often lain in bed like this, wondering why he couldn't seem to get anywhere in the world. The Klan had answered those questions for him. It had pointed to an enemy and supplied a plan that promised to lead, someday, to prosperity. But now the Klan provided no answers for the questions that stormed out of the darkness, like soldiers into battle, threatening to overwhelm him. He didn't remember falling asleep, but he must have, for when he opened his eyes again, the sun was shining in through the window beside the bed, and the house was silent and empty.

The second day of the charrette began promptly at 10 A.M., with the large group dividing into several smaller clusters to discuss in detail the issues brought up the previous day. C.P. put away his concerns from the night before and concentrated on leading a group discussion of interracial violence, the subject he had broached on Monday night. It was a surprisingly good discussion. Having survived the first day, several people felt freer to express themselves and began opening up. Yes, allowed one white student, interracial violence *did* sometimes occur. But it was a two-way street, he added, and besides, parents often blew small incidents out of proportion when race was concerned. C.P. was particularly interested in the comments of a small, wiry black woman who charged that teachers and the school administration treated her children as if they were stupid troublemakers—just because they were poor and black. The woman's complaint caught C.P.'s attention because he had been about to say the same thing about *his* children; they were treated badly because they were "poor white trash." Even more amazing, this experience happened to him repeatedly throughout the day. For the first time in his life, C.P. really listened to black people and he was stunned to hear, over and over, his own concerns coming from their mouths. When arguments erupted among kids at school, it was the working-class children—black and white—who were always blamed and punished. New supplies went to the suburban schools, while inner-city schools made do with worn-out equipment. Teachers spent more time with kids from "better" homes, and believed their excuses when papers were late or assignments lost. The poor kids were called "liars" and "cheaters." It had never occurred to C.P. that black children were treated as disdainfully as his kids were, and it puzzled him to hear it now.

By the end of the afternoon, everyone was exhausted. After his last session, C.P. headed down to the auditorium, where a few people were still talking. He spotted Ann sitting by herself and collapsed into a chair next to her.

"How you doing?" he asked.

If she was surprised by his friendliness, she didn't show it. She smiled at him. "'Bout wore *out!*"

"Yeah, me, too."

They chatted for a while about nothing in particular, neither of them in a hurry to go to dinner and just enjoying the pause between intense meetings. Before long they were alone in the large room.

"How're your kids?" C.P. asked Ann. "You got two, don't you?"

"Yeah, but my youngest ain't doing too good," Ann said. "She comes home from school every day crying."

"Why?"

Ann regarded him carefully before answering. "Don't take this personal, C.P. But her teacher's been saying her mama's a fool to be working with a Klansman. Other kids been fighting her over it."

C.P. stared at Ann openmouthed. "That's what's happening to my kids! But they're teased 'bout their daddy selling out."

Ann nodded. "Uh-huh. They say that 'bout me, too. But I told my girl this morning at breakfast that I'm doing this for her— so she'll have a place to stand in society. But she's afraid she'll get hurt over it."

"Ain't that something?" said C.P., incredulous. "Ain't that *something?*"

This led them into a discussion about all the difficulties they'd each had working on the charrette. They forgot their exhaustion in the excitement of discovering how similar their experiences were. Soon they were talking about other things, about how hard it was raising children without much money, and about how they were always having to tell their kids that they were just as good as kids from middle-class homes. About the problem of trying to convince their kids never to be ashamed of who they were, while all the time hiding their own shame for not being better providers. They talked about how teachers spoiled all of it by never letting the kids forget that they came from "impoverished households." It struck them how familiar each other's stories were. They were almost interchangeable. When Ann complained how rough it was living on a dirt street, C.P. quickly pointed out that he knew all about that because he had grown up in just such a neighborhood. And C.P. was moved to hear how, as a child, Ann's only dolls were the ones she made herself out of grass she pulled up, the tangled roots serving as hair. Some neighbor girls in the old mill village had played with those same grass dolls.

C.P. couldn't believe what he was hearing. But even more amazing to him was what he was saying—and to whom. He was sharing his most intimate grievances, all of his doubts and failures, with the hated Ann Atwater. The militant he usually referred to with a sneer as "that fat nigger." And yet, here they were, talking like old friends. As if she wasn't black at all, or he wasn't white, or as if all that didn't *matter*. He looked at her and it was as if he was seeing her for the first time. He was stunned by what he saw. Mirrored in her face were the same deeply etched lines of work and worry that marked his own face. And suddenly he was crying. The tears came without warning, and once started, he was unable to stop them. Ann was dumbfounded, but she reacted instinctively by reaching out and taking his hand in her own. She tried to comfort him, stroking his hand and murmuring, "It's okay, it's okay," as he sobbed. Then she, too, began to cry.

If anyone had walked into the auditorium just then, they would have found it hard to believe what they saw: the Exalted Cyclops of the Ku Klux Klan and Durham's most militant black leader sitting together, hand in hand, weeping copiously and oblivious to the world around them.

CHAPTER FOURTEEN

> As long as white people do not recognize
> themselves in black people, whites cannot know
> what it means to be human.
>
> —JULIUS LESTER

The single unifying element in the history of transformations in the West, from Saul's conversion on the road to Damascus to Kafka's cockroach, is the instantaneousness of the process— if the word "process" can be used at all to describe the psychological equivalent of a lightning strike. Jesus appears to Saul and the persecutor of Christians nonpareil cries out, "Lord, what wilt thou have me to do?" Gregor Samsa goes to sleep a human and awakens as an insect.

This was not C.P.'s experience. Just because he had discovered a commonality of experience between himself and Ann Atwater didn't mean that he would immediately leave the Klan and sign up with the NAACP. But still, it is no exaggeration to say that C.P. had been profoundly moved by the experience and even changed by it—although he himself could not have said how. Perhaps the best way of putting it is to say that a door previously unknown to C.P. had been opened to him. But he had not walked through it. And he did not want to. For the vision he saw through that doorway was not of some peaceable kingdom where lions and lambs dozed together in sunlit meadows, but of a hellish landscape befouled by miscegenation.

From that night on, C.P. wrestled more with his inner demons than with the outer ones the charrette had been convened to solve. The troubling interweave of class and race appeared to him in nearly every discussion. Problems he had always assumed to be purely racial turned out to have a hidden component. And some situations, C.P. was stunned to find, arose entirely out of class. In these cases, race had been an embellishment, a façade tacked onto a superstructure of class. The façade was old and exceedingly well crafted, and those who had erected it had long since died and had taken with them the memory of their achievement. But more commonly the two existed together, intimate, clinging, consanguine and insepara-ble. Class and Race: the South's—America's—Siamese twins. Each one was an entity in its own right, each possessed its own consciousness and a full set of limbs capable of autonomous movement. But they shared a single pulsing heart, and so they could not be uncoupled. C.P. was discovering, painfully and on his own, the truth elucidated by historian Edgar Thompson:

> [Race] came into the South . . . to do duty as an absolute, as a symbol more effective and lasting than language or religion to insure the continued economic, political, and social security of the classes of highest status. To be sure, it had to be shared with landless and impecunious whites, but this was not a complete disadvantage since these whites functioned as a buffer class to absorb the shocks of race conflict.

Suddenly, these lessons were everywhere. When C.P. stated that the reason black students didn't have good equipment in their schools was that they didn't care for things properly, Howard Clement drove him to a black school. There he saw for himself that the typewriters students used were simply old and worn-out. When the parent of one of the few black stu-dents at a white school complained that his child was margin-alized, C.P. heard a white working-class student point out that *he* also felt marginalized. There's a "privileged class" of wealthy white students, he charged. Those students dominated the student newspaper, added another poor white student. "They only write things about that one group."

In the few hours allotted to sleep each night, C.P. battled nightmare visions of betrayal and retribution. His dreams were filled with images of smoke and ruin, of land laid waste. His father appeared to him, dressed in faded overalls, bits of cotton fibers clinging to his hair. The son greeted his father, but the old man didn't recognize him and vanished without speaking. C.P. woke from these dreams terrified and gasping for air.

C.P. was certain he noticed a change in Joseph Butler's behavior. The Klan youth, who had worshiped C.P. and was attending the charrette meetings at his leader's request, now seemed hesitant to talk with him. At one small-group session, Butler was asked why he had left Durham High School to enroll in a private segregation academy. "I'm a racist and I cannot stomach integration," he answered. "That's why I went to a private school." He looked to C.P. for support and C.P. smiled in return, but Butler read the doubt in C.P.'s face and it caused him to draw back.

C.P. attempted to retreat into white supremacy. When Ann announced that she had invited the New Generation Singers, a black gospel choir, to perform after the Saturday-afternoon session, C.P. demanded equal time for the "white viewpoint."

"You got a Klan choir?" asked Ann, teasing.

But C.P. was in no mood for joking. "No, but I want to set up a display of Klan material in a classroom," he told her, coming up with the idea on the spot.

Bill Riddick tried to dissuade C.P., telling him that such a display in a black school would cause a riot. But C.P. would not give in. He felt that he had to do something to regain his credibility with the Klan, with poor whites in general, and, most of all, with himself. In his own mind, it became a test of his own commitment to "his people" and a test of Ann's and Bill Riddick's willingness to hear all sides. Sensing, but not fully understanding, C.P.'s obduracy, they gave in.

Joseph Butler was enthusiastic about working with C.P. on the display. Perhaps he had misread his leader's behavior. Butler called nearby Klan units for photographs and other materials related to Klan life. He worked diligently and with growing excitement to design an exhibit that would show exactly what the Klan was about. On the day that the display opened, C.P. and Butler sat defiantly at a table behind neat stacks of Klan literature while people walked around the room examining the exhibits. Small groups of blacks and whites came and went, most shaking their heads at what they saw. Few people said anything to the pair. C.P. was surprised when Elna Spaulding, wife of Asa T. Spaulding and the grande dame of the Mutual community, came through the door. She was an elegant woman, and a political activist in her own right, a founder of Women in Action for the Prevention of Violence, an interracial Durham organization dedicated to working for peaceful integration. She toured the room, carefully examining the photographs of Klansmen saluting flaming crosses, a display of Nazi armbands, and a pile of hate literature published by the National States' Rights Party. C.P. watched with growing discomfort as she circled the room slowly and with great dignity, as if she were an honored guest attending the opening of a show at a prestigious museum. When she was finished, she went up to C.P. and Joseph Butler, and smiled graciously at them both in turn. "You did a very good job putting this display together," she said in a voice that was as clear and brilliant as crystal. "Thank you so much for your efforts." Then she smiled again and walked regally from the room. C.P. and Butler avoided each other's eyes.

Later, C.P. was alone in the room when he heard loud whispers outside the door. He poked his head into the hallway and saw a group of black high school students standing a little way down the corridor. "Hey! There he is," a tall thin boy said, and pointed at C.P. The group fell into a sulky silence. From what little he had heard and from their gestures, he understood that they intended to tear up his display. Ann was meeting in a room down the hall at that time, and C.P. walked quickly over and found her. "Ann," he told her, "you're gonna have your gospel choir. And I'm gonna have my Klan display. Now there's a group of black kids fixing to rip it up. Either you do something about it, or I'm going to get my gun and protect my things." He walked out of the room and went back to his display.

He hardly had time to sit back down when he heard Ann's voice booming down the hallway as if through a bullhorn. "What you think you're doing?" she demanded. "Get away from there! Leave that alone!"

Ann planted her large frame in the doorway and lit into the

youths. "If you want to know where a person is coming from," she yelled, "you need to *read* this material, not tear it up! You got to *see* what makes him think what he *thinks!*" C.P. had seen Ann mad many times before, during protest marches and at City Hall. It occurred to him as he watched her in the doorway now that if someone had told him years before that someday she would be protecting his Klan material from a group of blacks, C.P. would have told them that they were crazy. Now he wasn't even sure what the word meant.

On Saturday night, the New Generation Singers filled the auditorium with their music. Ann gave herself up to the pious delight that hymn singing had always stirred in her ever since she was a child in the small wooden church down the road from her father's house. Her body swayed to the music, her eyes closed, her large hands smacking together on the downbeat.

"Yes, *Lord!*" she called out at one point, and as she did, her eyes came open for a moment. She saw C.P. standing nearby. He was staring straight ahead. His face was rigid and his hands were tethered to his side.

Poor man, she thought to herself, as she had several times during the past week. Ever since the night they had cried together in the auditorium, she saw how hard all of this was on him. She saw him suffering and wanted to ease his pain, but knew that that was beyond her power. Poor man, she thought again. She was about to turn away when a small movement caught her eye. She looked over and down at the floor. C.P.'s foot was counting out time to the music.

Why, C.P., she chuckled to herself. We 'bout *got* you!

After one of the final evening sessions, C.P. went home and wrote a short letter to his Klansmen explaining what he had been trying to accomplish through the meetings. In his nearly illegible longhand, he wrote and then tore up several drafts trying to find just the right words to convey his conflicted beliefs. "I wish all white kids could afford to go to a private segregated school," he finally wrote, "but I know most can't. I want to help those kids who are trapped in integrated schools." He did not discuss the new direction in which he wanted to take the Klan. Hard as it was for him to accept, he had come to believe that they had been fighting the wrong people for years. It wasn't that he loved blacks. He didn't, at least not as a group. And he still believed in social segregation. But he now realized that blacks simply were not the problem. How could they be? he reasoned. Except for a few executives over at the Mutual, blacks in Durham had no money or power. They could barely feed their own families. Their leaders had been unable to stop urban renewal from rumbling through the heart of the black community like a tank overrunning an enemy redoubt. C.P. had toured their crumbling and ill-equipped schools. He had visited the bleak housing projects and seen how people there were fighting each day for survival. These were the people who were supposedly oppressing whites? No, if any group was holding poor whites down, it was the wealthy white factory owners and businessmen who had called the shots in Durham since the days of Buck Duke—the same men who had been meeting behind the scenes with C.P. for years, slipping him a few dollars "for the cause" and telling him what a great job he was doing fighting the coloreds. He saw clearly now how those men had used him to keep poor blacks and poor whites fighting each other—while they kept control of the reins of power. And what, he wondered, had the Klan actually accomplished for white working people with the endless meetings and bitter fights against desegregation? *Not a damned thing*, he thought. All it had done was to make a miserable existence a little more miserable for poor and uneducated blacks—people with whom he had more in common than he had with the wealthy white citizens of Hope Valley and the other fashionable Durham neighborhoods.

C.P. knew better than to write any of this in his letter. He planned to reorient his unit one step at a time. First, he would wait for the response to his letter. Then he would tailor the speed and specifics of the changes according to what his people were ready for. C.P. grew excited thinking of what they could eventually accomplish: a thousand low-income whites marching and rallying to demand better housing and city services. *That* would shake up the Big Men! He finished the letter, wrote out more than a dozen copies, and mailed them to the most influential Klansmen. And then he waited for their replies.

But there were no responses—unless the increase in death threats counted. He understood then that no one was going to follow him in his work of re-creating the Klan. Just by meeting with blacks he had crossed the inviolable color line. C.P. slowly realized the implications of his transformation, seeing in broad but terrifying strokes the price he was going to have to pay. He had been born a nobody, a worker ant in the hive of the New South. Ridiculed by the same society that grew wealthy on the labor of his kind, C.P. had at last found a measure of self-respect and meaning in the Klan. What was it Ann had called what she was working for? *A place to stand.* Yes, that was what the Klan had provided him: a place to stand and feel he had a right to be there, a right to exist. And now he would have to give up that place. For what? he asked himself. And the answer returned to him like the tolling of a distant bell: merely for the truth.

He called his vice president in the Klan and told him to come by and pick up the keys to the Klavern. "I don't have any reason at all to go back," C.P. told him when he arrived.

"It's just as well you don't come back," the man agreed. "They'd probably kill you if you did."

It was the final night of the charrette. Some 300 participants and organizers gathered in the ornate ballroom of the Washington Duke Hotel, the sixteen-story fading dowager of Durham's glory days, to celebrate the completion of their work. On the afternoon before, C.P. and Ann had handed over to the School Board the recommendation, on a wide range of issues, hammered out over the last ten days. They argued that students should have a greater say on issues affecting their education and recommended that the School Board be enlarged to include four students—two black and two white. They proposed sweeping changes in the school curriculum, with an emphasis on individualized instruction, and, to deal with racial violence within the schools, the formation of a body to discuss and work out problems before they exploded. There were many more suggestions for changes, involving everything from discipline in the classroom to the choices of textbooks (which included the contributions of African-Americans) to the day-to-day operations of the downtown administration. As the co-chairs of a citizens' group, with no official recognition, all Ann and C.P. could do was turn over the suggestions and hope for the best, and that is what they did.

At the celebration, C.P. stood in a corner, sharing a drink with Bill Riddick, who was ebullient about the charrette. It had been a spectacular personal success for him. He had told a reporter a few days earlier that he had never seen anything like what was happening in Durham. The charrette was "the most intense I have ever seen. I have seen takeovers, I have seen blacks come in and say 'We don't want to talk to you white folks anymore,' but that thing . . . was the most intense I've ever seen. They were dealin' and dealin' and dealin'."

Shouting over the band, Riddick was telling C.P. about another charrette planned for next fall over at Winston-Salem. C.P. felt a tap on his shoulder. He turned around to find Ann's boyfriend, a tall middle-aged man with a small, neatly trimmed mustache, standing before him, nervously fingering his tie.

"Excuse me, Mr. Ellis," said the man. "Ann asked me to tell you that she'd like to dance with you."

C.P. looked across the room. He spotted Ann standing by herself near the stage. She was facing in their direction, but he couldn't tell if she was watching him.

C.P. turned to the man. "Look," he said. "I'm sorry. I'm real sorry, but I can't do that. I just can't. Tell her I'm sorry."

The man nodded, looking relieved to have fulfilled his duty, and walked back across the ballroom, threading his way past the many couples dancing there. He talked briefly with Ann and then he headed back in C.P.'s direction.

"Mr. Ellis," the man said when he arrived, even more nervous than before, yanking on his tie as if it were a noose, "Ann wants to know if you'd drink a toast with her."

C.P. smiled. "Tell her that I'd be glad to do that."

When the song ended, C.P. and Ann walked toward the center of the ballroom. People stopped talking throughout the room as they noticed the pair and watched as the co-chairs of the charrette came together and raised their glasses in the air.

"To the charrette," shouted Ann, her voice skipping over the polished wooden floor like a stone over the surface of a lake.

"To the charrette," echoed C.P., "and I hope it did some good."

Then they both drained their glasses.

Saying farewell to the crowd from the stage at the end of the evening, C.P. struggled to control his emotions. He looked down at the large group with whom he had spent almost twenty-four hours a day for the last ten days, and almost as many hours each day for several weeks before that. It had been, he said, the most intense and the most important few weeks of his life. He thanked them all for their efforts and urged them to keep working to make Durham "one of the more progressive places" in America—interrupting himself to laugh at the idea of a Klansman using the word "progressive" favorably.

"It's hard for me to believe that I'm saying some of the things I'm saying," he declared, and Ann, standing in the crowd, joined C.P. in his laughter. But as C.P. left his prepared remarks and talked in more personal terms, his voice becoming soft and hesitant as he struggled to convey something of what was happening inside him, Ann felt tears sting her eyes.

"Something . . . has happened to me," C.P. told the now silent room. There was a long pause, during which he swallowed several times. Then he added tentatively, "I think it's for the best."

He talked about how hard it had been to work with Ann at first, since she represented everything he had been taught to hate. "I used to think that Ann Atwater was the meanest black woman I'd ever seen in my life," he confessed, and the crowd laughed. But, he continued, talking to her had forced him to change his view. "She is trying to help her people just like I'm trying to help my people," he said.

He did not add that he was already on his way out of the Klan, ostracized by the very people he had been trying to help. And so only Ann, whom C.P. had confided in, understood the significance of his last melancholy words.

"Some say that by participating in the charrette, I've lost my effectiveness in the conservative community," he said with a small, sad smile. "That may be true. But I have done what I thought was right."

Then he gazed at the people gathered around him: liberals and conservatives, blacks and whites, men and women, middle-class and poor. He knew he would not meet many of them again, at least not in a way that allowed for the kind of intimacy that they had shared in the past days. And as he cut himself adrift, both from them and simultaneously from that other world he had known before them, he marveled: What an awful thing the truth is, and how comforting is a lie.

But there was nothing more for him to say and so he turned and walked off the stage.

It was late, the night before Christmas Eve 1972, and a damp, light snow that had been falling on Durham intermittently all day had now softened the industrial city's harsher edges and muffled the sound of trucks and cars which still rolled through town even at that late and lonely hour. Through the window, C.P. could make out the branches of a nearby sweet gum tree covered with several inches of snow. He walked unsteadily from the window and sat down in a chair across the room. He picked up an empty Pepsi bottle from the table beside the chair, stared at it for a second or two, and then, with all the strength in his muscular arms, swung the bottle in an arc, bringing it down full force on his head. The thick glass exploded on his skull, sending a spray of shiny pink-tinted shards throughout the room.

He had hoped to kill himself. But the act had not even caused him to lose consciousness. He stumbled to the bathroom and found a towel, which he pressed against the gash he had opened on the side of his head. It was soon saturated with blood. He got out another one. He was reaching for his third towel when he passed out from the combined effects of loss of blood and the fifth of whiskey he had drunk earlier. His wife found him the next morning collapsed into a bloody heap of towels. She thought at first that he was dead. When she revived him, he threw some clothes into a suitcase and drove himself out to the John Umstead Hospital. It was still early on Christmas Eve day when C.P. arrived at the hospital just north and east of town, on the other side of Falls Lake. The orderly who answered C.P.'s knock blinked into the dazzling sunlight.

"I need help," C.P. said, not knowing what else to say. The man looked at the blood on the side of his head and whistled in appreciation.

"I guess you do," he said. He took C.P. by the arm and led him inside.

For a time after the charrette, it had looked as if things might work out for C.P. When the national media heard about what had happened in Durham, he and Ann had become a hot story: America's racial "Odd Couple." They had been flown to New York to appear on *Good Morning America*. They had been interviewed together on *The David Frost Show* and featured in a television documentary about racial issues in the South. But soon the media had turned to other people and issues and Ann and C.P. were left to get on with their lives. Ann had returned to the institutions of the black community—social and political organizations like Operation Breakthrough and UOCI as well as the church. But C.P. had nowhere to go. He wasn't welcome in the Klan. As he had suspected on the last night of the charrette, he could not simply move over into the liberal world. He felt self-conscious around liberals. They were better educated and their larger vocabularies shamed him. They wore different clothes, listened to different music, and had different hobbies for recreation. And most of them seemed as uneasy around him as he was with them. He was far more comfortable around blacks, who seemed to accept him as he was, but he was still psychologically unprepared to mix with them on a regular basis and, even more importantly, there were few occasions that naturally brought him in contact with blacks.

The two blacks with whom he maintained close ties were Ann

and Howard Clement. He had developed a deep affection for Ann that was built on, but transcended, politics. When the two got together they hugged each other with an affection that was deep and genuine. C.P.'s wife also grew fond of Ann, and sometimes took produce from her garden over to Ann's house. C.P. considered Howard Clement one of his few close friends after leaving the Klan. When his wife had a heart attack soon after the charrette, C.P. called Howard in a panic, unable to think what to do. Howard called the hospital, which sent an ambulance out to C.P.'s house. When Mary Ellis had recovered, Howard had the couple over to his house for dinner. That night shattered more stereotypes for C.P. Howard's house was spacious and tastefully decorated and the food was something other than fried chicken and collard greens. But while C.P. was by now able to accept the fact that blacks didn't all think, eat, or talk in a certain way, there was no getting around the fact that Howard Clement, for all his radical politics, lived pretty much like any upper-middle-class Southerner. The color line no longer bothered C.P., but there remained the far less visible but just as substantial line of class separating himself from people like Howard Clement. Despite his respect and affection for Howard as a man, C.P. was uncomfortable around him, just as he was around the better-educated and wealthier white liberals.

He was plagued by guilt for "selling out" the poor white community. He spent hours in the back room of his house drinking whiskey and calling former friends in the Klan, trying to explain his actions. "Listen," he'd say, but no one would. They'd either hang up immediately or tell him he deserved to die for betraying his oath as a Klansman. In drunken frustration and rage, he punched holes in the Sheetrock wall by the phone. In time the wall resembled a lunar landscape upended, pockmarked with fist-sized craters. It was after one of these nights that he had finally tried to kill himself.

C.P. voluntarily committed himself to the psychiatric ward. The first doctor he talked with told him his problem was that he smoked too much and sent him home four days later with the recommendation that he cut down on cigarettes. C.P. searched out other therapists and finally found a young counselor over in Chapel Hill who seemed to understand what he was going through. After meeting with him for several sessions, the therapist told C.P., "Look, you haven't committed any crime. Why don't you just forgive yourself and get on with your life."

It sounded so simple, but it was what C.P. needed to hear. Driving home from the session, he decided that the man was right. He swung his car over onto the shoulder of the road and came to a stop. He turned off the engine and thought. What *had* he done that was so awful? He had changed. That was all. Was change a crime? Did it deserve a death sentence? He laid his head on the steering wheel and began to cry, softly at first, and then harder. He cried for himself and for his family—for his parents, who had lived their whole lives in a kind of dreamless and embittered sleep, haunted by phantasms and suckered by the empty promises of pitchmen. He cried for his children. Was it too late for them? Could he tell them he had been wrong, that he had lived the wrong life and was now changing? And, having told them, would it make any difference? Even if they believed him (and why would they?), what was his one frail voice against the thousands they would hear every day, singing the old familiar lies? But at least he had a chance now to raise his voice against the others, and for that he cried in gratitude. His tears were a mixture of anger, forgiveness, anguish, and exultation, the emotions overlapping and bleeding into one another, so that he was unable to separate them. When the tears at last subsided, he had no new answers to the questions that tormented him but they had lost their violence. He realized that the hatred that had turned his doubts necrotic had been draining imperceptibly from him over the last year, ever since Ann and Howard Clement and Bill Riddick and all the others at the charrette had treated him with respect, despite the fact that he preached the most vile racist hatred for them. They did it because they knew that whatever else he was, he was also a human being. And simply because of that fact, he possessed a certain dignity. They had known this simple truth all along, even if he hadn't, and now it was a gift they had given him.

He started up his car and pulled slowly back out onto the highway, heading home on a road that wound through ancient piney forests and fields nubbed with immature tobacco plants, passing the sprawling red-brick factories of the textile mills where the clatter of looms pierced and jarred the surrounding air, and finally coming into the white working-class neighborhoods of East Durham, with their tangled loves and poisonous hatreds, where each dawn the past strangled the present anew, but where, despite it all, C.P. knew he belonged.

He had found a measure of peace, that was all. But for a poor white son of the South, it was a good beginning.

Epilogue

C. P. Ellis

The charrette opened C.P.'s eyes to the problems of Durham's public schools. He ran for the Board of Education in 1972 with a campaign fund of just $85—and nearly won. Acutely aware of his own lack of education, C.P. enrolled in an adult high school equivalency class. He was one of only a few whites in the class, and was by far the oldest student. He received his diploma in 1973.

The following year he joined a campaign to unionize the maintenance staff at Duke, where he worked. After the International Union of Operating Engineers (IUOE) won the election, C.P. was elected chief steward of Local 465. In 1977, the former Klan leader was elected business manager by a four-to-one margin despite the fact that his opponent, the incumbent, was black, as were 80 percent of the union members. For the next eighteen years, C.P. worked full-time as an organizer for the IUOE, traveling throughout the state and rolling up an impressive record of victories for unionized workers. The same skills he had once used to further the ends of the Ku Klux Klan he now employed in the service of working-class people of all races.

In the 1980s, in an attempt to divide workers by race, professional union busters raised the issue of C.P.'s Klan past. C.P. recalls: "Most of the people I represented, if they heard this, they'd react: 'My God, what did we get into?' But once you set down and explain where you came from, how you got to where you were, what caused you to do what you did, 99% of them would say: 'Let's get on with it. We understand the situation you're in.'"

Black friends like Howard Clement and Joe Becton told workers about C.P.'s transformation. "I put the Good Housekeeping seal on C.P.," laughs Clement today. The divide-and-conquer tactic nearly always backfired. White workers understood the lure of the Klan and a majority of black workers, believing in redemption, accepted C.P.'s change.

C.P. retired in 1994. When asked what accomplishment he was most proud of, he answered without hesitation. "That would have to be the fact that I negotiated Durham's first paid holiday for Martin Luther King's birthday. Some white workers said, they didn't like King and weren't going to take the day off. We said, 'Okay, you idiots, go ahead and work on that day!' "

C.P. and his wife, Mary, now live in a small trailer park outside of Durham. He works part-time at a local auto-parts store.

Ann Atwater

Despite serious health problems (including a series of strokes and heart attacks), Ann continues her work on behalf of Durham's poor and working-class black community. In September 1975, she married Willie Pettiford. Six years later, she was hired as resident liaison at the Durham Housing Authority. Ann also returned to school and earned her general equivalency degree. Today, she is a deacon at the Mount Calvary United Church of Christ in Durham and remains active in church affairs. She and C.P. are often invited to speak about their experiences before college classes and various religious and civic organizations.

Bill Riddick

Riddick now heads a drug prevention program at the University of North Carolina at Chapel Hill. His only regret concerning the Durham charrette was that C.P. and Ann ended up working too well together. "I would have coached C.P. and Ann to have more conflict," he says. "I would have pushed for more substance. But otherwise, I was pretty satisfied. I walked away feeling that I had handled this tool effectively."

Ezell Blair, Jr. (Jibreel Khazan)

After graduating from North Carolina A&T, Blair left the state for a job in Massachusetts, where he continues to live, working with developmentally disabled adults. In 1968, he became a Muslim, later changing his name to Jibreel Khazan. Today, Khazan frequently lectures about the civil rights movement and his role in the lunch-counter protest. His thinking on race has evolved over the years. He finds the term "African-American" too limiting, since it doesn't reflect his white and American Indian heritage. If forced to label himself, he says he is "Afriyqaan-'Ur-Asian-American."

He has some bitterness about the continuing class system within the black community.

"In 1960," he says, "you couldn't get a ten-cent cup of coffee for one million dollars. You sat down and you went to jail where you were beaten half to death. You could have a Cadillac car, a hundred-thousand-dollar house, be president of the college. It made no difference. So, for those who had money, the civil rights movement paid off. They had their own African-American 'good ol' boy' system. Once the door was open, it was business as usual. They forgot about us—the people who helped them get their rights."

He is married and has three adult children.

Howard Fuller

Fuller left Durham in 1970 for Greensboro to work as a union organizer and to build the revolutionary school he had just started in Durham, Malcolm X Liberation University (MXLU). Frustrated with the decelerating pace of social change, and convinced of the need for more radical tactics, he joined the Revolutionary Workers League and changed his name to Owusu Sadaukai, Swahili for "one who clears the way for others." Funding for MXLU dried up after the FBI planted false stories about an arms cache at the school. After several trips to Africa, during which he met with nationalist and revolutionary leaders, Fuller returned to Durham in the 1970s, where he served as the business agent for the union local representing nonacademic employees at Duke University and Medical Center, while also working to "radicalize" workers into a revolutionary movement. A victim of one of the internal power struggles that characterized leftist organizations of this era, Fuller left Greensboro and moved back to Milwaukee, where he worked for a number of community service organizations, eventually earning a doctorate in the sociological foundations of education from Marquette University and becoming director of the Milwaukee County Department of Health and Human Services in 1988. In 1991, Fuller received national attention when he was named superintendent of the Milwaukee school system, the nation's seventeenth largest—despite a lack of elementary or secondary teaching experience. Fuller resigned that position in July 1995, citing differences with the School Board on a variety of issues. He is today Distinguished Professor of Education and Director of the Institute for the Transformation for Learning at Marquette University.

In Durham, Fuller is still remembered with affection as a charismatic leader. He returns the compliment: "Durham was the greatest learning experience of my life," he says. "If there's one place in America I'd go back to without hesitation, it would be Durham. I can't tell you what it meant to me. It was the people—Ann Atwater and the rest. They helped shape the fundamental beliefs that I hold today."

HOWARD CLEMENT III

Clement remains a top executive with the North Carolina Mutual and has served on the Durham city council for three consecutive terms. Each time, C.P. has campaigned for him in white working-class neighborhoods. Since the charrette, Clement and C.P. have moved in opposite directions on the political spectrum. Clement, a Republican, is far more conservative than C.P. on most issues. They remain close friends, however.

FLOYD McKISSICK

McKissick's tenure as national director of CORE (January 1966 through the fall of 1968) was a troublesome time, for both McKissick and the movement. Political and economic stagnation undermined many black Americans' confidence in the old tactics of the civil rights movement. McKissick spoke for disillusioned ghetto residents when he called nonviolence "a dying philosophy" that had "outlived its usefulness." Many questioned the validity of multiracial coalitions like CORE. Even the ultimate goal of integration itself was now challenged. Reflecting these changes, and attempting to steer the organization in a positive direction, McKissick moved CORE's headquarters from downtown Manhattan to Harlem and from there launched a series of inventive programs—all of which shared the same goal: the strengthening of an independent black community. Black nationalists such as Stokely Carmichael worked to purge longtime white activists from CORE's leadership. Although McKissick presided over the beginning of these changes, Joycelyn McKissick says her father never favored a blacks-only CORE.

"When he went into CORE the scream of 'Black Power' could be heard everywhere," she points out. "He was determined to keep it an integrated, multiracial organization, and I think he contributed to it staying that way for a long time."

McKissick left CORE in 1968 to form Floyd B. McKissick Enterprises, a consulting firm helping black-owned businesses. In a sense, McKissick had come full circle. He had begun his activist career as a follower of Du Bois, fighting to integrate interstate buses, and had ended up toiling in the fields of black enterprise, Booker T. Washington's domain. But there was really no contradiction in this journey. Like most black American leaders, McKissick was first and last a pragmatist. If whites were willing to live and work with blacks, fine; if they weren't, that was all right, too—blacks could prosper on their own, given a fair chance. His most ambitious project was the creation of Soul City, a wholly new community carved out of one of the poorest counties in rural North Carolina. Designed as a laboratory for black economic and political development, Soul City was planned to accommodate 50,000 residents. But a number of difficulties (including opposition by conservative whites) plagued the ambitious plan, and the community was never established on the grand scale that McKissick envisioned.

In 1990, McKissick fulfilled a lifelong dream when he was appointed as a judge for North Carolina's Ninth Judicial District. He died in April 1991 at his home in Durham at the age of sixty-nine.

LOUIS AUSTIN

Louis Austin died on June 12, 1971, just as the charrette was about to begin. He had published the *Carolina Times* for forty-four years. As he was dying, word spread throughout Hayti that he needed a blood transfusion. Within hours, a line of over sixty people formed at the hospital wanting to donate blood. "None of the uppity-ups came to give blood," recalls his daughter, Vivian Austin Edmonds, pointedly and proudly. "It was the street people."

Edmonds continues to publish the newspaper her father had built into a Durham institution. I asked her how Louis Austin would have responded to the question "What achievement are you most proud of?" She smiled and then, assuming a stern demeanor that was unquestionably her father's, she replied for him: "Pride goeth before the fall."

JOYCE THORPE

Thorpe, the single mother living in Durham public housing who was evicted after being elected head of the first independent tenants' organization (*see* Chapter Eight), sued the Housing Authority. The case was eventually heard by the U.S. Supreme Court, which in 1969 issued an equivocal ruling. As a result of Thorpe's case, however, the Department of Housing and Urban Development issued new regulations stating that public housing residents could not be evicted without cause and could appeal the action. On January 1, 1995, Thorpe was appointed chair of the Durham Housing Authority.

DOUGLAS MOORE

The former Boston University classmate of Martin Luther King, Jr., and leader of the 1957 Royal Ice Cream sit-in resigned his position as pastor of the Asbury Temple Methodist Church at the height of the lunch-counter movement he helped spark. Moore traveled to Africa, where he lived for several years. After returning to the United States, he served as a city councillor in Washington, D.C., where his uncompromising positions made him many friends and numerous adversaries.

Concluding that economics, not politics, held the key to black success in America, Moore started a new career as a corporate gadfly, disrupting stockholders' meetings with pointed questions about racial policies and hiring practices. Later, he became a businessman himself, and in 1991 Moore's energy supply company won a multimillion-dollar contract to sell natural gas to the Washington Gas Light Company—one of the largest contracts ever for a minority-owned business. As a former District politician, the fiery Moore had often been the subject of news stories in *The Washington Post*. He recently told a reporter for that paper, "Doug Moore has gone from the front page of the Metro section to the back of the paper on the financial page and that's exactly where I want to be."

JESSE HELMS

The former editorialist for television station WRAL, Raleigh-Durham, was elected to the U.S. Senate in 1972. From that post, he led the fight against creating a federal holiday to honor Martin Luther King, Jr. Helms was appointed chair of the Senate Foreign Relations Committee in 1995.

Wense Grabarek

Grabarek served as Durham's mayor from 1963 to 1971, and then returned to private practice as a CPA. He lives in Durham.

BIBLIOGRAPHY

Agger, Robert E. *The Rulers and the Ruled: Political Power and Impotence in American Communities*. New York: John Wiley & Sons, 1964.

Aitken, Jonathan. *Nixon: A Life*. Washington, D.C.: Regnery, 1993.

Anderson, Jean B. *Durham County*. Durham: Duke University Press, 1990.

Aptheker, Herbert. *A Documentary History of the Negro People in the United States*. Vol. 1: *From the Colonial Times Through the Civil War*. New York: Citadel Press, 1951.

———. *A Documentary History of the Negro People in the United States*. Vol. 2: *From the Reconstruction to the Founding of the N.A.A.C.P.* New York: Citadel Press, 1951.

———. *A Documentary History of the Negro People in the United States*. Vol. 3: *From the N.A.A.C.P. to the New Deal*. New York: Citadel Press, 1973.

———. *A Documentary History of the Negro People in the United States*. Vol. 4: *From the New Deal to the End of World War II*. New York: Citadel Press, 1974.

———. *A Documentary History of the Negro People in the United States*. Vol. 7: *From the Alabama Protests to the Death of Martin Luther King, Jr.* New York: Citadel Press, 1994.

Baines, Bruce. "Field Report," Congress of Racial Equality Papers, 1944–1968. Martin Luther King, Jr., Center for Nonviolent Social Change, Inc., Atlanta. May 25, 1963.

Bass, Jack, and Jack Nelson. *The Orangeburg Massacre*. Macon, Ga.: Mercer University Press, 1984.

Boyd, Harold Kent. "Louis Austin and the *Carolina Times*." Master's thesis, North Carolina Central University, 1966.

Boyd, William K. *The Story of Durham: City of the New South*. Durham: Duke University Press, 1925.

Branch, Taylor. *Parting the Waters: America in the King Years, 1954–63*. New York: Simon & Schuster, 1988.

Broderick, Francis, and August Meier. *Negro Protest Thought in the Twentieth Century*. Indianapolis: Bobbs-Merrill Company, 1965.

Burgess, M. Elaine. *Negro Leadership in a Southern City*. Chapel Hill: University of North Carolina Press, 1962.

Carey, Gordon. "Freedom Highways," *CORE-lator*, September 1963.

Cary, Jean. "The Forced Merger of Local 208 and Local 176 of the Tobacco Workers International Union at the Liggett & Myers Tobacco Company in Durham, North Carolina." Unpublished research paper, Duke University, 1971.

Cash, W. J. *The Mind of the South*. New York: Doubleday Anchor Books, 1954 (originally published 1941).

Chafe, William H. *Civilities and Civil Rights*. New York: Oxford University Press, 1980.

Chalmers, David M. *Hooded Americanism: The First Century of the Ku Klux Klan 1865–1965*. Garden City, N.Y.: Doubleday & Company, 1965.

"Chapel Hill Oral History Project." Duke University Oral History Program Collection, Manuscript Department, Duke University Library, 1974.

Clayton, Bruce. "No Ordinary History: W. J. Cash's *The Mind of the South*." In *The Mind of the South: Fifty Years Later*, edited by Charles Eagles. Jackson: University Press of Mississippi, 1992.

Cohn, David L. "Durham: The New South." *Atlantic Monthly*, May 1940, 614–19.

Connelly, Thomas L. *Will Campbell and the Soul of the South*. New York: Continuum, 1982.

CORE-lator. Congress of Racial Equality Papers, 1944–1968. Martin Luther King, Jr., Center for Non-violent Social Change, Inc., Atlanta.

Crow, Jeffrey J., Paul D. Escott, and Flora J. Hatley. *A History of African Americans in North Carolina*. Raleigh: Division of Archives and History, North Carolina Department of Cultural Resources, 1992.

Cunningham, James V. *Summary of Notes on Resident Participation in Durham, North Carolina*. Draft. North Carolina Fund Papers, #4710, 1966. Southern Historical Collection, University of North Carolina Library, Chapel Hill.

Du Bois, W. E. B. *The Souls of Black Folk*. Greenwich, Conn.: Fawcett Premier, 1953 (originally published 1903).

———. "The Upbuilding of Black Durham." *The World's Work* 23 (January 1912): 334–38.

Duke, James B. "Politics and Prosperity." *North American Review*, April 9, 1915, 521–29.

Durden, Robert F. *The Dukes of Durham*. Durham: Duke University Press, 1975.

Durham County Summary. Series 4.8, #6, file C-58, undated. Southern Historical Collection, University of North Carolina Library, Chapel Hill.

Forster, Arnold, and Benjamin Epstein. "Report on the Ku Klux Klan." Anti-Defamation League. North Carolina Archives, Department of Justice, Investigations into Subversive Organizations, Box 2, Ku Klux Klan, undated.

Franklin, John H. *The Color Line: Legacy for the Twenty-first Century*. Columbia: University of Missouri Press, 1993.

Frazier, E. Franklin. "Durham: Capital of the Black Middle Class." In *The New Negro*, edited by Alain LeRoy Locke. New York: A. & C. Boni, 1925.

Fuller, Howard. "Transcript of entire statement made by Howard Fuller before Durham City Council Meeting, July 17, 1967." North Carolina Fund Papers, #4710. Southern Historical Collection, University of North Carolina Library, Chapel Hill.

Furgurson, Ernest B. *Hard Right: The Rise of Jesse Helms*. New York: W. W. Norton & Company, 1986.

Hansberry, Lorraine. *A Raisin in the Sun and The Sign in Sidney Brustein's Window*. New York: New American Library, 1987.

Helms, Jesse. *Viewpoint*. WRAL-TV transcripts. North Carolina Collection, University of North Carolina Library, Chapel Hill.

Hodges, Luther. *Businessman in the Statehouse: Six Years as Governor of North Carolina*. Chapel Hill: University of North Carolina Press, 1962.

Howard, Bertie. *The Beginnings of Community Organization in Durham*. August 1968. Unreleased report. North Carolina Fund Papers, #4710. Southern Historical Collection, University of North Carolina Library, Chapel Hill.

——— and Steve Redburn. *United Organizations for Community Improvement: Black Political Power in Durham*. August 1968. Unreleased report. North Carolina Fund Papers, #4710. Southern Historical Collection, University of North Carolina Library, Chapel Hill.

Howard, Chris D. *Keep Your Eyes on the Prize: The Black Struggle for Civic Equality in Durham, North Carolina, 1954–1963*. History honors thesis, Duke University, 1983.

Hurder, Alex. "History of the Hoover Road Housing Project." December 1968. North Carolina Fund Papers, #4710. Southern Historical Collection, University of North Carolina Library, Chapel Hill.

Janiewski, Dolores E. *Sisterhood Denied: Race, Gender, and Class in a New South Community*. Philadelphia: Temple University Press, 1985.

Jones, Beverly W. "Race, Sex, and Class: Black Female Tobacco Workers in Durham, North Carolina, 1920–1940, and the Development of Female Consciousness." *Feminist Studies* 10 (Fall 1984): 441–51.

Karpinos, Ralph. *With All Deliberate Speed: The Brown vs. Board of Education Decisions, North Carolina and the Durham City Schools, 1954–1963*. Unpublished research paper. Duke University, 1972.

Keech, William R. *The Impact of Negro Voting: The Role of the Vote in the Quest for Equality*. Chicago: Rand McNally, 1968.

Key, V. O. *Southern Politics in State and Nation*. New York: Vintage Books, 1949.

Killian, Lewis. *Racial Crisis in America: Leadership in Conflict*. Englewood Cliffs, N.J.: Prentice-Hall, 1964.

King, Martin Luther, Jr. *Why We Can't Wait*. New York: Mentor Books, 1968 (originally published 1964).

Kinkead, Katharine T. "A Reporter at Large: It Doesn't Seem Quick to Me." *New Yorker*, April 15, 1961, 100–32.

Knight, Douglas. *Street of Dreams*. Durham: Duke University Press, 1989.

Korstad, Robert, and Nelson Lichtenstein. "Opportunities Found and Lost: Labor, Radicals, and the Early Civil Rights Movement." *Journal of American History* 75 (December 1988): 786–811.

Kostyu, Joel A., and Frank A. Kostyu. *Durham: A Pictorial History*. Norfolk, Va.: Donning Company, 1978.

Kramer, Reed. "The Durham Housing Problem and Duke University." Duke University Archives, Durham, May 1969.

Lester, Julius. *Hungry Mind Review*, St. Paul, Minn: Fall 1994.

Lewis, David L. *W. E. B. Du Bois: Biography of a Race, 1868–1919*. New York: Henry Holt, 1994.

Lomax, Louis E. *The Negro Revolt*. New York: Harper & Row, 1962.

Low, Augustus, and Virgil Clift. *Encyclopedia of Black America*. New York: Da Capo Press, 1984 (originally published 1981).

Marable, Manning. *How Capitalism Underdeveloped Black America*. Boston: South End Press, 1983.

McMillen, Neil. *The Citizens' Council: Organized Resistance to the Second Reconstruction, 1954–1964*. Urbana: University of Illinois Press, 1971.

Mebane, Mary E. *Mary*. New York: Viking Press, 1981.

Meier, August, and Elliott Rudwick. *CORE: A Study in the Civil Rights Movement, 1942–1968*. New York: Oxford University Press, 1973.

Mellon, James. *Bullwhip Days: The Slaves Remember*. New York: Avon Books, 1988.

Morris, Aldon D. *The Origins of the Civil Rights Movement*. New York: Free Press, 1984.

Morrison, Toni. *Song of Solomon*. New York: Alfred A. Knopf, 1977.

Murray, Pauli. *Proud Shoes*. New York: Harper & Row, 1978.

"News from Klansville." Newsletter. Folder I.B.K.K.K., Box 1, Department of Justice, North Carolina State Archives, Raleigh.

"News from the Rialto," photocopy of letter in author's possession, May 27, 1963.

Newton, Michael, and Judy Newton. *The Ku Klux Klan: An Encyclopedia*. New York: Garland Publishing, 1991.

North Carolina Fund Papers, #4710. Southern Historical Collection, University of North Carolina Library, Chapel Hill.

Parker, Gwendolyn M. *These Same Long Bones*. Boston: Houghton Mifflin Company, 1994.

Patton, Frances G. "The Town Bull Durham Built." *Holiday*, December 1959.

Phelps, Jake. Oral History Project, Special Collections, Duke University.

Piercy, Day. *The Greenberg Housing Controversy: A Case Study in Community Organization*. Unreleased report. August 1968. North Carolina Fund Papers, #4710. Southern Historical Collection, University of North Carolina Library, Chapel Hill.

Porter, Patrick G. "Origins of the American Tobacco Company." *Business History Review*, Spring 1969, 59–76.

Powell, William S. *North Carolina*. Chapel Hill: University of North Carolina Press, 1988 (originally published 1977).

Redburn, Francis Stevens. "Protest and Policy in Durham, North Carolina." Ph.D. dissertation, University of North Carolina, Chapel Hill, 1970.

Redburn, Steve. *United Organizations for Community Improvement: Black Political Power in Durham*. North Carolina Fund Papers, #4710, 1966. Southern Historical Collection, University of North Carolina Library, Chapel Hill.

Reddick, L. D. *Crusader Without Violence: A Biography of Martin Luther King*. New York: Harper & Brothers, 1959.

Rice, David H. "Urban Renewal in Durham: A Case Study of a Referendum." Master's thesis, University of North Carolina, Chapel Hill, 1966.

Roberts, Claudia, Diane Lea, and Robert Leary. *The Durham Architectural and Historic Inventory*. Durham: City of Durham and the Historic Preservation Society of Durham. 1982.

Rustin, Bayard. " 'Black Power' and Coalition Politics." *Commentary*, September 1966, 35–40.

Saunders, Doris. *The Kennedy Years and the Negro*. Chicago: Johnson Publishing Company, 1964.

Seeman, Ernest. *American Gold*. New York: Dial Press, 1978.

Sindler, Allan P. "Youth and the American Negro Protest Movement: A Local Case Study of Durham, North Carolina." Research paper. Duke University Archives, 1965.

Stanton, Bill. *Klanwatch*. New York: Grove Weidenfeld, 1991.

Stone, Ted G. *A Southern City and County in the Years of Political Change: Durham, NC, 1955–1974*. Master's thesis, North Carolina Central University, 1977.

Student Nonviolent Coordinating Committee Papers, 1959–1972. Martin Luther King, Jr., Center for Non-violent Social Change, Inc., Atlanta.

Symonds, Craig L. *Joseph E. Johnston: A Civil War Biography*. New York: W. W. Norton & Company, 1992.

Terkel, Studs. "Make New Sounds." *American Theatre*, November 1984.

Thompson, Edgar T., "The South and the Second Emancipation," in Allan Sindler, *Change in the Contemporary South*, Durham: Duke University Press, 1963, 106.

Time, "Cities: York's Charrette," May 11, 1970.

Trelease, Allen. *White Terror: The Ku Klux Klan Conspiracy and Southern Reconstruction*. New York: Harper & Row, 1971.

U.S. Congress. Senate. Committee on Interstate and Foreign Commerce. *Nomination of Luther Hartwell Hodges to Be Secretary of Commerce*. Hearings. 87th Cong., 1st Sess. Washington, D.C.: U.S. Government Printing Office, 1961.

U.S. President's Commission on Civil Rights. *To Secure These Rights*. Washington, D.C.: U.S. Government Printing Office, 1947.

Van Deburg, William. *New Day in Babylon: The Black Power Movement and American Culture, 1965–1975*. Chicago: University of Chicago Press, 1992.

Wallace, Patricia. "How to Get Out of Hell by Raising It: The Case of Durham, North Carolina." May 1967. North Carolina Fund Papers, #4710. Southern Historical Collection, University of North Carolina Library, Chapel Hill.

Washington, Booker T. "Durham, NC, a City of Negro Enterprises." *Independent* 70 (March 30, 1911): 642–50.

Waynick, Capus M., John C. Brooks, and Elsie W. Pitts, eds. *North Carolina and the Negro*. Raleigh: North Carolina Mayor's Co-operating Committee, 1964.

Weare, Walter B. *Black Business in the New South: A Social History of the North Carolina Mutual Life Insurance Company*. Durham: Duke University Press, 1993 (originally published 1973).

Weisbrot, Robert. *Freedom Bound*. New York: W. W. Norton & Company, 1990.

Wheaton, Elizabeth. *Codename Greenkill: The 1979 Greensboro Killings*. Athens: University of Georgia Press, 1987.

Williams, Juan. *Eyes on the Prize*. New York: Viking Penguin, 1987.

Williamson, Joel. *The Crucible of Race*. New York: Oxford University Press, 1984.

Wilson, Charles R., and William Ferris. *Encyclopedia of Southern Culture*. Chapel Hill: University of North Carolina Press, 1989.

Wolff, Miles. *Lunch at the 5 & 10*. Revised and expanded. Chicago: Elephant Paperbacks, Ivan R. Dee, 1990.

Woodward, C. Vann. *The Strange Career of Jim Crow*. New York: Oxford University Press, 1966 (originally published 1955).

Zinn, Howard, *The Southern Mystique*, New York: Alfred A. Knopf, 1964, 5.

ENDNOTES

EPIGRAPH

PAGE

xi can never be estimated: *Carolina Times*, 31 March 1956.

" it is filled with heroes: Howard Zinn, *The Southern Mystique*, (New York: Alfred A. Knopf, 1964), p. 5.

CHAPTER ONE

PAGE

15 "when they boast": "Letter from the Magnolia, Mississippi, Jail," in Aptheker (1994), p. 95.

16 "that will make Durham great": Crow, p. 128.

17 "like snow before the sun": Symonds, p. 335.

" fighting under such circumstances would be "criminal": Symonds, p. 354.

" signed articles of surrender: Kostyu, p. 29.

" troops in North Carolina, Georgia and Florida: Anderson, p. 125.

" The South's defeat was official: Kostyu, p. 29.

18 sold over five million pounds: Anderson, p. 139.

19 "business temples": Durden, p. 190.

" Jewish cigarette rollers from Poland: Anderson, p. 173.

" running into a stone wall: Boyd (1925), p. 87.

20 or his hated competitors': Durden, p. 59.

" "the Holy Ghost, and my son Buck": Durden, p. 158.

" wouldn't accept machine-rolled cigarettes: Durden, p. 27.

" replacing all hand rollers by 1888: Anderson, p. 175.

" 823 million in 1889: *Ibid*.

21 "seemed appalling to more conservative manufacturers": Porter, pp. 64–65.

" The photographs continued, however: Durden, pp. 60–61.

" "we will make them all consumers": Durden, p. 167.

" charged any other manufacturer: Porter, p. 69.

" the side of the Great Pyramid in Egypt: Durden, p. 18.

" a meeting with his four largest competitors: Durden, p. 48.

22 of the individuals in the room: Porter, p. 71.

" "to keep talking any length of time together": Francis S. Kinney, in Porter, p. 72.

" swallow up 250 smaller firms: Porter, p. 59.

" excepting only cigars: Durden, p. 62.

" makers of Bull Durham: Rice, p. 13.

22 to carve up his tobacco octopus: Porter, p. 76.
"   his giant holding company soon after its creation: Durden, p. 166.
"   the Dukes controlled all major textile mills in the Durham area: Janiewski, p. 74.
23 tobacco workers in Durham by a margin of two to one: Janiewski, p. 57.
"   formed three music schools: Anderson, pp. 283–85.
"   began its rise to the top of the Piedmont League: Anderson, p. 289.
"   "Magic City": Weare, p. 4.
"   "Progress, Success, Health, and Wealth": Anderson, p. 275
24 "sends its radiant beams out upon the world": Weare, p. 27.
"   from a city with its own jealous black elite: Weare, p. 4.
"   "resolve to go to Durham": Weare, pp. 4–5.
"   "friendly feeling between the two races of the South": Washington, p. 642.
"   "of any similar group in the nation": Du Bois (1912), p. 334.
"   "Negro clerks and agents": Washington, p. 642.
25 more than a quarter of a million dollars: Du Bois (1912), p. 335.
"   on Durham's prestigious Parrish Street: Weare, p. 117.
"   "all roads lead to . . . the North Carolina Mutual": Weare, p. 135.
26 in 1859 to a black mother and a white father: Weare, p. 52.
"   to Raleigh for a decent haircut: *Ibid.*
"   from the Royal Knights of King David: Weare, p. 30.
"   the Free Africa Society of the eighteenth century: Weare, p. 5.
"   had been secretary of the Royal Knights since 1883: Weare, p. 20.
"   before managing a black cooperative grocery: Weare, p. 59.
"   "He was strictly business": Weare, pp. 58–59.
27 "Give me a decent burial": Weare, p. 64.
"   "the white man's ice is cooler": Weare, p. 65.
"   charitable and service organizations: Weare, p. 200.
"   "undisputed leader of the black business world": Weare, p. 199.
28 "the character of the Negroes themselves": Boyd (1925), p. 278.
"   "because of his success or failure": Boyd (1925), p. 279.
"   "enterprising ones will either sink or migrate": Du Bois (1912), p. 338.
"   "They have been friendly to their enterprises": Frazier, p. 339.
"   "little public friction between the races": Patton, p. 217.
29 "between white and colored races of the South": Anderson, p. 305.
"   exceptions to the rule of racial comity: *Carolina Times*, 27 October 1962.
"   a region of blue sky and great wandering shadows: Du Bois (1953), p. 16.

CHAPTER TWO

PAGE
31 "completely apart from the rest of us": Aitken, p. 72.
37 toiled as unskilled laborers: Janiewski, p. 94.
"   "adorned with flower beds": Washington, p. 646.
38 "the meanest hut on a graded street": Murray, pp. 26–27.
"   lacking indoor plumbing: Crow, p. 130. A study conducted in the 1920s

found that 80 percent of black residents lived in substandard housing. In 1940, more than 5,000 dwellings in town still lacked indoor toilets; 10,000 had no bathtub.

" dead before the age of forty: Anderson, p. 307. In 1920, the death rate for Durham's white residents stood at 10 per 1,000 annually. For blacks, the figure was nearly 30 per 1,000. The death rate for blacks throughout North Carolina at that time was just 17.4 per 1,000. One of every three babies born to a black mother in Durham died within the first year. Surviving to adulthood was no guarantee of a long life. Where it was common to find black octogenarians in rural North Carolina, it was the exceptional black individual who lived to the age of sixty in Durham.

" the Durham Country Club (with a nine-hole golf course): Anderson, p. 275.

" "righteous rajputs and masters of machinery lived": Seeman, p. 7.

" shielded from the sun by a lace parasol: Kostyu, p. 44.

" "I want the best dog": Anderson, p. 268.

" "Capital of the Black Middle Class": Frazier, p. 339.

39 "has been advertised to death": Weare, p. 259.

" "between the two races of the South": Washington, p. 642.

" "and blacks for whites than ever before": Woodward, p. 96.

" "better than they are elsewhere in the South": Weare, p. 259.

" "they thought he was probably a nice man": Morrison, p. 8.

40 "bitter rivalries for meager advantage": Murray, p. 53.

" "the precarious balance in a household": Murray, p. 90.

41 "whose parents were black working class": Mebane, p. 220.

" "five-dollar bill from the president himself": Weare, p. 186.

" "Parrish Street Gang": Stone, p. 23.

" "sermon about the proletariat": Weare, p. 189.

" "too sporty for White Rock": Weare, p. 191.

42 attempts to "Mutualize" his church: Weare, p. 195.

" "offset this slight difference in rates": Weare, p. 99.

" in the "whites-only" section: Weare, p. 153.

43 "the opportunity to spend a dollar in an opera house": Aptheker (1951), p. 756.

" "ornamental gewgaws": Low, p. 842.

" "it will not be encouraged": Woodward, p. 95.

" "in all things essential to mutual progress": Aptheker (1951), p. 755.

44 "if need be, in defense of yours": *Ibid.*

45 on the ship of a Spanish explorer–slave trader: Crow, p. 1.

" "absolute power and authority over his negro slaves": Crow, p. 2.

" "to render the submission of the slave perfect": Crow, p. 49.

" "didn't go through slavery ain't got no idea what it was": Mellon, p. 290.

" blacks from gathering for any reason: Crow, p. 7.

46 "wrought in legible capital letters the word FREE": *Ibid.*

" "to the hearts and consciences of the people of our State": Crow, p. 78.

" "wiped from the statutes of the State": Crow, pp. 78–79.

" "impractical claims for social and political rights": Crow, p. 79.

" Southern blacks were abandoned by the North: Crow, p. 93.

46 "terror-driven assaults in the annals of modern history": Franklin, p. 6.
47 Thirty blacks were massacred that day: Low, p. 231.
"   "and white men will rule it": Crow, p. 115.
"   "Protect us with your vote": Janiewski, p. 91.
"   out of North Carolina heading for Western states: Crow: p. 93.
"   "Their names was slavery and freedom": *Ibid.*
48 "it was a word fitly spoken": Lewis, p. 175.
"   "the most distinguished Southerner since Jefferson Davis": Du Bois (1953), p. 43.
"   David Levering Lewis has pointed out: Lewis, p. 287.
"   "the evils of Get and Grab": Broderick, p. 55.
"   "the alleged inferiority of the Negro races": Du Bois (1953), p. 48.
49 "disaster to our children, black and white": Du Bois (1953), p. 51.
"   "the rise of the Negro American": Du Bois (1912), p. 334.
"   "black boys need education as well as white boys": Du Bois (1953), p. 51.
"   into speeches before white audiences: Aptheker (1951), p. 650.
"   who preferred loud suits to more conservative clothes: Washington, p. 642.
"   "Negro and all": Anderson, p. 222.
50 "call him a son-of-a-bitch under his breath": Weare, p. 52.
"   "a hatred hidden by fawning": Crow, p. 127.
"   primarily to counter Washington's influence: Broderick, p. xxi.
"   "Tuskegee machine": Low, p. 844.
"   attempt to destroy Du Bois and his movement: Crow, p. 126.
"   "there can be but one ending": Julian S. Carr, quoted in Weare, p. 40.
"   "settling down to development along safe lines": Weare, p. 96.
"   "What difference does it make to us who is elected?": Janiewski, p. 92.
51 "stop thinking we are the whole Republican party": Weare, p. 23.
"   "the opportunities that are open to them": Anderson, pp. 259–60.
"   "don't have a Charlie here, do we, ladies?": Weare, p. 138.
"   the effects of ignorance, crime, and poor work habits: Anderson, p. 430.
52 "following them with tear-dimmed eyes to their graves" Broderick, p. 6.
"   filled the air with patriotic songs: Anderson, p. 294.
"   needed no advice from outsiders: Anderson, p. 430.
53 to defuse a dangerous situation: Anderson, p. 303.
"   to integrate higher education in America: Crow, p. 159.
"   "going back Monday to pursue this cause": Boyd (1966), pp. 50–51.
"   to get "your people" off the street: Weare, pp. 250–51.
"   "heralded all the triumphs to come": Parker, p. 49.
"   "never ruffle the feathers of the oppressors": Crow, p. 150.
"   "things are pretty good for them": Weare, p. 259.
55 "respect and co-operation between the races": Korstad, p. 789.
"   "We feel we are the leaders instead of you": *Ibid.*
"   "But we had them at *our* library": Korstad, p. 791.
"   the largest affiliate in the state: Korstad, p. 792.
56 "he is to be found in the ranks of the labor movement": Korstad, p. 793.
"   "opportunity found and lost": Korstad, p. 786.
"   "a more aggressive leadership is needed": Anderson, pp. 369–70.

ENDNOTES

CHAPTER THREE

PAGE
59 "wealth is the basis of the classification": Duke, p. 521.
61 at the Metropolitan Opera House in New York City: Durden, p. 172.
" $320 for a year of hard labor: Janiewski, p. 111.
" to care for workers and their families: Anderson, p. 246.
" enforcing a 10 P.M. "lights-out" rule: Janiewski, p. 76.
" referred to as "my people": Anderson, p. 315.
" tennis courts and even a small zoo: Anderson, pp. 314–15.
62 "anything near even a living wage": Anderson, p. 316.
" based on the U.S. federal government: Janiewski, p. 76.
" served in this branch of "government": *Ibid.*
" firing the union activist they considered the "ringleader": Anderson, p. 312.
" "mere foam before passing gusts": Cash, p. 247.
  "and leave the city": Janiewski, p. 85.
63 futile attempt to oust the president: Janiewski, p. 86.
" religious movements, including snake handling: Anderson, p. 405.
" "Their world is bizarre": Int., Jack Shelton, 20 January 1992.
64 "shut out from their world by a vast veil": Du Bois (1953), p. 16.
65 "the colored laborer with the white laborer": Woodward, p. 63.
66 quickly attracted more than one million members: Low, p. 694.
" speaking from the same podium: Woodward, p. 64.
" offending white viewers in the South: Branch, p. 322.
" "put every man on his citizenship irrespective of color": Woodward, p. 63.
67 admired and supported by the Ku Klux Klan: Wilson, p. 1201.
" even in separate buildings: Jones, p. 443.
" where they earned low wages: Jones, p. 441.
" "white women over there wore white uniforms": Jones, p. 444.
" "working doing the lighter jobs": *Ibid.*
" "or live in the same town": Marable, p. 14.
" with few exceptions, hired only whites: Janiewski, p. 74.
68 in their relations with blacks: Williamson, pp. 291–95.

CHAPTER FOUR

PAGE
71 "whether of races or classes or creeds": Aptheker (1973), p. 422.
" "accepted by both races as being sound and sensible": Crow, p. 151.
74 "and it cannot be obliterated": Woodward, p. 96.
" The mistake was Couch's: Clayton, p. 20.
75 Richmond, Virginia, and Charleston, South Carolina: Woodward, p. 27.
" including Houston and Mobile: Broderick, p. 24.
" and sat down next to a white man: Anderson, p. 374.
" in front of the rear side door in a nearly empty bus: *Durham Morning Herald*, 1 June 1943.
" violating the Jim Crow law and fined five dollars: *Durham Morning Herald*, 5 June 1943.

75 sitting in the empty front section: *Durham Morning Herald*, 9 July 1944.
76 to find Council not guilty of any crime: *Durham Morning Herald*, 16 September 1944.
77 to sit in the back of the auditorium: Crow, p. 177.
" "with whites on an equal basis": Crow, pp. 177–78.
" "a restlessness which has a healthiness about it": *CORE-lator*, April 1952.
" "quite unfair to the theaters": *Ibid.*
78 for justice at home during wartime: Aptheker (1974), pp. 421–22.
" "how can you carry it to somebody else?": Aptheker (1974), p. 418.
79 "tracked down by the zeitgeist": Lomax, p. 89.
" Truman desegregated the military in 1948: Low, p. 259.
" "Separate educational facilities are inherently unequal": Williams, p. 34.
" "the law had rigidly denied it to them": Crow, p. 81.
80 to keep them racially homogeneous: Anderson, p. 284.
" 45 percent of black children were literate: Crow, p. 154.
" received state money for another thirty years: Crow, pp. 154–55.
" "in this county for the colored school children": Anderson, p. 284.
" attended school than did white children: Crow, p. 135.
" half the wage paid white teachers: Boyd (1966), p. 19.
" and only $21,000 for blacks: *Ibid.*
" one drinking fountain and no cafeteria: Anderson, p. 371.
81 "in a great state like North Carolina": Crow, p. 136.
" the addition was a rare and precious victory: Anderson, p. 367.
" finally admitted five black graduate students: Crow, p. 163.
" "but hurting his cash register": Kinkead, p. 111.
82 "based on race, color, creed, or national origin, from American life": U.S. President's Commission on Civil Rights, p. 166.
" role model for the nation and desegregate its schools ASAP: Branch, p. 113.
" "Thank God we've got good Federal judges": Woodward, p. 153.
" pledging resistance to forced school integration: Wilson, p. 817.
83 to accept desegregation, albeit unhappily: Chafe, p. 71.
" a symbolic "resolution of protest" against *Brown*: Woodward, p. 157.
" "cannot be accomplished and should not be attempted": Crow, p. 167.
" "we do it in a tuxedo and they wear suspenders": Chafe, p. 56.
" dubbed the "Businessman's Governor": U.S. Congress. Senate, p. 2.
84 from the state to local school boards: Crow, p. 168.
" close its public schools rather than desegregate: Stone, p. 33.
" by sixty radio and ten television stations: Hodges, p. 87.
85 "have ever been written or uttered in its behalf": *Carolina Times*, 13 August 1955.
" "and humiliations that go with segregation": *Ibid.*
" ridiculed his plan as a "Hodge-Podge": Stone, p. 31.
" "it will record him as the most stupid": *Carolina Times*, 3 November 1956.
" "would pay . . . for racial hatred": *Carolina Times*, 8 September 1956.
86 leaders expressed "shock and dismay": Howard (1983), p. 19.
" pledging to desegregate community schools: Chafe, p. 16.

" "next week in terms of compliance": Howard (1983), p. 20.

" "courtsuit by courtsuit, into contemporary society": Cunningham, p. 3.

" included two of the board's most ardent segregationists: Howard (1983), p. 21.

87 "in view in your next session": Aptheker (1951), pp. 7–8.

" he enrolled as a divinity student at Boston University: Int., the Reverend Douglas Moore, 12 July 1994.

88 "Just another Baptist preacher": *Ibid.*

" "in North Carolina in less than a year": Branch, p. 260.

" They wouldn't give up nothing": Int., the Reverend Douglas Moore, 12 July 1994.

" sat down in the white section and asked to be served: *Carolina Times*, 20 July 1957.

" "to get some ice cream or milk shakes": *Durham Sun*, 24 June 1957.

" all the way to the U.S. Supreme Court: Keech, p. 84.

89 opposed Moore's "radical" efforts: Howard (1983), p. 26.

" and, above all, civil manner: Chafe, p. 8.

" as long as they went in small groups: Howard (1983), p. 25.

90 "recoil from performing our solemn duty": *Carolina Times*, 15 June 1957.

91 "I don't approve of using children to do men's work": Reddick, p. 153.

" a "first-rate rabble-rouser": Branch, p. 217.

" "would ever get to the heart of the issue": Louis Lomax in Aptheker (1994), p. 55.

92 "my baptism in nonviolence": *New York Times*, 30 April 1991.

" (who became a family friend): Int., Joycelyn McKissick, 20 June 1994.

" the black Boy Scout troop which McKissick headed: Morris, p. 198.

" with Durham's older black leaders: According to McKissick's daughter Joycelyn, "Daddy knew C. C. Spaulding and respected him. I think C. C. Spaulding and Daddy had a kind of `hands off' policy. You do what you have to do and I'll do what I have to, and we won't know each other personally. He respected C.C. very, very much." Int., Joycelyn McKissick, 20 June 1994.

" as well as one for high school students: Howard (1983), p. 31.

93 "So make sure you're correct": Int., Joycelyn McKissick, 20 June 1994.

" "Nigger, Nigger, Nigger": *Ibid.*

" "Does Durham have less courage?": Kinkead, p. 102.

" "I should have been above that": Int., Joycelyn McKissick, 20 June 1994.

" first year of token integration: *Ibid.*

94 "they are changed by more concrete action": Howard (1983): p. 32.

CHAPTER FIVE

PAGE

95 "I'd like a cup of coffee, please": Wolff, p. 11.

" "on any prey that is weak and wounded": *Durham Sun*, 2 February 1960.

96 trembling in his dorm room: This and other details of the lunch-counter sit-in are from int., Jibreel Khazan (Ezell Blair, Jr.), 10 August 1994.

98 the waiter at the lunch counter in the bus station had refused to serve him: Raleigh *News & Observer*, 28 January 1990.

" "We don't serve Negroes here": Wolff, p. 11.

99 "That's why we can't get anywhere today": Wolff, p. 12.

" "the epitome of what we were fighting": Raleigh *News & Observer*, 28 January 1990.

" "We ought to do that here": Int., Callis Brown, 17 October 1994.

" "Oh my God, these kids have jumped the gun!": Int., Joycelyn McKissick, 20 June 1994.

" "would not want the publicity attendant to a long boycott": Wolff, p. 84.

100 and to coordinate plans to spread the sit-in: Branch, p. 273.

" to pass the word along to other black schools: Howard (1983), p. 31.

" "vicious practice of which they are the victims": *Carolina Times*, 6 February 1960.

" to an address on Durham's North Side: Morris, p. 200.

101 A CORE activist since 1951: Meier, p. 80.

" in Miami in April of that same year: Meier, p. 91.

102 had refused to reveal his occupation: *Durham Morning Herald*, 8 February 1960.

" local civil rights and religious organizations: *Durham Morning Herald*, 9 February 1960.

" their battle against segregated lunch counters: Morris, p. 198.

103 "such as the one that has prevailed since 1900": *Harper's*, June 1960.

" "broken the back of professional Uncle Tomism": Wolff, p. 161.

" students in Charlotte closed down eight lunch counters: *Durham Morning Herald*, 10 February 1960.

" to Chattanooga and Nashville, Tennessee, and Richmond, Virginia: *Carolina Times*, 27 February 1960.

" "You must tell Martin that we must get with this": Branch, p. 273.

" to put his blessing on the lunch-counter movement: *Durham Morning Herald*, 8 July 1990.

104 spilling outside onto the dew-soaked church lawn: *Carolina Times*, 20 February 1960.

" introduced King to the adoring crowd: *Ibid*.

" "destined to be one of the glowing epics of out time":*Ibid*

" "Fill up the jails" was King's new battle cry: Branch, p. 276.

105 "America is my home": *Carolina Times*, 20 February 1960.

" DeShazor's Beauty School and even Hillside High School: Sindler, p. 25.

" busy with exams or out of town on vacations: Kinkead, p. 108.

" "Peace without justice and equal opportunity is no Peace": *Carolina Times*, 27 February 1960.

" "at the movement churches rather than on the campuses": Morris, p. 200.

106 "very much like a church inside": Howard (1983), p. 67.

" at a country club for those of Durham's black elite: Anderson, p. 372.

" whom they deemed too accommodationist: Anderson, p. 432.

" black students integrating Durham's public schools: Anderson, p. 433.

" "In conclusion, we commend these students": *Carolina Times*, 20 February 1960.

107 to feed protesters returning from duty on the picket lines: Howard (1983), p. 36.
    " "and, you might say, personal lives already": Wolff, p. 115.
    " "behave himself and show he's a good citizen": *Ibid*.
    " "when he needs a nurse": *Carolina Times*, 25 June 1960.
    " "in a breakdown of law and order": Wolff, p. 114.
    " the Royal Ice Cream case as a precedent: *Durham Morning Herald*, 10 February 1960.
108 "it is unlikely that civic unity is being served": *Durham Sun*, 9 February 1960.
    " "racial issues ought to be resolved in good will": *Durham Morning Herald*, 10 February 1960.
    " hot soup spilled in their laps: Kinkead, p. 112.
    " chewing tobacco into a protester's face: Raleigh *News & Observer*, 28 January 1990.
    " by a group of white hoodlums at Walgreen's: *Carolina Times*, 7 May 1960.
    " tried to run down a group of picketers: Kinkead, p. 112.
    " "three cops just stomped me in the stomach": Int., Joycelyn McKissick, 20 June 1994.
109 "After all, who's got the bullets?": Int., Callis Brown, 17 October 1994.
    " study and prayer sessions that often lasted all night: Howard (1983), p. 51.
    " "You are on a mission of destiny": *Carolina Times*, 7 May 1960.
    " "the wherewithal to pay for goods and services": King, p. 136.
110 "they could all afford a nickel bar of soap": Branch, p. 230.

CHAPTER SIX

PAGE
111 "and often they need both": Williamson, p. 151.
    " THIS GENERATION WILL NOT TOLERATE SEGREGATION: Kinkead, pp. 125–26.
    " "and I'm ordering you to leave": *CORE-lator*, November 1962.
112 "by fusing into the white": Furgurson, p. 221.
118 the civil rights movement as nothing more than "anarchy": Furgurson, p. 213.
    " "agitators, opportunistic charlatans, and political phonies": Furgurson, p. 78.
    " socialized medicine was a Trojan horse for the Communists: Furgurson, p. 74.
    " a forum for advancing Red ambitions: *Ibid*.
    " "can be labeled and proved as Communists and sex perverts": Furgur"son, p. 78.
    " of the state's financial community, *The Tarheel Banker*: Wilson, p. 1188.
    " "men whose economic desires were in fact wholly the opposite": Furgurson, p. 72.
    " "is an *internal breakdown* in this country": Helms, 29 November 1961.
121 "God give us men!": *Kloran*, United Klans of America, Inc., Knights of the Ku Klux Klan, 1968, p. 10.

CHAPTER SEVEN

PAGE
125 "rest and peace compared to the South": Trelease, p. 210.
" pranks and good-natured tricks on each other: Trelease, p. 3.
" had made political alliances with the Republicans: Trelease, p. 10; Powell, pp. 154–55; Crow, pp. 154–55.
" a prominent state senator inside his county courthouse: Powell, p. 157.
" to floggings, to outright murder: Trelease, p. 189.
" finishing off one of the children by stomping him to death: Trelease, p. 192.
126 the Klan's new "political and pernicious" agenda: Trelease, p. 6.
" "the sooner such [an] organization is dissolved the better": *Ibid.*
" torched property belonging to their victimizers: Trelease, p. xix.
" "Like you did the other day": Crow, p. 67.
" who were all from the higher social classes: Williamson, p. 295.
127 "protect [their] families from the darkies": Trelease, p. 200.
" "better handled . . . open and above-board": Janiewski, p. 92.
" "in a lasting order with itself at the top": Williamson, p. 295.
128 most of them Catholics and Jews: Wilson, p. 1508.
" was introduced by Mayor John M. Manning: Anderson, p. 304.
" Henry A. Grady, a respected Superior Court judge: Chalmers, p. 92.
" and many more sympathizers: Newton, p. 431.
" "performed its task quietly and in a well organized manner": *Durham Morning Herald*, 8 July 1920.
" the crime for which he was killed: *Durham Morning Herald*, 11 July 1920.
" "the Klan had about gained political control of the state": Chalmers, p. 87.
" from his plush offices in Indianapolis: Chalmers, p. 163.
129 sent to jail for their night-riding activities: Newton, pp. 431–32.
" "a revived frankenstein, the Ku Klux Klan": *Carolina Times*, 3 November 1956.
130 "or what has become in our time "moderation": *Carolina Times*, 27 October 1956.
131 "the bedroom door of our white women to Negro men": Williams, p. 38.
" *Brown* v. *Board* decision as "socialistic": McMillen, p. 17.
" "and fall like Rome of old": McMillen, p. 243.
" with the Soviet hammer-and-sickle emblem: McMillen, illustrations.
" "shocking sexual activities and general depravity": Furgurson, p. 214.
" a staple feature in the organization's national magazine: Furgurson, p. 84.
132 "aggressive aristocracy": Key, pp. 211–23.
" and accepted black undergraduates the following year: Anderson, p. 437.
133 "I do not attend segregated movies. DO YOU?": Kinkead, p. 107.
" it was called the "buzzards' roost": *Ibid.*
" and lined up at the white ticket window: Phelps, #7, pp. 2-3.
" "segregation tomorrow, segregation forever": Woodward, p. 176.
" persuading white businesses to hire more blacks: Crow, p. 203.
" had little effect on job opportunities for blacks: Crow, p. 204.
" for positions other than custodial work: Howard (1983), p. 77.
" a boycott of goods made by slave labor: Aptheker (1951), p. 133.

134 larger NAACP campaign that included six Southeastern states: *Carolina Times*, 3 December 1960.
 " "where they are not treated with dignity": *Ibid.*
 " Ministerial Alliance refused to sponsor the measure: Howard (1983), p. 68.
 " letters about the boycott in the first week of March: Durham CORE chapter report, 9 March 1963, CORE papers.
 " to inform black shoppers: Howard (1983), p. 78.
 " secretly driving protesters to and from picket duty: Howard (1983), p. 60.
 " to back the effort: Howard (1983), p. 78.
 " students and other activists on the picket lines: *Ibid.*
135 "they should be counted out": *Carolina Times*, 20 April 1963.
 " "That was for public consumption": Int., Vivian Edmonds, 5 December 1994.
 " "have always had to play in order to survive": *Ibid.*
 " to host the event, but then backed out: Int., Joycelyn McKissick, 20 June 1994.
 " wasn't the proper place for the Nation of Islam minister to speak: *Ibid.*
 " that location was "unavailable": Howard (1983), p. 85.
136 "or a Malcolm Z": *Carolina Times*, 27 April 1963.
 " "We're supposed to be debating each other": Int., Joycelyn McKissick, 20 June 1994.
 " the school had banned Malcolm from the campus: *Ibid.*
 " "the Muslims desire separation of the races": *Carolina Times*, 27 April 1963.
137 they backed Malcolm all the way: Anvil, 15 March 1969.
 " peeling one off to pay the tab: *Ibid.*
 " to integrate the city's lunch counters and other facilities: Williams, p. 186.
 " Connor unleashed a furious preemptive strike: Williams, p. 190.
138 in the form of 500 state troopers: Williams, p. 191.
 " shrimp Newburg, and petits fours: *Durham Sun*, 11 May 1963.
 " "a glittering formal ball": *Durham Morning Herald*, 11 May 1963.
 " from Puccini's opera *Madam Butterfly*: *Durham Sun*, 11 May 1963.
 " the crowd booed him back inside: *Durham Morning Herald*, 11 May 1963.
 " half of the all-black East End Elementary School: Howard (1983), p. 87.
 " before the first Birmingham children's march: *Ibid.*
 " "an unbecoming and uncooperative spirit": *Durham Morning Herald*, 3 May 1963.
139 a courtesy Carr did not extend: Howard (1983), p. 102.
 " have an open mind and an open heart: Howard (1983), p. 104.
 " demonstration for election day, Saturday, May 18: Sindler, p. 36.
 " went ahead with the demonstration: Sindler, p. 40.
 " "VOTE TO MAKE DEMOCRACY MORE THAN A WORD": *Durham Morning Herald*, 19 May 1963.
 " were arrested and marched off to jail: *Ibid.*
140 slim margin of victory with their 2,418 votes: Howard (1983), p. 108.
 " Evans had left town earlier that day: *Ibid.*

140 that would have cost the city a million dollars: Howard (1983), p. 101.
  " struck some as formal and others as pompous: Howard and Redburn, p. 4.
  " wearing a red carnation in his lapel at all times: Anderson, p. 439.
  " endorsement of the Durham student protests: Howard (1983), p. 109.
141 had been arrested in the previous week: Meier, p. 217.
  " shouts of "Amen" punctuated Farmer's address: Howard (1983), p. 110.
  " which made him vulnerable to charges of discrimination: Howard (1983), p. 111.
  " more conservative blacks would tip off the authorities: Howard (1983), p. 110.
142 "eat at Howard Johnson's one of these days": Durham Morning Herald, 20 May 1963.
  " several hours to carry 700 protesters to jail: Ibid.
  " throwing firecrackers into the ranks of protesters: Howard (1983), p. 113.
  " from turning into a full-scale race riot: Howard (1983), p. 114.
  " thirty straight days of similar demonstrations: Waynick, p. 64.
  " "a powder keg": Durham Sun, 20 May 1963.
  " in his stiff speech, were negotiable: Sindler, p. 42.
143 theater had its first desegregated screening: "News from the Rialto."
  " when ordered to by the manager: Durham Morning Herald, 21 May 1963.
  " "the architects of chaos and disorder": Helms, 22 May 1963, p. 1.
  " "cheering on the agitators": Helms, 22 May 1963, p. 2.
  " voted to maintain its policy of segregation: Howard (1983), p. 114.
144 "then we will succeed": Durham Morning Herald, 21 May 1963.
  " and hurling the fruit at blacks: Howard (1983), p. 119.
  " turned around and headed quickly back downtown: Howard (1983), p. 120.
145 "encourage" the local franchise to desegregate: New York Times: 22 May 1963.
  " " mass demonstrations will not resume at any time": Durham Morning Herald, 9 June 1963.
  " Floyd McKissick, then a third-year law student: Phelps, #7.
  " agreed to attend the meeting: Howard (1983), p. 121.
146 and a unique multicolored ceiling of pressed tin: Roberts, p. 120.
  " "the seriousness and sincerity" of black resolve: Howard (1983), pp. 122–23.
  " reported back that the restaurants were indeed desegregated: Howard (1983), p. 122.
147 Rape's presence on the committee was the key to success: Howard (1983), p. 127.
  " whatever was necessary to end segregation: Howard (1983), p. 129.
  " "employ help without regard to race": Durham Morning Herald, 2 June 1963.
  " promising to follow suit: Carolina Times, 22 June 1963.
  " public swimming pool had also desegregated: Durham Morning Herald, 9 June 1963.
148 or the federal government would do it for them: Washington Post, 28 May 1968.

" to outlaw segregation in public places: Saunders, pp. 110–14.
" "discrimination furnishes grist for the Communist propaganda mills": Woodward, p. 132.
" added to the United Nations roster in just three months in 1960: Williams, inside back and front covers.
" for desegregating two city junior high schools in May: *Durham Morning Herald*, 9 June 1963.
" the practice of segregation in public education: Howard (1983), p. 148.
" targeting the recently desegregated businesses: *Durham Morning Herald*, 30 July 1963.
" Roy Harris, president of the national organization: *Carolina Times*, 3 August 1963.
149 "as a thief in the night to destroy local government": *Duke Chronicle*, 22 October 1963.
" "a spawning ground for Communism, the nation needs to know it": Helms, 1 August 1963, p. 2. The FBI had been illegally investigating these organizations for years without uncovering any such Communist conspiracies.
" "acceptable to all parties concerned": *Durham Morning Herald*, 9 June 1963.
150 "that's the easiest way to avoid giving it to them": *Anvil*, 10 August 1968.
" "mature facing of problems of human relations": *Durham Morning Herald*, 9 June 1963.
151 "some of the nation's most squalid housing": Cunningham, p. 9.
" "ran out of goals and then ran out of gas": Cunningham, p. 2.

CHAPTER EIGHT

PAGE
153 "It just doesn't work": Hurder, p. 25.
156 "North Carolina is *moving*!": Wallace, p. 2.
" to wear raincoats *inside* during bad weather: Wallace, p. 3.
" they considered him "not really black": Int., Howard Fuller, 20 September 1994.
157 he had forgotten how to dance: Howard (1968), p. 6.
" "just the right color brown to fill a job slot": Wallace, p. 2.
" "I wonder what will be the outcome? Who knows?": Aptheker (1951), p. 753.
158 to serve as a delegate to the Democratic County Convention: Anderson, p. 373.
159 "they weren't telling me anything": Wallace, p. 2.
" "deteriorating economic position of White or Negro labor": Agger, p. 352.
" "poverty was a punishment for sins": Agger, p. 353.
" members of a ruling "inner clique": Agger, p. 352.
" blacks to be genetically inferior to whites: Agger, p. 354.
" "and above all short on leadership": *Durham Sun*, 27 July 1967.
" only 800 earned over $3,000 a year: Howard (1968), p. 9.

160 "cycle of poverty lies within the community": Howard (1968), p. 5.
" "for self-help that might be offered him": Cunningham, p. 3-4.
" dedicated to empowerment and self-help: Howard (1968), p. 1.
161 the entire enterprise to blow up in his face: Howard (1968), p. 8.
" "to keep . . . doing . . . these . . . things": Int., Howard Fuller, 20 September 1994.
" encouraging the listeners to call out agreement for his words: *Ibid.*
162 that summer responded, "housing": Wallace, p. 5.
" lived in substandard housing: Crow, p. 130.
" in the Hayti area four decades later: *Durham County Summary*, p. 2.
163 "might seriously destroy or curtail their earnings": Anderson, p. 372.
" which oversaw housing issues: Piercy, p. 7.
" "family has extensive real estate interests in Durham": John Strange in Kramer, p. 29.
" "urban removal": Anderson, p. 409.
164 achieving this same exclusionary end: Low, p. 446.
" overturned this method of discrimination in 1948: Low, p. 447.
" "to live where your children would have playmates": *Anvil*, 10 February 1968.
" "You must keep up your home as well as he does": Helms, 30 August 1963, p. 2.
165 "evidence of natural racial distinctions in group intellect": Furgurson, p. 217.
" *"and to those submitting to racism"*: Hansberry, pp. 19–20.
166 "in one of the communities where the Youngers are going!" Terkel, p. 8.
" improvements to the dilapidated houses: Piercy, p. 8.
" by a whopping 25 percent in some cases: Piercy, p. 1.
" "made worth what you are charging": Piercy, p. 2.
167 "which are then allowed to deteriorate": Piercy, p. 3.
" high rents and summary evictions: This and other information about the origins of Operation Breakthrough are from Howard (1968).
169 "then we were really serious about what we were doin'": Wallace, p. 6.
" residents became disheartened: Redburn, p. 82.
170 Durham's turn-of-the-century White Supremacy Club: Int., Victor S. Bryant III, 27 July 1994.
" "get the children started in the right direction": *Ibid.*
" "approached things more on a racial basis": *Ibid.*
" "duplicated services of the other agencies": Cunningham, p. 6.
" "was a large problem within the organization": Int., Howard Fuller, 20 September 1994.
" "substandard property in the Edgemont area": Piercy, p. 20.
" "how could you have the enemy on the board?": Int., Howard Fuller, 20 September 1994.
" one less hamstrung by federal and local bureaucracies: *Ibid.*
171 "so much like a depressed backward country": Cunningham, p. 12.
" "something for you, for your dignity; it tells the truth": *Ibid.*

172 "federal intrusion" into Durham's affairs: Cunningham, p. 5.
" "The Future is in these young people": Cunningham, p. 7.
" "in subtle ways to defeat the cause": Boyd (1966), p. 51–52.
" "in their present economic and political straits": "Background Considerations for a Project in North Carolina," 30 May 1965, Student Nonviolent Coordinating Committee Papers.
173 when he had visited Durham back in 1910: Washington, p. 649.
" "likely come under similar pressure": Kramer, pp. 29–30.
" "since the last Cabinet meeting": Weare, p. 282.
174 "a colored man can't even get a loan up there anymore": Weare, p. 267.
" "is rushing to Fuller's bandwagon": Cunningham, p. 9.
" "many of the citizens of Durham are forced to live": Redburn (1970), p. 109.
175 "GREENBERG, MY HOUSE DOESN'T HAVE SCREENS": Piercy, p. 10.
" "CHILDREN SLEEP WITH RATS, MRS. GREENBERG": Piercy, p. 17.
176 "in undertaking to correct undesirable conditions": *Durham Morning Herald*, 26 June 1966.
" "then that's it": Piercy, p. 20.
177 "partisan fishing expedition": Piercy, p. 24.
" "black, polka dot or tweed who tries to keep you down": Wallace, p. 1.
178 "thought-control center for the Negro population of America": Helms, 25 September 1964, p. 1.
179 "a down-home lawyer who sounded black": Meier, p. 407.
" "more devoted to 'order' than to justice": King, p. 84.
" "We shall overrun": Weisbrot, p. 197.
180 "the Italians did it, why can't we?": Weisbrot, p. 201.
" "the ineffectiveness of the nonviolent movement": Crow, p. 207.
" "the term 'black power' means anti-white power": Weisbrot, p. 205.
" "Booker T. Washington and W. E. B. Du Bois": Rustin, p. 35.
" "they have deliberately tried to do to America": Helms, 4 August 1966, pp. 1–2.
" "Antipoverty Worker Urges Promotion of Black Power," Raleigh *News & Observer*, 1 August 1966.
181 "itself is certain to come to no good end": *Carolina Times*, 29 July 1967.
" insufficient manpower to get the job done: Piercy, p. 34.
" "in a desperate position and we will act accordingly": Piercy, p. 36.
" they would silently file out of the chamber: Piercy, pp. 40–41.
182 and skipped to other matters: Piercy, p. 41.
" "away from their leaking-roofed houses on this rainy night": Piercy, p. 42.
" many people simply drifted away from the ECC: Kramer, p. 24.
183 "won't tolerate further ghettoization": Memorandum, Wallace, 1968, p. 2, North Carolina Fund Papers.
184 "knows more than most bureaucrats in Washington": File, Ann Atwater, Series 4.8, #6, North Carolina Fund Papers.
" "in terms of problems with public and private housing": "U.O.C.I.," Pat Wallace, p. 10, North Carolina Fund Papers.

CHAPTER NINE

187 "do nothing, say nothing": Burgess, p. 22.

188 "I will not get the bloc vote!": Keech, p. 103.

" "or accept approval by the NAACP": Wolff, p. 147.

189 "personable," "easy to talk to" and a "go-getter: Raleigh *News & Observer*, 24 October 1965.

" "most active Klan state" in the country: Raleigh *News & Observer*, 24 October 1965.

" "the best run state organization": Forster and Epstein, p. 8.

" 112 Klaverns spread throughout the Tarheel state: Raleigh *News & Observer*, 24 October 1965.

" estimated 8,000 to 9,000 members: Forster and Epstein, p. 8.

190 "people in North Carolina are a bunch of joiners": Raleigh *News & Observer*, 24 October 1965.

" "BLOOD BANKS PEDDLE CONTAMINATED NEGRO BLOOD": "News from Klansville," 16 November 1967.

191 "and run the nigger off with a shotgun": Undated document in author's possession.

192 "not raised under a Communist, socialist society": Letter, Department of Justice, KKK, Box 2, Folder I. D. KKK:3 & 4, miscellaneous, North Carolina Archives.

193 Duke Forest, just outside of town: *Durham Morning Herald*, 27 April 1967.

" area in question, showed up that night: Kramer, p. 25.

194 "erected at the location on Bacon Street": *Anvil*, 21 July 1967.

" "We do not want any more projects in this area": *Anvil*, 18 August 1967.

" "turnin' down everything that will benefit Negroes": Fuller, p. 2.

195 "do things they wouldn't ordinarily do": Fuller, p. 3.

" "Right here in Durham will be another Vietnam": Redburn, p. 95.

" "Another 'Newark' Threatened Here": *Durham Morning Herald*, 18 July 1967.

" "We want action and we want it now": *Anvil*, 21 July 1967.

196 "the major and more complex problems": Memorandum, Dewitt Sullivan, 24 July 1967, p. 2, North Carolina Fund Papers.

" avoid inflammatory rhetoric: "Narrative of the events of Wednesday, Thursday, & Friday, July 19, 20, & 21 [1967]," Nathan Garrette, North Carolina Fund Papers.

197 "Let's go downtown and finish this meeting": Memorandum, Dewitt Sullivan, 24 July 1967, p. 3, North Carolina Fund Papers.

" "for all parties interested in public housing": *Durham Sun*, 20 July 1967.

198 "the voices of the poor whom we represent," Redburn, p. 97.

" "there would have been no march": Memorandum, Dewitt Sullivan, 24 July 1967, p. 3, North Carolina Fund Papers.

199 opening a large gash above his right eye: *Durham Morning Herald*, 21 July 1967.

" the young men to return to the rally: "Narrative of the events of Wednesday, Thursday, & Friday, July 19, 20, & 21 [1967]," Nathan Garrette, North Carolina Fund Papers.

CHAPTER TEN

PAGE

201 "they are the silent ones, the forgotten": *Anvil*, 10 February 1968.

202 "in all the brushfires last summer in Durham": *Anvil*, 4 November 1967.

" "responsible for any such tensions": *Ibid.*

203 1958 dynamiting of a Birmingham, Alabama, church: Stanton, p. 5.

204 "roofing tacks distributed upon all super highways": Knights of the Ku Klux Klan, SBI Reports, 1967, General Correspondence, Papers of Governor Dan Moore, North Carolina State Archives.

" "use bad language in the house if my wife's at home": Int., Joseph Butler, 14 July 1994.

206 Ponderosa Pistol Club, Hunters Club, Saddle Club: General Correspondence, 1966, Box 149-150, Papers of Governor Dan Moore, North Carolina State Archives.

" Lee County Improvement Association, Fine Fellows Club: Greensboro *Daily News*, 21 October 1964.

207 "scare the pants off the Mayor and leading businessmen": Cunningham, p. 9.

" " into a fiery jungle of violent lawlessness": Furgurson, p. 214.

" "the problem of the color-line": Du Bois (1953), p. 23.

" "ignorance and disease of the majority of their fellowmen": Du Bois (1953), p. 14.

208 "the most sinister political apparatus in our country": Aptheker (1994), p. 163.

" "There is a definite agitating element": *Durham Morning Herald*, 23 July 1967.

" "if problems . . . are not faced directly": *Durham Morning Herald*, 19 July 1967.

209 "and attempted to demand their rights": *Carolina Times*, 29 July 1967.

" "there would have been a leaderless mob": Letter to OEO Director Sargent Shriver, 25 June 1967, Series 4.8, #6, North Carolina Fund Papers.

" "a reminder of its ills until they are cured": Anderson, p. 443.

210 "shall not aid you in the preservation of peace": Redburn, p. 136.

" citing "fiercer than usual" opposition: Redburn, p. 137.

211 "as the councils formed by Operation Breakthrough": Cunningham, p. 7.

212 the manager "happened into" the apartment: *Carolina Times*, 16 November 1968.

" She died within hours: *Ibid.*

" "the despair of the tenants . . . is justified": *Ibid.*

" "Mr. Smooth-it-over": Cunningham, p. 9.

213 "sitting on a veritable powder keg": *Carolina Times*, 16 December 1967.

214 the date on which the black leader would be killed: Int., Howard Fuller, 20 September 1994.

215 such as grooming and good hygiene: Redburn, p.141.

" "Negroes who have jobs paying much less": *Anvil*, 23 March 1968.

" "They token us to death": *Ibid.*

215 "food is an important matter": *Carolina Times*, 24 October 1953.
" growing in size and intensity over the next few days: This and other details of the Orangeburg massacre are from Bass and Nelson, pp. 65–77.
217 "caused the violence and disorder": This and other details of the incident are from *Anvil*, 24 February 1968.
219 "equally for all people in the community": *Anvil*, 2 March 1968.
" "He has a proclivity for vexation": *Anvil*, 9 March 1968.
" "by the way they respond to [black] grievances": *Anvil*, 24 February 1968.
220 "less and less possible because they won't do anything": *Ibid.*
" voted to cancel the event altogether: Redburn, p. 142.
" "effective communication": Redburn, p. 143.

CHAPTER ELEVEN

PAGE
221 "broods fear": Du Bois (1953), p. 41.
222 "ring leader": *Durham Morning Herald*, 2 April 1968.
" "fellow traveller with known communists": Helms, 4 January 1968, p. 1.
" "spreading throughout the land": Furgurson, p. 214.
" "the threat of violence": Helms, 4 January 1968, p. 1.
" "non-violence is on trial": *Durham Morning Herald*, 5 April 1968.
223 "not able to think clearly": *Ibid.*
" "people were going to get killed": Int., Howard Fuller, 20 September 1994.
" the house in which Powell slept: *Ibid.*
225 "difficult time for our nation": *Durham Sun*, 5 April 1968.
" "terrible tension at Memphis": Helms, 5 April 1968, p. 1.
" "he provoked it": *Ibid.*
" "the murder of Dr. King": Helms, 5 April 1968, p. 2.
" pass through checkpoints: *Durham Morning Herald*, 7 April 1968.
226 "to love and serve humanity": *Durham Sun*, 9 April 1968.
" the back of the local graveyard: *Ibid.*
" rousing chorus of "Dixie": *Durham Morning Herald*, 10 April 1968.
" no injuries were reported: *Durham Morning Herald*, 8 April 1968.
227 to await a substantive reply: *Anvil*, 13 April 1968.
" forced Knight to resign: Knight, p. 140.
" "beer, basketball games and studying": *Duke Chronicle*, 29 April 1968.
228 "fine building like at Duke": Janiewski, p. 83.
" "for the employees at Duke": *Duke Chronicle*, 29 April 1968.
" "fullest sympathy and support": *Ibid.*
" "all should emulate": *Ibid.*
" Negro community at a crucial hour: *Ibid.*
229 "to attack these problems": *Ibid.*
" diatribes against Jim Crow: Aitken, p. 72.
" anti-integrationist "Southern strategy": Wilson, p. 1197.
" "coalition among themselves": *Anvil*, 24 February 1968.
" when Knight "felt better": *Anvil*, 13 April 1968.
" "wrought a revolution": *Duke Chronicle*, 29 April 1968.
" "you have been overcome": *Anvil*, 13 April 1968.

" "I'll say it was a victory": *Duke Chronicle*, 29 April 1968.

230 "blacks can never quit": *Ibid.*

" "mock hearing" concerning grievances: *Durham Morning Herald*, 7 May 1968.

" involving DHA property: Redburn, pp. 149–51.

231 "it has failed to act": *Durham Morning Herald*, 2 July 1968.

" segregationist Charles Steel: *Anvil*, 10 August 1968.

" list of eighty-eight demands: Redburn, p. 162.

" of all of Durham's ills: Redburn, p. 180.

232 "for whites only": *Carolina Times*, 23 November 1968.

" "like a prayer meeting band": *Carolina Times*, 24 August 1968.

" "suffered more violence than Durham": *Durham Morning Herald*, 4 September 1968.

" "meeting last Tuesday night": *Carolina Times*, 7 September 1968.

233 tossed by a black Santa Claus: Redburn, pp. 182–183.

234 "have what they want?": *Anvil*, 10 August 1968.

" "this town without fighting": *Carolina Times*, 23 November 1968.

" "could not support the boycott": *Carolina Times*, 21 December 1968.

" around a million dollars: Redburn, p. 166.

235 "more or less the way it goes": File: Ann Atwater, Series 4.8, #6, North Carolina Fund Papers.

" "preserving its current status": Redburn, p. 203.

236 last place in the nation: *Anvil*, 2 May 1967.

" "economic exploitation of another": Edward McConville, "The Prophetic Voice of C. P. Ellis," *The Nation*, 15 October 1973, p. 365.

" Joseph Butler: Int., 14 July 1994.

238 Joseph High . . . county sheriff, Marvin Davis: Int., Joseph Butler, 14 July 1994; int., C. P. Ellis, 31 July 1994.

239 before the police stepped in: Weisbrot, p. 289.

241 bullets dipped into wet sand" Int., C. P. Ellis, 7 December 1993.

" "try and get him off": Int., E. Carter Harris, 27 July 1994.

242 found C.P. not guilty: "State of North Carolina vs. Claiborne Paul Ellis," File #70-C R-16626, Superior Court Records.

" "if they were identified": Trelease, p. 201.

CHAPTER TWELVE

PAGE

245 because they fought each other: Aptheker (1994), p. 106.

246 only 9,000 students: *Durham Morning Herald*, 13 May 1984.

247 "view of the local communities": *Durham Morning Herald* (undated), August 1970.

" to help schools in this effort: *Durham Morning Herald*, 13 May 1971.

248 "undermined the process": Int., Bill Riddick, 22 June 1994.

250 "their use in his community!": *Time.*

253 "would give some answers": *Durham Morning Herald*, 21 May 1971.

" "on the part of white people": Crow, p. 123.

" "Right on, brother Ellis": Int., Howard Clement III, 20 June 1994.

254 "before and changed my mind": *Durham Morning Herald*, 21 May 1971.
  " "what you're talking about": *Ibid.*
257 "they call it 'Save Our Schools'": *Durham Morning Herald*, 4 June 1971.
259 "you got me": *Durham Morning Herald*, 11 June 1971.

CHAPTER THIRTEEN

PAGE
261 "what it was really like": Mebane, p. 5.
265 "you people to come": *Durham Morning Herald*, 15 June 1971.
266 "more neutral than that": *Durham Morning Herald*, 19 June 1971.
269 to take care of black troublemakers: Int., John Meyers, 13 April 1995.
  " "I intend to do it": *Durham Morning Herald*, 3 July 1971.
270 "can say we didn't try": *Carolina Times*, 3 July 1971.
  " "to accomplish its plans": *Carolina Times*, 17 July 1971.
272 "There he goes again": *Durham Morning Herald*, 20 July 1971.
  " "females against their will": *Durham Sun*, 20 July 1971.
  " "by whites against blacks": *Durham Morning Herald*, 20 July 1971.
  " "that we're all alike!": *Ibid.*

CHAPTER FOURTEEN

PAGE
277 "what it means to be human": Lester, p. 26.
278 "the shocks of race conflict": Edgar T. Thompson, "The South and the Second Emancipation," in Allan Sindler, Change in the Contemporary South (Durham: Duke University Press), 1963, p. 106.
  " "about that one group": *Durham Morning Herald*, 22 July 1971.
284 "and dealin' and dealin'": *Ibid.*

INDEX

Atwater-Ellis relationship (*cont.*)
  friendship, 275–76, 281, 285,
    287–88
  toast to charrette's success,
    284–85
Austin, Louis, 50, 54, 106, 129, 232
  black elite and, 172
  Black Power movement, 180–81
  black unity issue, 134–35
  BSC boycott, 231–32
  Citizens' Councils and, 129–30
  civil rights movement, support
    for, 89–90, 91
  death of, 296
  employment issues, 215
  Fuller, defense of, 208–9
  higher education, desegregation
    of, 53
  housing issue, 213
  lunch-counter protests, 99, 104,
    107, 109
  McKissick, J., and, 93
  Malcolm X and, 135–36
  Operation Breakthrough, 161
  school desegregation, 84–85

Baez, Joan, 228
Baltimore Afro-American, 39
Baraka, Amiri, 165
Barden, Graham, 96
Becton, Joe, 245–46, 250–51, 252,
    256, 258, 259, 291
Big Men, 132
Birmingham, Ala., 137–38
Black Christmas, 233
Black community of Durham
  black uplift issue, 50–53
  conservative leadership, 53–54
  divisions within, 39–42, 54–55
  economic relations, 49
  elite's "dual personality," 172–74
  Hayti slums, 31, 36–38, 156
  King, affection for, 221
  landlord-tenant relations, 156,
    158, 173
  religious establishment, 41–42
  solidarity within, 42
  See also Durham, N.C.; Housing

in Durham; North Carolina
    Mutual Insurance Company;
    Operation Breakthrough;
    United Organizations for
    Community Improvement
Black nationalism, 229
Black Power movement, 177–81, 295
Blacks
  black uplift issue, 42–45, 47–53
  Durham, positive attitude
    toward, 23–24, 28, 38–39
  "free Negroes" within slave soci-
    ety, 45–46
  history of challenges to racial
    oppression, 77–79, 87
  housing aspirations, 164–66
  labor movement, 54–56
  oppression following Civil War,
    46–47
  slavery, 40, 45–46, 52, 87
  See also Black community of
    Durham; Civil rights move-
    ment
Black Solidarity Committee for
    Community Improvementm
    (BSC), 231–32, 233–34
Blackwell Durham Tobacco Com-
    pany, 19, 21, 22
Blair, Ezell, Jr. (Jibreel Khazan), 95,
    96–99, 293
Boulware, C. E., 182
Brady, Thomas Pickens, 131
Branch, Taylor, 104
Broughton, J. Melville, 71
Brown, Callis, 99, 100, 108–9
Brown, Nathaniel, 181, 182
Brown v. *Board of Education*, 79,
    81, 82, 131, 246
Bryant, Victor S., III, 170
Bull Durham Smoking Tobacco, 18
Buses, desegregation of, 71–72,
    74–76, 88, 92
Busing programs, 239
Butler, Joseph, 236–38, 239, 266,
    279

Cabinet Committee on Education,
    247